NATIONAL TRAILS *of* AMERICA

Contents

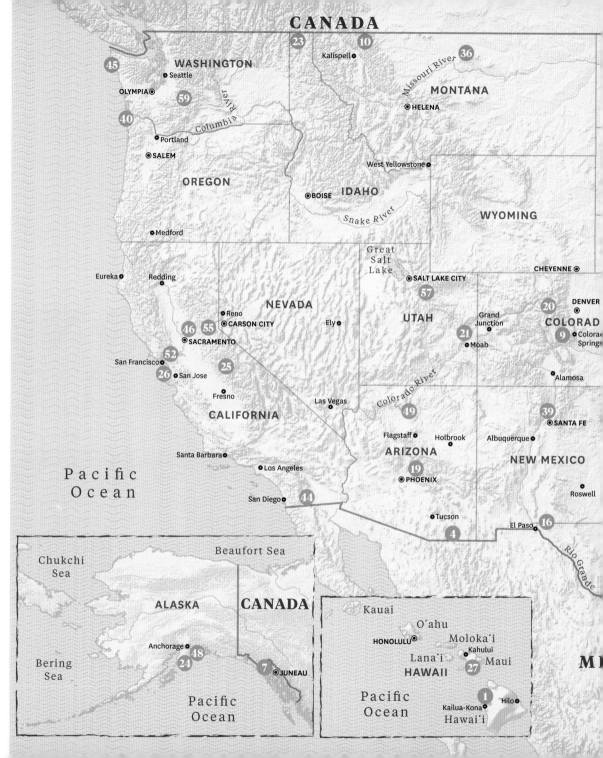

CANADA

NORTH DAKOTA
⊙ BISMARCK

MINNESOTA
Duluth
Grand Portage
Lake Superior

SOUTH DAKOTA
⊙ PIERRE

Rapid City

Missouri River

Minneapolis ⊙ ST. PAUL
WISCONSIN
MADISON ⊙
Milwaukee

Lake Michigan

MICHIGAN
LANSING ⊙
Detroit

Lake Huron

Lake Ontario
Rochester
Buffalo
Lake Erie
Cleveland

MONTPELIER
VERMONT
CONCORD
NEW HAMPSHIRE
AUGUSTA
MAINE

ALBANY ⊙
NEW YORK
BOSTON ⊙
MASSACHUSETTS
HARTFORD ⊙
New Haven
PROVIDENCE
RHODE ISLAND
CONNECTICUT

Atlantic Ocean

NEBRASKA
Omaha
LINCOLN ⊙

IOWA
⊙ DES MOINES

Chicago

Fort Wayne

ILLINOIS
⊙ SPRINGFIELD

INDIANA
⊙ INDIANAPOLIS

OHIO
⊙ COLUMBUS
Cincinnati

Toledo

Pittsburgh
PENNSYLVANIA
HARRISBURG ⊙
Philadelphia
TRENTON
NEW JERSEY

New York

KANSAS
TOPEKA ⊙
Kansas City
St Louis

MISSOURI
JEFFERSON CITY

WEST VIRGINIA
⊙ CHARLESTON

MARYLAND
Baltimore
ANNAPOLIS
WASHINGTON, DC

Arkansas River
Wichita

KENTUCKY
FRANKFORT ⊙
Louisville
Lexington

Ohio River

VIRGINIA
RICHMOND ⊙
Norfolk

OKLAHOMA
OKLAHOMA CITY
Tulsa

ARKANSAS
LITTLE ROCK

TENNESSEE
⊙ NASHVILLE
Memphis

Tennessee River

Greensboro
Durham
⊙ RALEIGH
NORTH CAROLINA
Charlotte

TEXAS
Lubbock
Fort Worth ⊙ Dallas
Odessa

Mississippi River

MISSISSIPPI
⊙ JACKSON

ALABAMA
Birmingham
MONTGOMERY

GEORGIA
⊙ ATLANTA

COLUMBIA
SOUTH CAROLINA

AUSTIN ⊙
San Antonio
Houston

LOUISIANA
BATON ROUGE
New Orleans

TALLAHASSEE ⊙

Jacksonville

Gulf of Mexico

FLORIDA
Orlando
Tampa
St. Petersburg
Miami

MEXICO

Laredo
Corpus Christi

Atlantic Ocean

Isla de Mona

PUERTO RICO
Bayamon ⊙ SAN JUAN

Ponce

Vieques

Caribbean Sea

1 Ala Kahaka Trail
2 American Discovery Trail
3 Appalachian Trail
4 Arizona Trail
5 California Trail
6 Captain John Smith Trail
7 Chilkoot Trail
8 C&O Trail
9 Colorado Trail
10 Continental Divide Trail
11 Crawford Trail
12 Cumberland Trail
13 Derby Wharf Trail
14 East Coast Greenway
15 El Camino Real de los Tejas
16 El Camino Real de Tierra Adentro
17 Flordia Trail
18 Freedom Trail
19 Grand Enchantment
20 Grays Peak
21 Hayduke Trail
22 Ice Age Trail
23 Idaho Centennial Trail
24 Iditarod Trail
25 John Muir Trail
26 Juan Batista Trail
27 Kaupo Trail
28 Lewis & Clark Trail
29 Long Trail
30 Maah Daah Hey Trail

31 Mormon Pioneer Trail
32 Mountain to Sea Trail
33 Natchez Trace Trail
34 Natural Bridge Trail
35 New England Trail
36 Nez Perce Trail
37 North Country Trail
38 Old Rag
39 Old Spanish Trail
40 Oregon Coast Trail
41 Oregon Trail
42 Overmountain Trail
43 Ozark Highlands
44 Pacific Crest Trail
45 Pacific Northwest Trail
46 Pony Express
47 Potomac Heritage Trail
48 Resurrection Pass
49 Rim to Rim Trail
50 Santa Fe Trail
51 Selma to Montgomery
52 Sierra High Route
53 Star Spangled Banner
54 Superior Hiking Trail
55 Tahoe Rim Trail
56 Trail of Tears
57 Union Pacific Rail Trail
58 Washington Route
59 Wonderland Trail
60 El Yunque

Foreword

Last summer I spent several hours hiking along the shores of Loch Ness in Scotland on the South Loch Ness Trail. It was something of a fulfillment of a dream. I'd wanted to visit the lake since I was a child, when I, like many of my generation, had become convinced by news reports and television shows that a mysterious long-necked monster lived in its dark waters. By the time I first gazed out across the lake in middle age, I knew better, but I'll admit I couldn't keep myself from half-searching for a sign of it. The story of Loch Ness ran deep within me, though I'd grown up thousands of miles away, but once I started to walk, everything changed. Each step erased my idea of Loch Ness and replaced it with what it actually was – the dozens of gorgeous and comical sheep who grazed near its shore, lifting their heads to watch me zigzag past them on the trail; the forested hills that climbed above the lake and opened up to rocky and windy knolls; the frigid water that lapped onto a stony spit of beach, where I squatted to submerge my hand in the lake in which I once believed a monster lived.

This has always been my favorite way to travel. At footspeed. Everywhere I've gone in the world, the thing I most love to do is walk. Whether wandering through cities or trekking through the wilderness, experiencing a place at a pace achievable only by the efforts of my own exertions creates a sense of intimacy like nothing else. The slope of the land, the clamor of the streets, the way the flowers or the buildings or the mountains look when you round that bend, the smell and sound and sight and feel of that particular spot, there and then, with nothing between you and it – that's the gift we get when we wander on foot or bike or beast. We don't only take in the view; we are taken in by it.

This book is about the love of that kind of travel. Of the sort we do when we venture down the most interesting paths. The sixty trails that are featured in these pages represent an astonishing range of landscapes, habitats, and climates that span the United States, but what they share in common is an open invitation to discover them one step at a time. Some of the trails pass through America's most rugged wilderness, some are urban walks, and others weave through the territory between the two worlds. Several of the trails described in this book commemorate important, sometimes difficult events in our nation's history – the civil rights movement, the American Revolution, the forced relocation of the Cherokee Nation; others celebrate and protect the beauty and diversity of our natural environment. These trails pass through national parks, historic town squares and seaports, vast deserts and tropical rain forests. The shortest trail in this book is less than a half a mile; the longest is 6800.

Every one of these trails tells a story of a place, a time, a people – and most powerfully, if we allow them to, they teach us about our connection to each other, to history, and to the land. By exploring these trails, we become part of that story. Our perception of the places they pass through morphs from the idea we had of them to the understanding of what they actually are by sheer force of the fact that by setting foot on them we will forever know how it felt to be there. The impenetrable mountain range becomes the rainy day you sweated up its muddy slopes. The history lessons you learned about the Klondike Gold Rush or the Spanish explorers or the Ice Age become the things you saw, smelled, didn't know, but learned. The lake with the monster becomes the lake that once held your hand.

I hope you will venture onto some of these trails and savor reading about them all. This book is a glorious journey all its own. Happy trails.

By Cheryl Strayed
Oregon, 2019

➔ Hāpuna Beach.

01

Ala Kahakai National Historic Trail

This 175-mile trail on the lush Big Island honors and protects Native Hawaiian culture and natural resources. Still in development, it traverses the coast from kiawe forest and beaches to petroglyph grounds and fishponds.

Ala Kahakai Trail

Hawai'i, also called the Big Island, is twice as big as the other Hawaiian islands combined, and its dramatic terrain will surprise you and take you to extremes. The island's history can be readily found along its coastal and *mauka to makai* (mountain to shoreline) trails, a network imprinted by the hands and feet of Hawai'i's original Polynesian settlers and their descendants. The main coastal or *Ala Loa* (long path) trail formed the backbone of the trail network that supported communication and commerce between *ahupua'a* (land districts). In recognition of the importance of the coastal trail, the Ala Kahakai National Historic Trail was added to the National Historic Trails register in 2000. Once circumnavigating the entire island, the coastal trail corridor, rich in historic sites, now stretches 175 miles from Upolu Point in North Kohala along the coast, rounding *Ka Lae* (South Point) and heading northeast and into Hawai'i Volcanoes National Park.

The Highways Act of 1892, signed into law through the auspices of Queen Lili'uokalani and the legislature of the Kingdom of Hawai'i, dictated that any trail in existence at that time was a public right-of-way. This has become a critical tool for the establishment of trail segments for the Ala Kahakai National Historic Trail and the state's Nā Ala Hele trail system, which coincides with the Ala Kahakai at various points. When complete, the Ala Kahakai Trail will be the cordage that binds the island canoe together. The 175-mile trail includes four national park units and traverses 220 active ahupua'a. The NPS and community volunteer groups work closely with lineal descendants who have

Sleep here...

South Kohala's 'Gold Coast' doesn't just offer opportunities for feeling the ancient mana *(spiritual essence) at Pu'uhonua O Hōnaunau National Historical Park. As you head toward the ocean, rolling emerald golf course slopes edge onto condo complexes and electric-teal pools. Whatever your feelings are on resorts, this is where you'll find some of the area's best beaches, and the grand hotels are directly on the trail path.*

 Hāpuna Beach State Recreation Area
The Hāpuna Beach State Recreation Area in Waimea has four-person A-frame cabins that you can rent through the Hawaii state website. It's the perfect spot to bask in the rays and one of only a small number of camping options on the island.

 Spencer Beach Park Campground
Permits for camping at Spencer Beach Park, directly next to Pu'ukohola Heiau National Historic Site, can be obtained through the County of Hawai'i website. The campground has full facilities, plus beach access and a nighttime security guard.

 Mauna Kea Beach Hotel
This grand hotel on the Gold Coast is understated and quietly confident of its reputation. At first glance it might not wow you, but there is history here. Rooms are regularly renovated and nicely maintained. The hotel's crowning jewel is simply its location on Kauna'oa Bay, which contains some of the island's best beaches.

 Fairmont Orchid
Elegant and almost formal (for Hawai'i), the Orchid never lets you forget that you're at an exclusive, luxury hotel. The architecture may be continental, but the gorgeous grounds are buoyantly tropical.

Toolbox

 When to go
Summer is fairly hot and dry, and the cooler fall, winter and spring months are rainier, with changeable weather such as flash floods, high surf and winds. The trail status along the coastline of Hawai'i Volcanoes National Park should be checked in advance, as access can be limited by volcanic activity.

Getting there
The NPS is currently working with the entities along the planned route to establish trail segments. The existing official segments are best accessed through the parks and historic sites along the route. All national park access points have info, water and restrooms. Flights usually land at Kona International Airport.

Practicalities
Start: Pu'ukoholā Heiau National Historic Site
End: Hawai'i Volcanoes National Park
Length: 175 miles (with interruptions)
Dog friendly: No
Bike friendly: No
Permit needed: Not on official segments
States covered: Hawai'i

➡ Sunset at Hāpuna Beach;
Left: Kohala Coast.

The trail follows the coast.

ancestral ties to the trail, its ahupua'a and its cultural resources, and who wanted the chance to manage their shoreline areas. The trail is a viable cultural corridor and a living source of Hawaiian history, as well as a treasure trove of ocean wildlife, native plants and birds.

The trail begins at a sacred site, the Pu'ukoholā Heiau, a massive temple built by Kamehameha I (1758–1819) and the hands of thousands, stone by stone. The heiau was dedicated to Kamehameha's war god Kukai'ilimoku and is thought to have been instrumental in Kamehameha's success in unifying Hawai'i Island and, ultimately, the entire island chain. Just north of the heiau is Pelekane Bay, where sharks often gather over the site of a submerged temple. In August, at the annual Ho'oku'ikahi i Pu'ukoholā Heiau Establishment Day Hawaiian Cultural Festival, visitors can experience living Hawaiian history.

As the trail meanders south, it passes through kiawe forest and along the shore, with spectacular panoramas of the azure Pacific and majestic Maui. There is a sense of timelessness as you imagine fisherfolk perusing fishing grounds for signs that it was time to throw the net, and in winter you may see humpback whales frolicking. Yet the trail also passes by massive beachside resorts. It's an apt reminder of how Hawai'i plays hosts both to modern tourist infrastructure and indigenous cultural touchstones.

Later, the trail crosses the entrance to the Puakō petroglyph field. With more than 3000 petroglyphs, this preserve is among the largest collections of ancient lava carvings in Hawai'i. The carvings might not make sense to you, but viewed together, they are fascinating and worth a visit. The petroglyphs are a window into the history of the area's residents and are a recording of births and other important events.

On the opposite end of the trail is the fearsome, elemental Hawai'i Volcanoes National Park, its geothermal activity a constant guessing game. The park is a micro-continent of thriving rainforests, volcano-induced deserts, high-mountain meadows, coastal plains and plenty of geological marvels in between. While other national parks in the US are home to active volcanoes, Kīlauea holds the distinction of being one of the world's most active volcanoes. Mauna Loa, also within the park's boundaries, is the world's most massive shield volcano. It's hardly surprising that Native Hawaiian culture, religion and mythology place a large emphasis on vulcanism. Halema'uma'u crater on Kīlauea is believed to be the home of the goddess Pele, creator of the Hawaiian Islands. Stop at the Kīlauea Visitor Center first. Extraordinarily helpful (and remarkably patient) rangers and volunteers can advise you about volcanic activity, air quality, road closures and hiking-trail conditions.

It's best to experience the trail in segments for now; the national park access points are well marked and provide a way to experience Hawai'i's unique environment and culture up close. The hike is often scorching, but you can turn back at any point, and the path's shoreline-hugging nature means plenty of opportunities to cool off with a swim.

Highlights

Even among the Big Island's many wonders, the path of the Ala Kahakai trail is something special. While South Kohala resort visitors have access to part of the same shoreline, walking its length reveals a wilder, more untamed Hawai'i.

SHORELINE ECOSYSTEMS
Hikers will find anchialine ponds, which provided the ancients with drinking water. These ponds contain small fish, mollusks and opai'ula, small red shrimp.

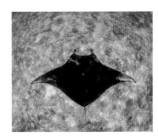

KAUNA'OA BAY
There are vibrant coral reefs at either point of this bay, which is home to the Mauna Kea Beach Hotel. Manta rays gather at the north end at night.

HĀPUNA BEACH STATE RECREATION AREA
Kick off your shoes and walk with the ocean lapping at your feet, or stop in the shade of the kiawe trees for a snack.

BIRD-WATCHING
Be on the lookout for black-crowned night herons perching on rocks or flying along the coast. Also look for shoreline birds such as the Hawaiian stilt.

HAWAI'I VOLCANOES NATIONAL PARK
Its two active volcanoes testify to the ongoing birth of the islands. With luck, you'll witness the primal power of molten earth meeting the sea.

Resources

01 National Park Service Websites

Hawai'i Volcanoes
National Park:
www.nps.gov/havo
Kaloko-Honokōhau
National Historical Park:
www.nps.gov/kaho
Pu'uhonua o Honaunau
National Historical Park:
www.nps.gov/puho
Pu'ukoholā Heiau National
Historic Site:
www.nps.gov/puhe

02 Other Trail Resources

Ala Kahakai National
Historic Trail
Comprehensive
Management Plan:
www.nps.gov/alka/learn/
*management/upload/ALKA_*
CMP_low-resolution.pdf
Ala Kahakai Trail
Association:
www.alakahakaitrail.org
Nā Ala Hele Trail and
Access Program:
hawaiitrails.hawaii.gov/
trails/#/trail/ala-kahakai-
trail/5

⬆ Shoreline in Pu'uhonua O Honaunau National Historical Park in South Kona, Hawai'i with Mauna Loa in the distance. Left: Hawai'i Volcanoes National Park.

Hike this...

175 miles of trail is a lot to bite off, but the still-in-progress Ala Kahakai is best done in sections anyway, jumping off from nearby park access to some of the area's best beaches and numerous ancient Hawaiian sights.

➔ A green turtle relaxing on the beach

01
South Kohala Beaches

This 15-mile stretch of signature beaches takes you past pristine shoreline. Start at the southern end of Spencer Beach Park and pass thick kiawe groves to reach white-sand Mau'umae Beach. The trail turns right and travels by private residences until it reaches the Mauna Kea Beach Hotel, on Kauna'oa Bay. At the south end of the beach, walk or wade around a rock wall and an overhanging tree to pick up the trail on the other side, or head uphill and turn right on a paved road to rejoin the trail on the other side. Continue along the shoreline to the north end of Hāpuna Beach State Recreation Area. From here, look for the Ala Kahakai Trail sign and follow the trail uphill to Wailea Beach and Puakō. From Puakō, the easiest way is to walk along the road to Pani'au, where the trail continues to Holoholokai Beach Park. Walk the Mauna Lani Hotel grounds, past a lava field, to the Hilton Waikoloa golf course, pass the Waikoloa Beach Marriott and on to 'Anaeho'omalu Beach.

02
Kaloko-Honokōhau National Historical Park

This 1160-acre national park may be the Kona Coast's most under-appreciated ancient Hawaiian site. Hidden among lava fields lies evidence of the innovations that allowed Hawaiians to thrive in this hostile landscape: fish traps, lava planters used to grow taro and other staples, and the ahupua'a between Kaloko and Honokōhau that gives the park its name. There are also heiau, burial caves and petroglyphs. From the visitors center, take the Ala Mauka Makai Trail for 0.7 miles to Honokōhau Beach, where it will intersect with the Ala Kahakai National Historic Trail. At this point turn right and head north along the white-sand beach for 1.2 miles to the Kaloko Fishpond, where the massive rock retaining wall is being completely rebuilt in the traditional way (without mortar) so it can once again be fished. To continue, head inland on an unpaved road for 0.2 miles, where it intersects with the Ala Kahakai Trail, and continue north 1.5 miles to Wāwahiwa'a Point.

03
Pu'uhonua o Honaunau National Historical Park

Two trails originate in the Pu'uhonua o Honaunau National Historical Park, in South Kona: the coastal trail and the '1871 trail,' the latter a widening of the *ala loa* to accommodate horses, which were first brought to the island by Captain George Vancouver. About a mile along, the trails meet and continue on to Ho'okena Beach Park, where there are showers, camping and beach access. Pu'uhonua o Honaunau was once a place of refuge where, if a *kapu* (law) breaker reached the enclosure, they would be sheltered from punishment.

Today the park is dedicated to preserving and perpetuating Hawaiian culture. In 1993 the *Mauloa*, a traditional coastal sailing canoe, was constructed in the canoe house here using traditional materials and techniques, from sennit cording made of coconut fiber braided together to lauhala sails. The native plants along the trail provided the needed raw materials, such as the hala tree, whose leaves are used to weave mats and baskets.

02
American Discovery Trail

Covering 6800 miles from coast to coast, the multiuse American Discovery Trail (ADT) connects cities, forests and rural areas in 15 states from Delaware to California.

One of the allures of the American Discovery Trail is its appeal as an old-fashioned trail, the kind of trodden path used for getting from one town to the next before motorized travel. Except this path has tens of thousands of places to discover from sea to shining sea.

Starting at the shoreline of the Atlantic Ocean in Delaware and stretching to the California coast, the ADT is a 6800-mile transcontinental phenomenon that passes through 15 states, connecting dramatic natural sites to lively urban areas including Washington, DC, Chicago, St Louis, Kansas City, Denver and San Francisco.

Because the ADT is the first coast-to-coast trail that links other national trails, such as the Appalachian, Pacific Crest, Lewis & Clark and Santa Fe trails, its supporters call it the backbone of the nation's trail system. The nonprofit organization that manages the ADT, the American Discovery Trail Society (ADTS), says on its website that the ADT offers adventurers 'the opportunity to journey into the heart of all that is uniquely American – its culture, heritage, landscape and spirit.'

The ADT, which was first conceived of in 1989, is so different from other national trails that the US Congress has struggled for decades to make it official, mainly because it doesn't fit other designations in the National Park Service's National Trails System: Historic, Scenic or Recreation trails. In other words the ADT isn't just about history, scenery or recreation; as the name says, it's about the discovery of all those things and more.

Take a 360-mile section that traces the

■ Chimney Rock formation at Capitol Reef National Park.

Sleep here...

ADT thru-hikers rely on hostels, motels and hotels more than other long-distance hikers because much of the trail passes through private and municipal property where camping isn't allowed. Still, places to stay along the route run the gamut from backwoods camping in wilderness areas to luxury hotels in cities and resort towns. Here's a sampling of the more offbeat options.

Phoenix Hotel, California
Hotels in the Bunkhouse Group are wonderfully weird and sustainable; its Phoenix Hotel in San Francisco is a 1950s-era motor court frequented by musicians and intrepid travelers.

Dolly Sods Wilderness, West Virginia
Monongahela National Forest in West Virginia has the highest elevations along the ADT east of the Rockies. In the forest, the trail crosses the Dolly Sods Wilderness, with rustic campsites near waterfalls and swimming holes – 'nuff said!

St Meinrad Archabbey, Indiana
If clean sheets in the abbey's guest rooms are too luxurious, ask if you can camp on its scenic grounds in St Meinrad, Indiana (65 miles west of Louisville). Bonus: buffet-style meals cost $8 in the dining room.

Trail Angels, Everywhere
Seasoned backpackers who live near the trail are known to invite ADT thru-hikers to pitch tents on their property or even to stay in their homes. Check the ADTS website's contact info for state coordinators, look for blog posts recommending them, or trust in happenstance.

Toolbox

When to go
Since the ADT spans the nation's midsection east to west, hikes can be more challenging in the winter; finish mountainous sections before the snow comes.

Getting there
The American Discovery Trail Society (ADTS) website has state-by-state details, including contact information for state coordinators who can field queries and give advice.

Practicalities
Length in miles: 6800+ miles, including the southern route (5057 miles) and northern route (4834 miles)
Start: Cape Henlopen State Park, DE
End: Point Reyes National Seashore, CA
Dog friendly: Varies by individual trails and sites.
Bike friendly: The vast majority is bikable, and a few people have hiked/biked the entire length, but evaluate local restrictions and conditions.
Permit needed: Varies; check the ADTS website.
States covered: CA, CO, DC, DE, IA, IL, IN, KS, KY, MD, MO, NE, NV, OH, UT, WV

'bootheel' of southern Indiana along the Ohio River. Westbound from Cincinnati, the ADT follows the hills and dales from one Hoosier town to the next – places called Canaan, French, Vienna, China, Friendship and Sassafras – punctuated along the way by the relative hubbub (and amenities) of small cities like Madison, Corydon and Evansville. In between the town and cities are numerous state parks and forests, as well as Hoosier National Forest, that offer backcountry hiking and camping. Leaving the comfort of one town takes you past meandering trails, wilderness and back roads to another; cresting every ridge could reveal a splendid vista such as a steamboat plying a bend in the Ohio River.

This is an American walkabout through the heartland of the country, where 19th-century architecture means log cabins and Greek Revival mansions, where local lore means a lottery game called straws, the best fried bologna sandwiches this side of Italy or deathly serious Midwestern euchre tournaments.

Some people might wonder why you'd take such a hike. As one Hoosier resident put it, 'You mean you're walking to Madison? You know, you can get there by car.' He has a point. Much of the ADT never strays far from well-traveled roads, making many of its interesting sights accessible by car, whether you're marching along Military Road past Civil War forts outside of Washington, DC, or strolling on the Embarcadero in San Francisco.

But in southern Indiana, as in other places, a car wouldn't give you the thrill of hiking limestone canyons, tallgrass meadows, dazzling glens, and rare forests of poplar, sycamore, hickory, white oak and black walnut. And those forest trails lead to caves, waterfalls, Abe Lincoln's boyhood home and an Indiana monastery in St Meinrad that's unchanged since 1854.

Similar discoveries are all along the trail. Several people have completed thru-hikes of the entire route (including at least one by horse and one by running), but almost all other explorers take the ADT in chunks. Because it is the most accessible trail in the country, with 36 million Americans living in the ADT corridor, a hike along any part of it – even, say, the 1.5 miles from Fredonia to Artist Point in southern Indiana – is a hike of national scope, a glimpse of how even disparate regions in the nation are connected.

Like many trails, the ADT is a work in progress. It began in 1989 when *Backpacker* magazine and the American Hiking Society proposed a nonmotorized, east–west transcontinental trail. Since then, state coordinators with the ADTS have worked with local groups and governments to map and maintain the trail. While bills to officially designate the ADT have been introduced during almost every session of Congress since the 1990s, they've died in committees. In 2019 the effort gained new momentum when a law was passed authorizing the placement of ADT signs on federal lands.

The American Discovery Trail might not always be noticed by the small communities along its route, but for believers, the trail is a throwback to the original purpose of hiking, in which you hit the road not just for the physical challenge but also for the chance to connect to other ways of life. It's a chance to live the trail's mantra: Hike Your Own Hike.

Highlights

The only coast-to-coast trail in the country, the ADT has it all: cities, mountains, deserts and plains. Crossing the entire nation from Delaware to California (or vice versa), the wonders and discoveries are endless. Here are some favorites.

CINCINNATI
Historic neighborhoods and river vistas highlight the ADT's passage through Mount Adams in the heart of scenic Cincinnati, Ohio, and across the Roebling Suspension Bridge into Kentucky.

ANGEL MOUNDS
The culture of Native Americans from the Mississippian period is well-preserved at Angel Mounds State Historic Site along the Ohio River in southwestern Indiana.

KATY TRAIL
A prime example of how the ADT incorporates rail trails (rail tracks converted to multiuse paths), the Katy, as it's called, follows 240 crushed limestone-surfaced miles of the former Missouri–Kansas–Texas Railroad through Missouri.

CAPITOL REEF NATIONAL PARK
Red rock country, petroglyphs, narrow canyons and deserts – this is the rural, remote and rugged terrain of Utah.

THE PEOPLE
'This trail opens you up so much to trust people, to talk to people.' –Joyce and Peter Cottrell, the first to backpack the entire ADT.

Aerial of the Katy Trail near Pilot Grove, Missouri.

Resources

O1 American Discovery Trail Society
discoverytrail.org
The website has links to affiliated trails, parks and points of interest along the way. GPX files are available for $7 per state, as are Data Books, which include turn-by-turn instructions. The website also includes 'Trail Tales' from people who have hiked, biked, run and ridden on horseback the entire ADT.

O2 *American Discoveries: Scouting the First Coast-to-Coast Recreational Trail*
Now out of print, Ellen Dudley and Eric Seaborg's 1996 title shows the ADT's origins.

Hike this...

Depending on what part of the country you find yourself in, the terrain of the shorter day hikes on the ADT varies wildly. The below options are a great sample of what some of these regions have to offer.

➡ The Front Range in Rocky Mountain National Park. Opposite page, from left: The ADT's end in Point Reyes; Sculptured Beach, Point Reyes National Seashore.

01

North Bend Rail Trail, West Virginia

Administered by West Virginia State Parks, the North Bend Rail Trail gives a strong sense of the ADT's mission by turning what was once B&O rail infrastructure and making it an escape from everyday life. At 72 miles long, and incorporating 10 historic rail tunnels and 38 bridges, the crushed limestone bed of North Bend Rail Trail permits usage by bikers and horseback riders as well as hikers, and the flat terrain makes it doable for the whole family.

In 2018, the North Bend Rail Trail acquired land to extend to Corning Park in Parkersburg, West Virginia, adding a new continuous link on the ADT's path from Pittsburgh to Parkersburg; work is now underway to finalize work on the trail extension along a former CSX rail line. Taking this path is a wonderful way to get to know the scenic Mountain State better.

02

Colorado's Front Range and Rocky Mountains

Colorado might be home to the most challenging – and scenically spectacular – part of the ADT. The backcountry segment between Denver and Utah crosses six national forests, the Continental Divide (three times) and 15 mountain passes higher than 9000 feet, as well as many resort towns. Along the Front Range, many excellent day trips are possible. The route passes through the foothills between 5000 and 9000 feet, putting travelers in or near Pikes Peak Greenway, Garden of the Gods and Platte River Greenway, all connected to Colorado Springs and Denver via the ADT. The 24 miles from Canon City to Cripple Creek ('the world's greatest gold camp') features a 5000ft elevation gain. As it can snow any day of the year at higher elevations, July and August are strongly recommended.

03

Redwood Creek Trail, California

After crossing the University of California Berkeley campus and taking a ferry across San Francisco Bay, the ADT passes through San Francisco and into Marin County. Experience Muir Woods via the Redwood Creek Trail loop, featuring 1500ft in elevation gain over 10.5 miles. It's often quieter than other regions of Muir Woods. The trailhead climbs up the salmon-spawning Redwood Creek of the trail's name through beautiful meadows to meet Dipsea Trail, part of the Bay Area Ridge Trail network and known as the site of the annual Dipsea race, the second oldest footrace in the country. More ambitious hikers can choose to trek up to Mount Tamalpais State Park's Pantoll Ranger Station by the Stapelveldt Trail instead, while those with less time can opt for a stroll to Muir Beach.

On the Appalachian Trail at Carver's Gap.

© Craig Zerbe / Getty Images

03
Appalachian National Scenic Trail

The world's longest hiking-only footpath is a classic bucket list trail, a 2190-mile wilderness pilgrimage from the southern Blue Ridge Mountains to the wilds of Maine.

The Appalachian Trail – the AT – is a world unto itself. For thru-hikers (people walking the entire stretch of almost 2200 miles) the trail will be home for between five and seven months, on average. When you get back to civilization, you'll be changed, and we're not just talking about weight loss and boulder-like quads. A piece of your soul will be forever wild.

The very language used on the trail sets the AT apart from the rest of the world. As a thru-hiker, you'll shed your name for a 'trail name' – ideally something with a winking double meaning, given to you by a fellow hiker. You're a thin guy who loves to swim in every river you cross? Hello, Skinny Dip. Are you a Wisconsinite who tells goofy jokes? We dub you Cheesy. A NOBO is a northbound (Georgia to Maine) hiker, while a SOBO is the opposite. A Trail Angel is a person who helps out hikers, whether giving rides to town or leaving snacks by a campground.

The community is central to the AT experience. Several thousand aspiring thru-hikers start out each year, most heading north. Only about a fifth of them will make it. Those who remain after a few hundred miles begin to bond, meeting up at overlooks and sharing campsites and rustic shelters. They track each other's progress by looking at signatures in shelter logbooks. Strangers become hiking partners. Hiking partners become lifelong friends.

Day after day you'll trek through green tunnels of leaf canopy, ford creeks pulsing with fish and salamanders, and balance on granite ridges above the tree line. You'll feel the sun on your back as you gaze down at the patchwork fields of Virginia's Shenandoah Valley. You'll be dazzled by the golden afternoon light of the Berkshires in

Sleep here...

The huts and lean-to shelters on the AT itself are well-loved by thru-hikers, but due to the trail's path along the heavily-populated Eastern Seaboard, there are plenty of places to partake in a mattress, hot water and a meal.

Trail Shelters
The trail has more than 260 rustic shelters available on a first come, first served basis. Many are mere lean-tos, while others are closed and have actual bunks and outhouses. Heavy-use areas may require a permit, registration or a fee.

Shaw's Hiker Hostel, Maine
In a big white clapboard house, this friendly hostel in Monson, Maine, is at the edge of the 100-Mile Wilderness. Wash clothes and fuel up on breakfasts before plunging back on the trail.

Big Meadows Lodge, VIrginia
In Virginia's Shenandoah National Park, this 1930s rock-and-timber park lodge is a favorite with day hikers. It has a restaurant and shop, plus junior ranger programs for the kids.

White Mountains Huts, New Hampshire
In New Hampshire's White Mountains, eight rustic lodges run by the Appalachian Mountain Club offer cooked meals and cozy bunks, ideal for short-term hikers traveling light. Prebooking is essential.

Toolbox

When to go
Northbound thru-hikers start in Georgia between late March and mid-April. Southbound hikers leave from Maine between late May and mid-June. For day or overnight hikers, late spring through early fall is the most pleasant time for the majority of the trail.

Getting there
The southern terminus at Springer Mountain, Georgia, is 22 miles from the town of Dahlonega and 90 miles from the Atlanta airport. The northern terminus at Mt Katahdin in Maine is 17 miles from Millinocket and 90 miles from the Bangor airport.

Practicalities
Length in miles: 2190
Start: Springer Mountain, GA
End: Mount Katahdin, ME
Dog friendly: Yes, except Great Smoky Mountains National Park (NC, TN) and Baxter State Park (ME)
Bike friendly: No
Permit needed: No
States covered: GA, NC, TN, VA, WV, MD, PA, NJ, NY, CT, MA, VT, NH, ME

➡ Hiking the Appalachian Trail near Burnsville, North Carolina. Left: On the trail near the North Carolina–Tennessee border.

Atop Moxie Bald, Maine.

Massachusetts, and awed by the foliage.

You'll also slog 20 miles through ankle-deep Blue Ridge mud, the rain and fog drawing a gray veil across the scenery. You'll wake up one summer morning to find snow falling in the White Mountains of New Hampshire. You'll crawl along Maine ridges in the whipping wind and grip tree roots for balance, pulling off your pack to squeeze beneath boulders.

No matter what, a day will likely come, whether it's day 10 or day 100 on the trail, when you'll want to pull off your boots and head for the nearest Greyhound station.

But then something will stir your soul. A rainbow over the waterfall. A meadow spangled with white yarrow and fire pinks. The sight of a moose grazing at sunset. An impromptu swim with new friends in a glass-clear mountain pond. Suddenly you'll feel fortified for another day on the trail.

Along the way, hikers stop for an occasional hit of civilization at towns near the trail. These 'town days' mean repairing gear, gorging on diner pancakes, sleeping in an actual bed, and re-upping food supplies. Which brings us to the topic of food, a thru-hiker obsession. A hiker can burn upward of 5000 calories a day, so planning a calorie-dense yet lightweight food supply is an art. Think Pop-Tarts smeared with peanut butter, ramen swimming in olive oil, tortillas stuffed with salami. Even then, most thru-hikers still lose a substantial amount of weight.

Amazingly, this trail that feels as ancient as time is less than 100 years old. Starting in the early 1920s, a planner and conservationist named Benton MacKaye began promoting the idea of a 'great trail' down the East Coast. He was soon joined by grassroots organizers and volunteers, who mapped promising territory, coordinated with government officials and blazed trails. By 1937 these trails connected Maine to Georgia. In 1968 President Lyndon Johnson signed the National Trails System Act, designating the AT an official National Scenic Trail and bringing it under the management of the National Park Service (NPS).

Though thru-hikers number in the four digits, the trail sees as many as three million visitors each year. These are day hikers, overnight campers, people on multiday or multiweek trips, or simply those stopping to stretch their legs during a mountain road trip. All this wear and tear means maintenance, much of which is done by volunteers from the dozens of AT conservation clubs, maintaining trails and building shelters.

The trail, you see, is part of Americans' shared heritage, a true 'footpath of the people,' as the NPS calls it. It's the antidote to our teeming cities, our stressful jobs, our computer-focused lives, our alienation from the land and from each other. Here, in the ancient Appalachian Mountains, people of all stripes – men and women, young and old, dentists and students and chefs and mechanics – come together to share Snickers bars and Band-Aids and jokes. And together they walk, one foot in front of the other, for 2190 miles.

Yet it's also the perfect trail for the beginner long-distance hiker. There are backcountry cabins, service roads where the trail-weary can make an easy escape, and close proximity to towns and airports for any emergencies. Start with section hikes to test out the backpacking life, and before you know it, you may be strapping your boots for the entire length of this incredible trail.

Highlights

The granddaddy of the 'Triple Crown of Hiking,' and definitely the most user-friendly, the AT is a great place to start a thru-hiking career, as it's so convenient to civilization. Plus there are pages and pages of history and literature every step of the way.

CLINGMANS DOME
Legend says that on a clear day you can see seven states from the tower atop this North Carolina–Tennessee border mountain, at 6644ft the highest point on the AT.

HARPERS FERRY
This historic West Virginia Civil War town is the AT's rough midway point; tradition says thru-hikers must stop here and gobble a half gallon of ice cream.

TRAIL DAYS
The southwestern Virginia trail town of Damascus hosts a Trail Days festival each May, with some 20,000 hikers gathering for parades, concerts, workshops and gear expos.

MCAFEE KNOB
Photos of the AT's most Instagram-famous spot show hikers posing on a rock ledge hundreds of feet above the Roanoke Valley. Sunsets here are mind-blowing.

MT KATAHDIN
The final challenge for NOBO hikers, climbing Maine's highest peak means a hands-and-feet scramble up boulder-strewn slopes. The reward? Spectacular views.

Resources

O1 Appalachian National Scenic Trail
www.nps.gov/appa
The National Park Service's info-packed site about the trail has up-to-date warnings and closure announcements.

O2 Appalachian Trail Conservancy
www.appalachiantrail.org
This nonprofit works to protect the trail; its headquarters is in Harpers Ferry.

O3 The Trek
www.thetrek.co
This website and online community dedicated to long-distance hikes has tons of articles to help plan AT thru-hikes.

O4 *A Walk in the Woods*
Bill Bryson's classic memoir of his AT fumbles is just as funny now as it was in 1997.

The summit of The Horn on Maine's Saddleback Mountain. Left: The first sign of the Appalachian Trail at its Southernmost point near Springer Mountain in Georgia.

Hike this...

It's estimated that two to three million people trek a portion of the Appalachian Trail annually, thanks to easy-to-access day hikes up and down its length, and section hiking is a popular tactic for vacation-pressed hikers. Try the below routes for a shorter taste of this mammoth trail.

▶ Hikers on the Appalachian Trail near Bakersville, North Carolina.

01
Anthony's Nose, New York

This short but oh-so-steep climb makes for an excellent day hike from the New York metro area. Though it's only 2.6 miles roundtrip, the staircase-like start means plenty of quad burn. Once you chug up the first half mile, the trail flattens considerably. Meander upward through the birch and pine forest toward the summit, a stony clearing with postcard views across the Hudson River, including the 1924 Bear Mountain suspension bridge that carries the AT across the mighty Hudson and into (you guessed it) popular Bear Mountain.

Pack a lunch to eat on the sun-warmed rocks while enjoying the river views. It's a good choice for families with kids, provided they're willing to hump up the start (or you're willing to carry them!). The origin of the peak's odd name is unknown – it may be in honor of St Anthony, or perhaps for a large-schnozzed Dutch settler. The AT trailhead is located off 9D; an alternative approach heads up from Rt 202.

02
Presidential Range, New Hampshire

Home-cooked meals. Evening entertainment. Convivial strangers who share your love for the outdoors. And we haven't even mentioned the gorgeous mountain views. Sold? Yep, day hiking between the eight huts maintained by the Appalachian Mountain Club (AMC) in the White Mountains is one of the most enjoyable outdoor adventures in New England; just make your reservation as many as nine months out.

The first hut opened more than 125 years ago and today they are going strong. The huts dot a 56-mile stretch of the Appalachian Trail, which is reached by a network of trails unfurling from the Highland Center at Crawford Notch, the Pinkham Notch Visitor Center and various roadside pull-offs. These trails all swoop along the Presidential Range, with streams, waterfalls, wildlife sightings, alpine views and plenty of trees along the way. A small but dedicated 'croo' maintains each hut. Set along 50 miles of the trail, they provide respite for some 30,000 hikers annually.

03
Lemon Gap to Max Patch, North Carolina

Max Patch, a beloved mountain bald (a treeless, grass- or shrub-covered mountaintop, common in the southern Appalachians) in North Carolina, is an easy 1.5-mile loop from the parking lot. But if you'd prefer to avoid the crowded lot and sink your feet into something more substantial, try the 10.5-mile out-and-back route from the Lemon Gap trailhead just north of the mountain. You'll hike through dense forest, crossing creeks and stopping to rest on rocks plush with moss, pausing to listen to the tinkling of nearby waterfalls. In spring you'll pass stands of blooming rhododendrons and hillsides bejeweled with wildflowers.

The star of the show is Max Patch, its vast, sunny meadow filled with picnickers, Frisbee-throwers and photographers, with everyone reveling in the 360-degree mountain views. Watch out for lightning storms, which can rumble through with little warning, and start early if you want to avoid the crowds. Dogs are welcome here if leashed.

→ The Sonoran Desert at sunrise.

04

Arizona National Scenic Trail

Clocking in at 800 miles, the Arizona Trail spans the incredible scenery of this state from the Mexican border to Utah, traversing two national parks and no fewer than 10 mountain ranges.

One of the nation's most rewarding long-distance trails, the Arizona National Scenic Trail (AZT) climbs and descends rugged mountain ranges and the world's grandest of canyons, repeatedly crossing mountain peaks, deep gorges, forested landscapes, riparian corridors and countless wilderness expanses. While it occasionally teems with iconic saguaro cacti and other prickly Sonoran Desert succulents, it offers 800 miles of so much more. If the word 'desert' preceded by the word 'vast' describes your preconceived image of the AZT, you may not be grasping the Arizona Trail's full, sweeping diversity.

To challenge your assumptions, let's begin at the Mexican border. Here, where a barbed-wire fence separates the US from Mexico, the AZT trailhead perches at a breezy 5900ft in elevation. Less than 6.5 miles from its start, the footpath rockets immediately to the top of Miller Peak at 9090ft, a place capped in deep snow for much of the winter. At its lowest, the AZT briefly dips to 1650ft just outside of Superior, but the overall average elevation hovers around 5000ft. And so goes the AZT, up and down, over and over, for nearly 800 miles.

In northern Arizona's high country, the trail is crowned with firs, patches of aspens and the world's largest stand of ponderosa pines. South of Flagstaff the AZT dives into what resembles a shag carpet of juniper-chaparral woodlands. Sedona's red rocks intermingle with dramatic canyon fissures and endless ribbons of distant purple mountains – several of which you'll summit along your path. Eventually, these mesas descend into an alien desert floor, colored toy-soldier green with bountiful

Sleep here...

The AZT is remote throughout its length (and proud of it), passing through few population centers. However, there are 29 designated gateway communities along the AZT, and accommodations and AZT discounts are available in each. Thru-hikers can mail packages to themselves in all the communities nearest the trail, which have resources and respite for day hikers too. Listed below are a few accommodation options.

Stage Stop Inn, Patagonia
At mile 50 on the AZT, the Stage Stop Inn was once a bona fide, rootin' tootin' stagecoach stop along the historic Butterfield Trail. Several places to eat are nearby. Arizona Trail discounts are available.

Pine Creek Cabins, Pine
Clean cabins with a kitchenette in Rim Country's Pine at mile 460. THAT Brewery nearby offers the perfect nightcap opportunity for a tired, thirsty hiker.

Copper Mountain Motel, Superior
This family-run motel at mile 300 close to Boyce Thompson Arboretum State Park promises a 'swanky, irresistible vibe that makes each guest feel like a celebrity.'

Jacob Lake Inn, Jacob Lake
Off mile 760, Jacob Lake Inn is 2 miles from the trail but worth the detour, with rooms, a restaurant, a store and the best cookies north of the Grand Canyon.

Toolbox

When to go
South-to-north thru-hikers strike out in spring, taking advantage of cooler, wetter conditions in southern desert stretches. Starting from Utah? The logic is reversed. Begin in fall to beat the high-elevation snow and tackle the deserts as winter descends.

Getting there
Both border trailheads are remote. Fly into Tucson to reach Coronado National Memorial. In the north, the closest gateway communities are Page, Arizona, or Kanab, Utah.

Practicalities
Length in miles: 800
Start: US–Mexico border within Coronado National Memorial, AZ
End: Arizona–Utah border, 20 miles from Kanab, UT
Dog friendly: Yes, except in national parks and Pusch Ridge Wilderness
Bike friendly: Yes, with exceptions like the Grand Canyon; the trail is designed with mountain bikers in mind
Permit needed: Yes for the Grand Canyon, no otherwise
States covered: Arizona

The southern Coyote Buttes from the northern end of the AZT in the Kaibab National Forest. Left: Arizona–Mexico Border starting point in Coronado National Memorial.

➡ Toroweap Overlook,
North Rim, Grand Canyon
National Park.

life. Saguaros cover the landscape like stubble on a chiseled jaw. Lush paloverdes, their bark a bright lime hue, fill the washes and canyons. The rocky soils hide beneath endless prickly pear cacti, teddy bear chollas and jojobas. Creosote bushes climb the hills, smelling of rolling thunder and desert rain.

To fully explore the length of Arizona, it is necessary to explore its depths. The Grand Canyon contains a kaleidoscope of eco-zones. Dropping from the rim to the river, you'll move from snow-patched, mixed conifer forest through ponderosa pine, through a juniper-oak woodland and a sagebrush plateau and finally into desert scrub, complete with shocking heat. The average 60-day thru-hike across the state requires leaping and climbing and stumbling through every one of these systems, but at the Grand Canyon you can experience them all in a single day. It's as if someone took the full, sweeping diversity of the Arizona Trail and collapsed it into, well, a CliffsNotes version (it's so good, you can delve deeper into the Rim-to-Rim Trail on p258).

Close your eyes and imagine for a moment taking 8 or 10 weeks to thru-hike these roadless vistas. Only your two feet pull you forward during the course of changing seasons. You have enough time between the endless risings and settings of Arizona's fiery sun to actually stop and smell the wildflowers and cactus blossoms, and to really taste water in your throat, the liquid precious and hard-won between moments of natural scarcity. You flush unsuspecting javelinas, bobcats and coyotes from their shady resting spots as you pass, occasionally stepping over giant black bear scat. You stand atop the summit

you've just ascended and turn and see nothing but nature. You rest in silence with a sense of smallness and insignificance, imagining a planet without us, and dare to ponder your miraculous but minuscule part in the cosmos.

Broken into 43 distinct passages, the AZT offers serious long-distance trekkers and casual day hikers countless opportunities to be transported back in time to landscapes unburdened by the trappings of modern humanity. The solitude that so many hikers seek in the wilderness (and that is sometimes elusive along other National Scenic Trails) can still be found in abundance. Whether you're thru-hiking, day hiking or slowly completing the trail in segments, countless trailheads offer convenient access.

Water is the thru-hiker's single greatest challenge, but numerous resources and strategies abound all along the trail to help thirsty explorers cope. Supplies you cache for yourself along the route will be left alone. Apps allow hikers to communicate info to each other about the location and quality of water along the way.

The Arizona Trail owes its legacy to Flagstaff schoolteacher Dale Shewalter, who envisioned an interconnected, nonmotorized path between Mexico and Utah in the 1970s. He finally walked the length of the state on foot in 1985, exploring routes that might be suitable for his vision. Thanks to his advocacy, that vision was gradually embraced by cities and towns, state parks, national forest managers and the National Park Service. Avid hikers, bikers and horseback riders throughout the state took ownership of this national amenity and connected all the dots, much to our benefit.

Highlights

Arizona's ancient beauty reminds you that human affairs are short-lived. The majestic Grand Canyon, the saguaro-dotted deserts of Tucson and the ability of life to thrive in seemingly inhospitable terrain all bring new perspective to hikers.

NORTH RIM, GRAND CANYON
Closed seasonally to cars, the North Rim may feel like yours alone if you make it here on your own feet.

SONORAN DESERT
This desert dominates the southern half of the AZT. Try hiking it by moonlight, and you might find the trail bustling with active wildlife.

WORLD'S LARGEST PONDEROSA FOREST
From the Grand Canyon's South Rim to the Mogollon Rim, the AZT cuts through 203 miles of ponderosa pine country.

WHITE CANYON WILDERNESS
Your experience in this vast wilderness includes the perennial Gila River. Keep an eye out for mountain lion tracks as you scramble the arroyos.

PUSCH RIDGE WILDERNESS
Hovering above Tucson at 6000ft, the forested wonderland of stately rock formations feels like a labyrinth. Bring a good map!

Resources

O1 Arizona Trail Association (ATA)
www.aztrail.org
Since 1994, the official voice for the trail.

O2 *Your Complete Guide to the Arizona National Scenic Trail*
An authoritative guide by Matthew J Nelson, the ATA's Executive Director.

O3 *Arizona Trail: The Official Guide*
This 2005 out-of-print paperback by Tom Lorang Jones is still invaluable.

O4 Arizona Trail App
Search for Guthook Guides to get this $9.99 app with complete access to maps and info.

O5 Grand Canyon National Park
www.nps.gov/grca
Learn about current trail conditions here.

Arizona desert landscape at sunrise. Left: Saguaro in front of the Superstition Mountains.

Hike this...

Think Arizona is nothing but heat and flat sand? Think again. This 800-mile trail explores deserts, mountains, canyons, and cultures from Mexico to Utah. Endlessly snaking from the state's southern border to the northern border are grueling mountain switchbacks... and, okay, some beautiful desert too.

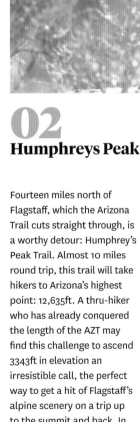
⬒ A coyote relaxing on a rock in Arizona's desert.

01
Picketpost Trailhead

Head east of Phoenix to the Picketpost trailhead of the Arizona Trail for an out-and-back day hike through the saguaro cactus of Tonto National Forest, with stunning views of the Superstition Mountains and beautiful wildflowers in spring. Follow US 60 east to marker 221 to find the Picketpost trailhead off FR 231; from here, the trail runs south through Alamo Canyon. Those wanting to make the loop of Picketpost Mountain can follow the Arizona Trail on its west side before linking up with the east-side trail for a roughly 9-mile journey; otherwise, opt for a 3.9 mile out-and-back option. It's a path well suited to equestrians, bikes and dogs, but keep an eye out for rattlesnakes, and know that trail markings can be missed. In addition, be aware that portions of the trail can wash out during heavy rains (and bring lots of your own water for hot dry days, as always in this Southwestern state). The Picketpost trailhead parking lot is open from dawn to dusk.

02
Humphreys Peak

Fourteen miles north of Flagstaff, which the Arizona Trail cuts straight through, is a worthy detour: Humphrey's Peak Trail. Almost 10 miles round trip, this trail will take hikers to Arizona's highest point: 12,635ft. A thru-hiker who has already conquered the length of the AZT may find this challenge to ascend 3343ft in elevation an irresistible call, the perfect way to get a hit of Flagstaff's alpine scenery on a trip up to the summit and back. In winter skiers hit Humphrey's Peak for its slopes and powder (not on the trail, of course), and cold season hikes demand snow poles, good shoes for ice and extra attention to the weather forecast. In summer it's an easier trip, but it's not a trail for novices, as the elevation can cause altitude sickness and the climb is significant. Yet its views of the Kachina Peaks Wilderness in the Coconino National Forest make it one of the most scenic viewpoints in the San Francisco range, which are the remnants of an extinct stratovolcano and important mountains in local Native American cultures.

03
Butterfly Trail

The highest peak in the Santa Catalina Mountains and an AZT highlight, Mt Lemmon (9157ft) is in one of the region's Sky Islands. Here, beautiful pine forests exist just a few miles away from the desert cactus below. Hikers can drive up to Mt Lemmon's Upper Butterfly trailhead for a 4.6-mile one-way hike (10 miles out and back) to Novio Falls along the Arizona Trail's detour of the Pusch Ridge Wilderness Bypass. Three miles into the trail, it passes the remains of a 1957 plane crash on the site.

Past Novio Falls, the AZT continues toward Mt Bigelow. Part of section 11b on the trail, it can be found off General Hitchcock Hwy/Mt Lemmon Hwy, itself a beautiful scenic drive; amateur astronomers can take the highway up to Mt Lemmon SkyCenter's observatory after their exercise, though the strenuous climb that is the trip back to the trailhead (all uphill) may leave you ready to call it a day. Bring plenty of water and don't come during the extensive snowy season.

05

California National Historic Trail

→ Horseshoe Springs Wildlife Management Area, Utah. Right: California Trail route on Snowshoe Thompson Trail, Humboldt-Toiyabe National Forest, California.

Follow the 49ers and find your fortune, or at least an unforgettable vacation, on this trail from the Midwest to the Golden State.

In the days when California was part of Mexico – that is, before 1846 when the US came to effectively control it, even if Mexico didn't renounce its claims officially until 1848 – the few non-Latino residents were vastly outnumbered by Mexicans and Native Americans. Then on January 24, 1848, a glittering speck of gold dust found in the American River drastically changed the course of this region's history. James Marshall and John Sutter managed to keep their discovery secret for two months, but once it was confirmed in San Francisco, and then in newspapers across the nation, the California Gold Rush began. Before its end, some 500,000 people would travel to California.

While some of those would-be prospectors came from other countries, among them China and Mexico, where mining had long been central to the economy, the majority were from other states in the US. Few had any knowledge of mineralogy or prospecting. Instead, most were farmers – though there were also blacksmiths, lawyers, doctors and others – drawn by tales of men scooping up a handful of soil and finding their fortune, and of mules weighed down by the gold panned in one day. The lure of gold made the westward movement in these years the largest mass migration in American history.

Some Americans – especially those coming from the East Coast – traveled to the Golden State by sea, but the overland route was the more obvious one for others, especially those departing from the center of the country. The path they followed became known as the California Trail, a network of roads that, in its eastern half, follows the older Oregon Trail. After

Sleep here...

As befits a National Historic Trail, there are plenty of nostalgic, stately hotels along this route , perfect for keeping the history-filled theme of the days going where you rest your head at night. But backpackers or car campers will find some scenic options under the great big (starry) sky, too.

Eldridge Hotel, Kansas
Emigrants to California may have stayed at the Free State Hotel, which once stood on this site in Lawrence, Kansas. The current building dates from 1925, though it was restored in 2005.

Sloanes General Store & The Inn at Alcova, Wyoming
This simple but welcoming 10-cabin property in Alcova, near Devil's Gate and several other landmarks on the trail, is in an especially photogenic corner of Wyoming.

Camping at Antelope Island, Utah
The California Trail passed by Utah's Great Salt Lake, and on Antelope Island you can sleep among bison and bighorn sheep under the many stars at this designated International Dark Sky Park.

Gold Hill Hotel, Nevada
The oldest hotel in Nevada is still a little younger than the California Trail; it opened in Virginia City in 1861. Still, its saloon and historical rooms offer an Old West atmosphere.

Toolbox

When to go
To avoid winter storms that may result in some road closures, late spring, summer and early fall are the ideal times to explore the trail.

Getting there
Independence, Missouri, is next to Kansas City, which is served by many flights each day. St Joseph, Missouri, another starting point, is just an hour's drive away. San Francisco, at the opposite end, has a busy airport.

Practicalities
Length in miles: 1000 (5000 including alternate routes)
Start: Independence, MO (one of several starting points, along with St Joseph, MO, and others on the Iowa–Nebraska border)
End: Sacramento, CA (one of many end points in CA, OR and WA)
Dog friendly: Yes; portions
Bike friendly: Yes; portions
Permit needed: Some campgrounds
States covered: CA, CO, ID, KS, MO, NE, NV, OR, UT, WY

beginning in the Midwest, it crosses two mountain ranges (the Rockies and the Sierra Nevada) and then ends at various points in California, as well as in Oregon and Washington.

The California Trail, or at least portions of it, were mapped before the Gold Rush by trappers and earlier settlers who were headed to Oregon. The first recorded party to use at least part of the trail to reach California was in 1841, and the first wagon crossing of the Sierras was in 1844. Traffic on the trail, however, reached new heights with the 49ers – as those in the first wave of the Gold Rush called themselves.

As the crow flies, the distance of the California Trail is a mere 1000 miles; however, if all the different branches are added up, the trail includes more than 5000 miles. Retracing its route takes you through 10 states and nearly half the country. Exploring it today gives a glimpse into one of the early chapters in the settling of the American West, before the arrival of the railroads and the Indian Wars that would be a dominant part of the later 19th century. That said, much of what would unfold on the Great Plains was foreshadowed in the fate of California's indigenous peoples.

Given the trail's length and its many different branches, hiking or even biking its entirety is impossible for most travelers. Even if you were interested in pulling off that feat, some 2000 miles of the trail are now on private land; securing permissions to visit all those stretches would be near impossible. Instead most people today drive its length – Auto Tour Route signs from the National Park Service mark the route – stopping along the way to explore some sections that are open to the public

on foot. Those can range from a historic site a few hundred feet from the road to others that require full days or even multiday hikes to explore.

The most obvious place to start is in Independence, Missouri, where many migrants assembled. The National Frontier Trails Museum there provides an overview of the California Trail and the westward migration more broadly. In Kansas City, at Minor Park, you can see swales where wagons gathered to cross the Blue River. Many sights along the way look largely as they did when the westward migrants made their trip, like the Shawnee Methodist Mission of 1839, a National Historic Landmark in Fairway, Kansas, and Chimney Rock, a geologic formation in western Nebraska.

The landscapes along the trail are expansive and dramatic, whether it is the big skies of the Great Plains or the peaks of the Rockies and the Sierras. Most stretches of the trail have one aspect in common, however – graves and memorials to those killed in raids, by cholera (a scourge of the migration, especially the 1852–60 third cholera pandemic along the Platte River) or by other hardships. The memories of those settlers live on thanks to these monuments, some grand and others humble, and the survival of the California Trail itself, though the memories of the Native American populations they displaced are harder to find. The trail largely became irrelevant after 1869; the opening of the transcontinental railroad cut the travel time from Omaha to California to seven days. Yet captured by the myth of the pre-railroad West wagon trains, thousands of Americans still retrace the route of those early pioneers each year.

Highlights

While the trail largely became irrelevant after 1869 and the opening of a transcontinental railroad, thousands of Americans still retrace the route of those early pioneers each year, drawn by its iconic Western vistas.

INDEPENDENCE
This starting point of the California Trail in Missouri has a number of sites related to the trail, as well as the Harry S Truman National Historic Site, the home of the 33rd president.

SCOTTS BLUFF NATIONAL MONUMENT
The 800ft-tall rock outcropping in Nebraska was a landmark for Plains Indians, and nearby Mitchell Pass became a symbolic gateway to the West for emigrants.

HORSE CREEK TREATY GROUNDS
Near Morrill, Nebraska, a roadside marker indicates where around 12,000 Plains Indians from 13 nations negotiated the Horse Creek Treaty of 1851, guaranteeing the safety of overland travelers.

SUTTER'S FORT
This 1841 fort in California was built by John Sutter of Sutter's Mill, where the first flecks of gold were found. Today it's a living history museum.

FORT LARAMIE
This fur trading outpost in Wyoming was purchased by the US Army in 1849 to protect emigrant trails. It became the most important federal presence on the Northern Plains.

Scotts Bluff National Monument.

Resources

01 California National Historic Trail
www.nps.gov/cali
The National Park Service's trail overview includes downloads of maps and detailed PDFs for some states, as well as links to national parks on or near the trail.

02 Oregon–California Trails Association
www.octa-trails.org
This independent nonprofit has an interactive map of both the Oregon and California Trails and a searchable database of documents (subscription required).

03 *Ken Burns Presents: The West*
The third and fourth episodes of this 1996 PBS TV series cover the California Gold Rush and the years when the California Trail was at its peak.

➜ Chimney Rock National Historic Site, western Nebraska. Left: David C Haddenham's cabin at Fossil Butte National Monument, built in 1918.

Hike this...

With over 5000 miles of trail to choose from across ten states, it can be hard to pick just one path. Make it a road trip and visit these attractions with your hiking boots in tow.

➔ Scenic wonders of Lassen Volcanic National Park in California.

01
Chimney Rock National Historic Site, Nebraska

This rock formation of alternating layers of clay, ash and sandstone rises 286ft above the Nebraska plains below. Because sections of the California, Mormon and Oregon Trails overlap – and Chimney Rock sits next to one such meeting point – it has become an icon of all three routes and of the westward migration generally. The rock served as a dramatic signpost for travelers on the trails.

This is a great starting point for a driving tour of the California National Historic Trail, but as befits a path that was blazed by wagons, the hiking opportunity here is more an opportunity to stretch your legs. Rattlesnakes in the area make it impossible to get too close to Chimney Rock itself, but the visitors center offers excellent vantage points as well as a short film about the overland migration and the area's geologic history. There is also a small cemetery with the graves of some pioneers who never reached California. Think too of the Oglala Sioux who preceded them.

02
Fossil Butte National Monument, Wyoming

History did not begin with the discovery of gold in California, of course. Get a glimpse of that prehistory where the trail passes by Fossil Butte National Monument. This sagebrush desert area in Wyoming was once, 50 million years ago, covered by a 900-sq-mile lake. After the lake dried up, the remains of the fish that lived there fossilized, creating one of the richest vertebrate fossil deposits in the world. The national monument itself occupies only some 13 sq miles of the former lake, but some of the best-preserved fossils have been found there and are displayed in the visitors center. The park has five trails, two maintained and three not. While the hikes are short, at under 4 miles each, they offer opportunities to travel back millennia. Trailside panels cover the area's geology, though no fossils are visible from the trails. The 2.5-mile Historic Quarry Trail loop might be the best option, though the mesas get hot in summer, while in winter, many park roads close from November to May.

03
Lassen Volcanic National Park, California

Nearly 1000 miles of the California Trail (counting all its different branches) are in California itself. Two routes, the Lassen Trail and the Nobles Trail, pass near Lassen Volcanic National Park, home of Lassen Peak, which rises to an elevation of 10457ft. It's the southernmost active volcano in the Cascades Range. The park has around 150 miles of trails with day or longer hikes of varying lengths and difficulty. Note, however, that many trails are covered in snow even into summer. If you visit in August or September, you'll have the best chance of finding most trails open. Keep your eyes open for the elusive Sierra Nevada red fox – this is one of only two places where they can be found. For a relatively easy out and back, the 6.8-mile Manzanita Creek passes through meadows. Hikers looking for a challenge can take on the 5-mile round-trip Lassen Peak Trail, starting at the trailhead from an elevation of 8500ft and climbing steeply to the summit, where the smell of sulfur lingers.

06

El Camino Real de los Tejas National Historic Trail

One of several royal roads in New Spain, this one ran through what is now the southern part of Texas. It remains a link to the history of Texas and Louisiana long before either state came into existence.

The historic San José mission in San Antonio, Texas. Right: The Lower Falls at McKinney Falls State Park in Austin, Texas.

As with some other historic trails in America, El Camino Real de los Tejas is not one route from point A to point B. Instead it was composed of many different paths used by traders, missionaries and settlers for some three centuries across shortcuts and detours. This road was, for a long time, a work in progress.

The Camino Real's origin is commonly dated from 1686 to 1690, when it was mapped by Alonso de León, the governor of the state of Coahuila, an area adjacent to Texas on the other side of the Rio Grande. Many trails that became the basis of this Camino Real (the words mean 'royal road'), however, had been followed by Native Americans for centuries before the arrival of the Spanish. The route established by de León, and modified by other explorers who followed in the 18th century, would eventually stretch from Mexico City, the capital of the viceroyalty of New Spain, to Natchitoches on the western side of the Mississippi River, in territory that was controlled by the French until the Louisiana Purchase in 1803.

For centuries this route was the spine of Spanish and later Mexican Texas. The road connected missions and ranchos as well as roadside towns, some of which, like San Antonio, would grow into major cities. As was the fate of many of America's historic trails, it was eventually superseded by other routes – alternative stagecoach trails, then the railroads and eventually highways. Today, Texas State Highway 21 and Highway 6 in Louisiana largely follow the main branch of the original road. Unlike the original Camino Real, the National Historic Trail that goes by the same name stops, for obvious political reasons, at the

Sleep here...

The so-called King's Highway threads its way from the Rio Grande at the Mexico border, across East Texas, to reach Natchitoches and the Mississippi River. Along the way, it passes through some of the most important early Texan settlements, several of which still boast digs that retain their 19th-century character.

🏠 La Posada Hotel, Laredo
The historic hotel on the banks of the Rio Grande in Laredo has views into Mexico and incorporates portions of an 18th-century hacienda and a 19th-century convent.

🏠 Landmark Inn, Castroville
You can spend the night at a historic site when you check into this hotel in Castroville, Texas. Dating to 1849, it was established as a roadside tavern serving travelers en route to San Antonio.

🏠 Bastrop State Park, Bastrop
These 14 cabins in Bastrop, Texas, were built by the Civilian Conservation Corps and became a model for other CCC projects, helping earn the park its status as a National Historic Landmark.

🏠 Hotel Emma, San Antonio
The 19th-century Pearl Brewery, just north of downtown San Antonio, has been reborn as a culinary and cultural destination, complete with its own 146-room hotel.

© Oleg Kovtun Hydrobio / Shutterstock / Shutterstock; © Tricia Daniel / Shutterstock

Toolbox

📅 When to go
You might want to avoid the height of summer, when South Texas gets hot and humid. In almost every other season of the year, you can expect temperatures ideal for exploring the state.

🧭 Getting there
Laredo, Texas, has a large airport, though there are more options if you check out Corpus Christi and San Antonio, both under three hours from Laredo. The closest large airports to Natchitoches, Louisiana, are Alexandria and Shreveport, both about an hour away.

🎒 Practicalities
Length in miles: 2500
Start: Laredo, TX
End: Natchitoches, LA
Dog friendly: Yes; portions
Bike friendly: Yes; portions
Permit needed: Some campgrounds; also, unless clearly marked, some of the historical route crosses private land, and requires permission from the owner
States covered: Texas, Louisiana

→ The Rio Grande, dividing line between the USA and Mexico.

US–Mexico border. The main route ends, or begins, at Laredo, though other branches stop at the border in nearby Maverick and Zapata counties. Travelers today are unlikely to travel the entire route on foot or even by bike, much less stagecoach. You'd need to have accumulated many vacation days to make the full 2500-mile journey. Since the road runs parallel to two highways, it is a popular driving option, and a trip along it passes through different regions of Texas. The early Spanish history of the Lone Star State comes to life on a journey along the old Camino Real.

Traveling west to east, the Camino Real starts in Laredo, a South Texas city founded in 1755 by Spaniard Don Tomás Sánchez. This is the portion of the state with the deepest ties to Mexico, which is just on the other side of the Rio Grande. Off and on, the states of Texas and Coahuila were united, though their separation in 1835 would become permanent once Texas became its own country and was later incorporated into the US. San Agustin de Loredo Historic District is filled with buildings from the Spanish and Mexican periods, as well as later structures often built in Colonial and Mission Revival styles. Even more than other Texas border towns, Laredo has always been tightly entwined with its sister city to the south, Nuevo Laredo, and time spent here makes the Spanish past of the state feel more vivid.

There is no formal auto trail route to take east, but historic markers indicate local tour routes as well as the original route. The San Antonio–Goliad region is dominated by those two cities, and it has some of the most impressive reminders of the days of Spanish and Mexican rule. Haciendas, missions and presidios dot the landscape here. Five 18th-century missions in San Antonio, including the famous Alamo, have been recognized as a Unesco World Heritage Site. The presidio in Goliad, now a National Historic Landmark, was also built in the 18th century, and its chapel is one of the oldest continuously used churches in the US.

Texas' capital, Austin, sits in the Brazos region near one of the road's branches, though it was founded in 1837 (and incorporated in 1839), late in the period when the Camino Real was actively used. As in the region to its west, this area has a number of historic Spanish missions: Nuestra Señora de la Candelaria, San Ildefonso and San Francisco Xavier de Horcasitas are among them. You may also want to include some natural landmarks on your itinerary, like McKinney Falls State Park in Austin. The Homestead Trail takes in the remains of Thomas F McKinney's 1850 homestead, one of the early settlers and traders on the Camino Real de los Tejas who pushed for Texan independence from Mexico.

The trail's final stretch brings travelers to Natchitoches in modern-day Louisiana. This area was once part of New Spain, and Los Adaes, now a state historic site, was the site of the first capital of Texas. After the territory was ceded to France, the residents relocated to San Antonio, the new capital of Texas. No original buildings remain at Los Adaes, but you can visit the site of the old presidio. This stretch of the trail also has sites associated with a civilization that flourished long before – the Caddo Indians. Leave some time at the end of your journey to enjoy Natchitoches as well as Nacogdoches in Texas, both historic and atmospheric towns.

Highlights

In a relatively young country, many of the best sights along the Camino Real de los Tejas date from before the USA even existed, whether from the Spanish era or the Mound Builder culture of the Caddo Indians.

TREVIÑO–URIBE RANCHO
The fortified house in San Ygnacio, Texas, at the western end of one branch of the trail was built in the 1830s and provides a glimpse of life in Mexican Texas.

SAN ANTONIO MISSIONS NATIONAL HISTORICAL PARK
These four Texas missions from the 1700s are still active. An ideal way to explore them is by the hiking and biking trail that connects the missions with the Alamo.

PRESIDIO NUESTRA SEÑORA DE LORETO DE LA BAHÍA
Construction on the presidio in Goliad, Texas, began in 1749, but the landmark has been restored to its appearance in 1836, the year of the Texas Rebellion.

MCKINNEY FALLS STATE PARK
Many visitors to this park in Austin come for the 13 miles of trails and the namesake falls. It also includes a portion of the Camino Real and an 1850 homestead.

CADDO MOUNDS STATE HISTORIC SITE
The three mounds in Alto, Texas, part of the Caddo Indians Mound Builder culture, were constructed about 1200 years ago; the site sustained tornado damage in 2019.

07

El Camino Real de Tierra Adentro National Historic Trail

America's oldest trade route swings past missions, mountains, pueblos and hot springs on a 404-mile journey along the Rio Grande through Texas and New Mexico.

The Organ Mountains in southern New Mexico near Las Cruces, New Mexico. Right: Claret cup cactus in bloom, Hueco Tanks State Park and Historic Site, Chihuahuan Desert, near El Paso, Texas.

As you trudge up the scrubby Point of Rocks Trail, sweaty from the heat and huffing from exertion, curiosity builds about the view from the summit ahead. The rocky overlook surveys the Jornada del Muerto, a 90-mile expanse of desert once feared by travelers on El Camino Real de Tierra Adentro.

Loosely translated as the 'Dead Man's Journey,' the desert's evocative name dates to 1680, when a band of Spanish traders discovered human remains along the route. They believed the bones were the remains of Bernardo Gruber, a German trader on the run from Spanish Inquisitors, who had accused him of witchcraft. The poor fellow escaped the Inquisition, it seems, only to lose his life along a stretch of wretched terrain far from his homeland. Its bareness hits home when you reach the summit and see what lies to the north: a vast scab of desert scrub and red-baked sand reaching to the horizon. No shade. No river. Little hope.

El Camino Real de Tierra Adentro (Royal Road of the Interior, in English) was a trade, communication and settlement route linking Mexico City in the south with trading hubs in El Nuevo Mexico, known today as New Mexico. The road stretched more than 1600 miles, bordering the Rio Grande for much of its journey. Spanish explorers built out the route in the 1500s, traveling on ancient footpaths used by the region's native people.

Spanish nobleman and explorer Juan de Oñate established the full length of the trail in 1598 when he ventured north with a 2-mile-long caravan of wagons, livestock and colonists. The trail originally ended at Ohkay Owingeh Pueblo, 30 miles northwest of Santa Fe. Today what is now a shorter National Historic Trail links El Paso,

Sleep here...

Merchants, soldiers, missionaries and immigrants usually covered about 20 miles a day, spending each night in a paraje (inn or campsite). Today's lodging offerings have quite a few more amenities than those in 1600, but many retain a distinctly Southwestern feel that goes back to the world of the Tierra Adentro, the Spanish Colonial version of an interstate highway.

 Aguirre Spring Campground, Las Cruces
Flanked by the jagged Organ Mountains, this popular Las Cruces campground has expansive views of the Tularosa Basin. The 55 sites are first come, first served.

 Hotel Chaco, Albuquerque
Rooms blend contemporary amenities with traditional and modern Native American motifs and soothing earth-colored tones. This Albuquerque hotel is inspired by the Ancestral Puebloan site of Chaco Canyon in northwestern New Mexico.

 **Riverbend Hot Springs, Truth or Consequences**
Spring-fed hot tubs with their own decks overlook the Rio Grande at this small resort and spa in Truth or Consequences, New Mexico. Local artists decorated the rooms.

 La Fonda, Santa Fe
Santa Fe's loveliest historic hotel sprawls through a Pueblo Revival–style building just off the famous Plaza. Retaining its beautiful folk-art windows and murals, it's both classy and cozy.

Toolbox

 When to go
Expect gorgeous weather and loads of fiestas in late summer and early fall. The Festival of the Cranes is on the Rio Grande in November, and Santa Fe hosts the Spanish Market in July and the Santa Fe Indian Market in August, two major arts and crafts events.

Getting there
El Paso sits beside I-10 in west Texas, 12 miles south of the New Mexico border. Fly into El Paso International Airport or fly into Albuquerque International Sunport, New Mexico, located at the junction of I-40 and I-25.

 Practicalities
Length in miles: 404
Start: El Paso, TX
End: Santa Fe, NM
Dog friendly: Varies by location
Bike friendly: Limited sections; the Santa Fe greenway connector is best
Permit needed: Generally no, but some of the trail runs on private or reservation land and requires permission to traverse.
States covered: Texas, New Mexico

Texas, with Santa Fe, New Mexico; the latter became the Spanish regional capital in 1610.

Although few traces of the original trail remain, the missions, pueblos and museums along its route provide historical and cultural background. These sites reveal the intriguing blend of Native American, Spanish and American culture still evident along this corridor today. El Camino is easily explored by car, but hiking trails along the way give a sense of the features and terrain that travelers in the past encountered.

The trail kicks off in El Paso, which is as far west as you can get in the Lone Star State. This once-sleepy city thrums with trendy boutique hotels, a young-but-thriving brewery scene and a vibrant arts culture. The city retains strong ties to its past, however, and the roots of its culturally mixed heritage can be seen at the Ysleta and Socorro missions. Located near the Rio Grande, the two congregations are the oldest in Texas, established by Spanish refugees and Pueblo Indians fleeing here after the Pueblo Revolt in 1680.

The drive on I-10 and I-25 from El Paso to Las Cruces, New Mexico, has few challenges, but El Camino in its heyday served up a host of obstacles for wagons and livestock. In Las Cruces you'll find hints of the hardships at the New Mexico Farm & Ranch Heritage Museum, which explores 4000 years of regional farming. The frisky horses, ornery cattle and skittish sheep here look particularly unsuited for long-distance caravanning! Almost 30 miles north of Las Cruces, the Rio Grande bends west. From here, caravans would leave the river – before a challenging stretch of riverside terrain – to shoot straight north across the level Jornada del Muerto. To follow their journey, leave I-25 at exit

32 to find the Point of Rocks and Yost Escarpment trailheads, where you'll find interpretive signage and desert scenery that vividly evokes the past.

About 4 miles north of the Yost Escarpment, County Rd A039 doubles as the entrance to Spaceport America, where a 2.7-mile paved 'spaceway' runs parallel to El Camino. The spaceport was planned as the starting point for long-distance journeys of the future, hurling civilian astronauts into the heavens to points beyond. Though the property is open only by guided tour, you can drive to the eye-catching *Genesis* sculpture, an arc-shaped landmark studded with glass that sparkles under the moonlight.

Today descendants of the region's Ancestral Puebloans occupy 19 distinct reservations and pueblos in north central New Mexico. Acoma Pueblo is home to a mesa-top village known as Sky City, one of the longest-inhabited communities in North America. Touring the village with an Acoma Puebloan guide is a gripping way to hear a less frequently shared perspective about El Camino's history. While it's easy to envision caravans of settlers on the Royal Road, or the construction of adobe missions, it may be harder to grasp the full impact of the colonizers' oppression of early Native Americans – until you hear the stories firsthand.

The trail received a 14.7-mile extension in 2018 with the opening of a hiking-and-biking connector to the Santa Fe River Greenway southwest of downtown. But Santa Fe Plaza, the commercial and cultural heart of the city, remains the trail's dazzling end point, sitting under crisp blue skies at the base of the Santa de Cristo Mountains.

Highlights

From missions and pueblos to the Rio Grande Valley, from the bubbling hot springs of funky Truth or Consequences to the bone-dry desert, this royal road hosted trade and cultural exchange. Time has wrought some changes, but preserved much.

EL PASO MISSION TRAIL
This 9-mile trail links two mission churches and a presidio chapel. Of the three sites, the best known is Ysleta Mission, the oldest continually active parish in Texas.

SPACEPORT AMERICA
This spaceship hangar and runway near Truth or Consequences, New Mexico, is readying for commercial space launches by Virgin Galactic. Facility tours are available.

WHITE SANDS NATIONAL MONUMENT
Ethereal white dunes undulate across the Tularosa Basin between Las Cruces and Alamogordo in New Mexico. Come here for dune sledding and the sunsets.

INDIAN PUEBLO CULTURAL CENTER, ALBUQUERQUE
Run by New Mexico's 19 pueblos, this cultural center has fascinating displays on the Pueblo Indians' collective history.

PALACE OF THE GOVERNORS AND NEW MEXICO HISTORY MUSEUM
Bordering the Santa Fe Plaza, a sprawling adobe complex holds the centuries-old Palace of the Governors and a well-curated history museum.

Resources

O1 El Camino Real de Tierra Adentro National Historical Trail
www.nps.gov/elca
The NPS website on the trail provides current information about the route with history summaries and an interactive map.

O2 New Mexico Office of the State Historian
dev.newmexicohistory.org
The state history website summarizes the history of El Camino Real de Tierra Adentro.

O3 Bosque del Apache National Wildlife Refuge
www.fws.gov/refuge/ bosque_del_apache
A federal agency manages the refuge, and the website gives details about its trails.

O4 Santa Fe Tourism
www.santafe.org
Everything you need to know about visiting the city is on its official site.

O5 *Following the Royal Road: A Guide to the Historic Camino Real de Tierra Adentro*
Hal Jackson's book includes eyewitness narratives about the trail.

Sunset over the snow-capped peak of Santa Fe Baldy in the Sangre de Cristo Mountains near Santa Fe. Previous page: The historic San Elizario Presidio Chapel in El Paso.

Hike this...

Colonial New Mexico's only link to the rest of New Spain, once the longest road in North America, wends through beautiful territory from start to finish.

➡ *La Puerta del Sol* sculpture, Tomé Hill Park on El Camino Real de Tierra Adentro.

01
Jornada del Muerto Trails

Hundreds perished while crossing this 90-mile waterless expanse of desert stretching between Las Cruces and Socorro. So why did travelers continue to take this desert route and not follow the Rio Grande? North of Las Cruces, the river bends west. By cutting north here, across the desert, caravans saved days of travel. The level terrain was also easier for wagons and livestock, despite the lack of forage or water. Yet approached carelessly, the shortcut was deadly.

Today visitors can get a taste of the scenery via the safety of the 0.5-mile Point of Rocks Trail, a loop that climbs to the summit of a rocky hill with expansive desert views, a landmark that marked the last 10 miles before reaching water again. The scrubby 3-mile round-trip Yost Escarpment Trail leads to a section of the actual El Camino Real, ending atop a steep hill known as an escarpment – a tough climb for cargo-bearing wagons. Both trailheads are on Sierra County Rd A013.

02
Bosque del Apache National Wildlife Refuge

Bird-watchers and aspiring photographers, cut your engines. A 14-mile scenic drive loops through this wildlife refuge south of Albuquerque, but you'll want to experience the magic of the forested wetlands here by foot. Or you can sit quietly in one of the many viewing decks – prime vantage points for observing the migrating birds that roost at this 57,000-acre oasis by the Rio Grande on their annual migrations.

It's estimated that more than 100,000 sandhill cranes, snow geese and ducks stop by in winter. In the days of the Camino Real de Tierra Adentro, caravans leaving the nearby Jornada del Muerto would immediately beeline for the river to quench their thirst and replenish their water supplies. The Point of Lands Overlook takes in the Rio Grande, the refuge, the Jornada and Black Mesa. Short trails lead to boardwalks, observation decks, wetlands, cottonwood forests and a desert garden. To hike in the Chihuahuan Desert, take the 2.2-mile Canyon NRT.

03
Albuquerque Trails

Tucked between the Rio Grande and the Sandia Mountains, Albuquerque still feels wild. At sunset you might even hear the howl of a coyote in the distance. Cyclists, joggers and pedestrians can scan for turtles and roadrunners along the 16-mile Paseo del Bosque, a multiuse trail that runs through a cottonwood forest beside the Rio Grande. Hit the side trails for extra exploring. West of the river, short hikes lead to ancient rock carvings at Petroglyph National Monument. Bird's-eye views of the city await as you ascend the Sandia Mountains on trails in the Elena Gallegos Open Space. For another way into the Sandias, mix up the thrills (and get spectacular views) by riding the Sandia Peak Tramway to the summit of the 10,378ft Sandia Crest. Descend by foot on the 8-mile La Luz Trail. If you plan on hiking down (or up), a one-way ticket costs $15. Hikes throughout the area during October's International Balloon Fiesta have the added benefit of views of the craft.

08

Captain John Smith Chesapeake National Historic Trail

→ Great Blue Heron catching a fish on a Chesapeake Bay beach at sunset; Right: Maryland's Thomas Point Shoal Light in the Chesapeake Bay.

The English explorer John Smith was the first European to explore and map the Chesapeake Bay. This water-based trail incorporates the many rivers and creeks that pour into the vast watershed, making it the only National Historic Trail best explored by boat.

The Chesapeake Bay estuary is the crown jewel of the mid-Atlantic region, and Native American occupants as well as Colonial settlers appreciated it accordingly. Mapping the bay, an area of almost 4500 sq miles, was a tremendous undertaking, one that makes up the other half of Captain John Smith's notoriety. Today Smith is best known for the embellished, often-changing tale of Pocahontas persuading her father, Chief Powhatan, to free Smith after he was captured by Powhatan. However, the captain's exploration of Chesapeake Bay on an expedition that was the first to map the area is just as significant. His charts would be used by other sailors for some 70 years. As Smith also plotted the locations of Native American settlements, the charts remain an invaluable historical resource to this day. It is this period of Smith's life, the summer of 1608, that inspired the National Historic Trail, established in 2009.

Unlike many historic trails, this one doesn't really have start and end points; instead it consists of different branches that extend into all the rivers and estuaries that drain into the Chesapeake Bay, as well as a route along the length of the bay itself. The start and end points given here as Cooperstown and Suffolk are more accurately simply the northernmost and southernmost points on the trail. Are you wondering how the trail extends all the way up to Cooperstown? That is where the Susquehanna River begins, making its way south through New York and Pennsylvania before finally draining into Chesapeake Bay.

The other distinction of this trail is that it consists primarily of water routes. While you can visit many of the key locations by driving to them, to experience the region

Sleep here...

The Chesapeake communities of Virginia and Maryland offer their own pace. Its friendly villages are often working waterfront communities that still survive off the bay and its tributaries, and boating, fishing and crabbing are integral to local life. Although increasingly destinations for daytrippers and gentrifiers as well, they still offer a watery escape for visiting kayakers, birders and armchair historians.

 Susquehanna State Park, Maryland

At the northern end of Chesapeake Bay, this Maryland state park on the Susquehanna River has 69 campsites as well as some 18th- and 19th-century historic sites.

 The Inn at Brome Howard, Maryland

The 1840s inn is on the grounds of St Mary's City, a National Historic Landmark and living history museum focused on life in 17th-century Maryland.

 Janes Island State Park, Maryland

This state park in Crisfield on Maryland's Eastern Shore, just north of the Maryland–Virginia border, offers full-service cabins by the water as well as campsites.

Hotel Cape Charles, Virginia

The charming historic district of Cape Charles, Virginia, is of much later date than Smith's era: most buildings date from the late 19th and early 20th centuries. This hotel is a good base for exploring the town.

Toolbox

 When to go

April to October are the best months. Some campsites and other businesses are only open seasonally, and if you are going to explore the region as Smith did, kayaking and canoeing are simply more pleasant when the temperatures are warmer.

Getting there

While technically this trail extends as far north as Cooperstown, New York, most of its trails and historic and other sites are on or near the Chesapeake Bay. Airports in Washington, DC (Dulles and Reagan National) and Baltimore (BWI) are the most convenient starting points.

Practicalities

Length in miles: 3000
Start: Cooperstown, NY
End: Suffolk, VA
Dog friendly: Some sites
Bike friendly: Some sites
Permit needed: Some campgrounds
States covered: DC, DE, MD, NY, PA, VA

Sunset at Columbia, Pennsylvania, overlooking the Susquehanna River.

as Captain John Smith did, you need to get out on the water. At a minimum, that means taking ferries or scenic day cruises on the National Historic Trail's waterways. If you are really serious, rent a boat (if you don't have your own) for a multiday exploration of the bay and the water trails that lead to it.

There are myriad options when it comes to exploring the trail, though whichever ones you choose, the Zimmerman Center for Heritage in Wrightsville, Pennsylvania, is a good starting point. It stands at the spot of the last known settlement of the Susquehannock Indians, which consisted of a stockade protecting 16 or so longhouses, each housing 50 people. While the buildings no longer stand, the center gives an overview of the Susquehannock tribe and the central role that the river played in their lives and those of other Native Americans in the Chesapeake Bay region. The mile-long heritage trail that runs through the adjacent Native Lands Park fits a lot of history into a small space. It introduces not only the Susquehannock people but the Seneca and Shenks Ferry people as well.

If you are exploring the trail by car, among the places you may want to include on your itinerary is Virginia's First Landing State Park, where the earliest Jamestown settlers first set foot on North American in 1607. The park's 19 miles of trails through cypress swamp, maritime forest and dunes offer a glimpse of how this part of America would have looked four centuries ago. Historic Jamestowne, also in Virginia, has unearthed some of the original James Fort, where Smith would have planned his exploration of Chesapeake Bay. Ask one of the docents here to share the real

story – not the Disney version – of the relationship between John Smith and Pocahontas, daughter of Tsenacommacah chief Powhatan.

If you are seeing the region by boat, whether that is a canoe, kayak or motorboat, the James River is the southernmost of the waterways that are part of the trail. Running for 110 miles from Virginia's capital, Richmond, to the bay, the river passes key sites including Jamestown as you paddle its length. The 355-mile-long Potomac Heritage Trail is equally historic, going through Washington, DC, and then to Alexandria, Virginia. You'll paddle by Fort Washington, which long defended the nation's capital, and Point Lookout, infamous as a prison camp for 52,264 Confederate soldiers. The trail includes smaller waterways too, such as the 20-mile Sassafras River Water Trail on Maryland's Eastern Shore. Dramatic cliffs line both sides of the river here, and bald eagles can often be spotted overhead. Note that this is a popular destination among weekend boaters, so if you schedule your visit on a weekday, you'll find fewer people. Whenever you go, the creeks off the river offer quiet serenity.

The Captain John Smith Chesapeake National Historic Trail is more like a buffet than a set menu. It is what you make of it, and the routes you choose will vary depending on your interests. Birders will likely pick different water trails than history buffs. Some sections are better suited to motorboats, while others are better for kayakers. Before you get too far in planning your trip, also check out the Star-Spangled Banner National Historic Trail (p278). While that trail's focus is the later War of 1812, much of it overlaps geographically.

Highlights

This trail may be historic in nature, and includes the home of the first permanent English settlement in North America, but most of all, it's a way to appreciate the Chesapeake estuary's unbroken miles of bird-dotted wetlands and serene waterscapes.

CHESTER RIVER WATER TRAIL
This 50-mile water trail in Maryland begins in wooded hills and makes its way down to farmlands and tidal inlets. It makes for a peaceful day of kayaking.

BLACKWATER NATIONAL WILDLIFE REFUGE
Mostly tidal marsh near Cambridge, Maryland, the refuge is home to a rotating cast of migratory birds, viewable from 20 miles of water trails.

POWHATAN CREEK BLUEWAY
Paddle along this 23-mile creek, a tributary of the James River in Virginia, and you will be following the waterways that composed the territory of Tsenacommacah.

STRATFORD HALL PLANTATION
This stately home on the Potomac in Stratford, Virginia, was home to two signers of the Declaration of Independence and the birthplace of Confederate leader Robert E Lee.

ELIZABETH HARTWELL MASON NECK NATIONAL WILDLIFE REFUGE
A birding favorite, this 2276-acre refuge near Lorton, Virginia, includes trails along the shoreline and marshes.

09
Chilkoot Trail

Follow in the footsteps of thousands of Gold Rush 'stampeders,' who traversed this steep and wild 33-mile trail in Alaska and Canada for the promise of wealth at the end.

→ Historic St Andrews Church on Lake Bennett at the end of the Chilkoot Trail.

The Chilkoot Trail is one of the most popular and storied trails in Alaska. During the Klondike Gold Rush that began in 1896, miners trekked this route in a winding, single-file line up and then down Chilkoot Pass to reach the Yukon goldfields in Canada. Long before the days of recreational hiking made this route attractive, prospectors streamed up its snowy path. Bent over with the weight of their tools and provisions, the stampeders, as they were called, faced disease, exhaustion and frostbite.

The trail was first used as a trade route by the Tlingit, an Alaska Native group. Chilkoot Pass was one of only three paths in what is now Southeast Alaska that could be traversed year-round, so it was a valuable resource. In the late 1800s, expeditions hired local Alaska native people to carry gear; but when the Gold Rush hit, the locals were effectively shoved out. Tramlines were built to shuttle goods up Chilkoot Pass, which was steep, rocky and slippery – quite rough for humans carrying loads. Stampeders short of funds might work as packers to earn money, carrying supplies over terrain that was too steep for pack animals. The trail was so crowded that on April 3, 1898, an avalanche between Sheep Camp and the Scales at the base of the so-called 'golden staircase' before the Pass killed at least 63 people. The Palm Sunday Avalanche would be the deadliest event of the Klondike Gold Rush.

The trail starts in Dyea, 10 miles out of Skagway, Alaska. This quiet, wooded spot was once a bustling Gold Rush hub. At one point the town had thousands of residents, but once the railroad was completed to Skagway, making the Chilkoot Pass unnecessary, Dyea was abandoned. At

Sleep here...

Accommodations in Skagway make much of the town's Gold Rush history, as well as its access to natural attractions. It's the National Park campgrounds on and off the Chilkoot Trail that are the real stars. Reserve in advance for the Chilkoot Trail, and show up at the Dyea Campground near the trailhead first come, first served. Off season (Labor Day to Memorial Day), there are no fees, but fewer facilities.

Chilkoot Trail Campgrounds
There are nine backcountry campgrounds along the trail itself, several with warming huts, tent platforms and outhouses. Your Chilkoot Trail reservation will include selecting your campgrounds as part of the permit process. You can also camp at the trailhead in Dyea and the trail's end in Bennett.

Sheep Camp
The last campground before Chilkoot Pass, Sheep Camp has a ranger station and several hiker huts for comfortable shelter. It's the most popular campground on the trail.

Chilkoot Trail Outpost
Across the road from a National Park campground and half a mile from the head of the Chilkoot Trail, the cabins at Dyea's Chilkoot Trail Outpost were crafted out of local Sitka spruce and are a great spot to rest up and enjoy some s'mores before taking the pass.

Skagway Inn Bed and Breakfast
Built in 1897, the Skagway Inn has been a brothel and boardinghouse over its lifetime, with the turn-of-the-century decor to prove it. The Inn is located directly in the Klondike Gold Rush National Historic District.

Toolbox

When to go
June, July and August are the best times of year to hike the trail, though you'll need a permit during these months. If you go any earlier or later, you risk snow and freezing temperatures.

Getting there
The trail starts 10 miles outside of Skagway, Alaska, at the abandoned townsite of Dyea off the Klondike Hwy; Skagway is the southernmost point of the Klondike Hwy. At the trail's end you can take the train back into Skagway from Bennett in British Columbia. Many arrive in Skagway on cruises, and it is also the most northern stop of the Alaska Marine Highway. If flying, there are regularly scheduled flights on bush planes from Juneau International Airport.

Practicalities
Length in miles: 33
Start: Dyea, AK, US
End: Bennett, BC, Canada
Dog friendly: Yes
Bike friendly: No
Permit needed: Yes
States covered: Alaska, British Columbia (Canada)

➡ Montana Peak rises up from Lake Bennett, Carcross, Yukon Territory. Right: Alpine flowers on the Chilkoot Trail.

the same time, the Gold Rush ended, having lasted only a few years. Today the only evidence that Dyea existed, let alone boomed, is some Ozymandias-like crumbled pier pilings and a few gravesites in the quiet woods. The road that links Skagway and Dyea wasn't created until the 1940s, so the abandoned boomtown didn't see visitors again until then. Today the old townsite and the trail are part of the Klondike Gold Rush National Historical Park, headquartered in Skagway.

On the Canadian side, the trail ends in Bennett, British Columbia. Bennett was the end of the line when the White Pass & Yukon Railroad opened, but the line eventually continued to Carcross in the Yukon Territory. Today only the bright-red rail depot and a refurbished Presbyterian church remain at Bennett, and you can hop on the train here back to Skagway.

After 1899, the Chilkoot Trail was mostly forgotten and overgrown; the buildings along it were dismantled and used for other purposes. The modern hiking trail wasn't completed until 1968, nearly 10 years after Alaska became a state. Today it is considered a living museum, with remnants of its Gold Rush past scattered alongside the trail.

The hike begins close to sea level in a coastal rainforest, staying mostly flat for the first 8 miles. On a sunny day, light dapples the mossy ground in this section, and the Taiya River rushes alongside you as it hurries back to Dyea. At Canyon City the trail starts to climb. Many hikers spend their first night here. Canyon City, a tent settlement that grew where stampeders crossed the river, is now an official tent site for hikers with a free log cabin for cooking.

Another 5 miles of hiking gets you to Sheep Camp, the last campsite on the US side of the trail. Hundreds of Gold Rush stampeders would camp here on any given night, as it was also the last place for firewood until the trail descends back into the forest. Today it's home to a backcountry ranger station, complete with a ranger who'll prep you for the big climb ahead of you.

After Sheep Camp comes Chilkoot Pass itself. Steep and rugged, the trail climbs the stampeder's 'golden staircase' of 1500 steps carved into the wintry snow and ice, gaining 1000ft in the last half mile. Hiking will be easier if there's still some snow on the ground; otherwise it's a rocky balancing act. A tidy shelter cabin greets you at the summit of the pass, where you can rest your legs and refuel for the downhill grind. Thankfully, that lasts only about a half mile, and the rest of the hike is relatively gentle. Descend past several alpine lakes resting in rocky bowls to Happy Camp at mile 20.5, or head on further to Deep Lake at mile 23. Both spots have tent platforms. The trail continues down another 10 miles, passing Lindeman City. Here stampeders often sailed up Lindeman Lake to Bennett, but you'll need to skirt the lake on foot.

Once in Bennett, you can ride the railroad that essentially killed the Chilkoot Trail for decades. The railroad was built over the White Pass Trail instead of the Chilkoot Trail, and its portside destination of Skagway thus became the Gold Rush's favored seaside boomtown.

You'll need a permit to hike the trail; reservations usually open in November for the following summer. Only 50 hikers per day are permitted. Don't forget your passport, as you'll be crossing the border into Canada (and crossing back to the US on the White Pass & Yukon Route Railway).

Highlights

Sometimes known as the 'Last Great Adventure' or the 'Meanest 33 Miles in America,' the Chilkoot Trail is an unforgettable way to get in touch with Gold Rush history on the path to the Klondike.

GOLD RUSH ARTIFACTS
A steam boiler, an old cookstove and a gas engine winch are some of the larger artifacts left along the trail. Smaller pieces are scattered throughout.

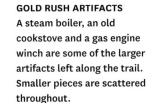

DYEA
Once a bustling boomtown, Dyea is now a ghost town. Search for the townsite's remains scattered in the overgrowth and pay your respects at the graves of miners.

WHITE PASS & YUKON ROUTE RAILWAY
Built to provide faster and easier access to the Yukon goldfields, the railroad now offers an incredibly scenic journey and a comfortable post-hike commute to Skagway.

CHILKOOT PASS
The highlight of the trail has a summit shelter and stunning views. Imagine climbing it in winter with gold-mining gear on your back.

CANVAS BOATS
Near Chilkoot Pass are nearly 50 abandoned canvas boats. Their origins are unknown, but they've been there for over a century.

10

Chesapeake & Ohio (C&O) Canal National Historical Park

This former commercial transport route is now a beloved, beautiful recreational area for cyclists, walkers and hikers that also has educational stopovers for history lovers.

➡ The C&O Canal walking trail makes its way through the Georgetown neighborhood of Washington, DC. Right: A hiker on the Billy Goat Trail.

In its day, the Chesapeake & Ohio Canal was both an engineering marvel and a commercial disaster. Today, it's one of the nicest national parks in the mid-Atlantic. Visitors to the 184.5 miles of preserved, accessible nature along the winding Potomac River have a Supreme Court justice to thank for its existence. In 1954 the US government was poised to turn the defunct C&O Canal into an extension of the George Washington Memorial Parkway. But Justice William O Douglas was determined to protect the region's historic elements, natural beauty and abundant wildlife, and he believed that anyone who had experienced the canal towpath would feel the same. Douglas organized an eight-day hike that included *Washington Post* reporters; their experience swayed reporting on the issue and hence public opinion.

Today the nearly five million annual visitors to the Chesapeake & Ohio Canal National Historical Park can discover the 'strange islands and promontories through the fantasy of fog...discover the glory there is in the first flower of spring, the glory there is even in a blade of grass,' as Douglas described in his ode to the towpath's natural wonders.

Completed in 1850, the C&O Canal was cut alongside the Potomac River to transport coal, limestone and other goods from the Allegheny Mountains to the port of Georgetown, now an upscale neighborhood of Washington, DC. It was built mainly by indentured laborers, working in tough conditions, over more than 20 years. Meant as a competitor to the Erie Canal, the rail system slowly stole away business in the early 20th century, and devastating floods resulted in damage the canal couldn't recover from. Today the canal itself has mainly been drained and

Sleep here...

Quite unlike a backpacking trail or excursion into the wilderness, the C&O towpath cuts through not just the densely populated capital but also through small communities. Those hiking or biking along the canal can drop in at free campsites, and drive-in sites are available along the way, along with unique historic lockhouses and inns.

C&O Canal Campsites
Dozens of primitive hike/bike campsites are available about every 5 miles along the C&O towpath. All are first come, first served and have water pumps, grills and picnic tables. Drive-in campsites require reservations and have more amenities – showers, RV hookups and even pools or horse/bike rental services.

Three Otters Eco Retreat Center
Just across the Potomac from the C&O Canal National Historical Park, this eco retreat center near Berkeley Springs, West Virginia, offers charming riverfront accommodations from April to October. Book and get unplugged (there's no wi-fi).

Bavarian Inn
A luxury resort in West Virginia's oldest town, quaint, artsy Shepherdstown, the European-style Bavarian Inn has plenty of amenities for visitors, including an on-site brewpub, a beer garden and an infinity pool.

Canal Quarters
Six former lockhouses, the Canal Quarters, are available for rent along the towpath. These historic buildings, once home to the lockkeepers who oversaw stretches of the canal, can each sleep groups of up to eight. Reserve well in advance.

Toolbox

When to go
Although the towpath trail is open year-round, spring, summer and fall are the best times to explore the C&O Canal. Some trails are inaccessible in winter, and many campsites and regional accommodations close from November to March.

Getting there
The C&O Canal runs through three states and passes through several small towns, but Washington, DC, is the most natural access point. The US capital is home to two major airports and is easily accessible by bus and train from Philadelphia and New York City.

Practicalities
Length in miles: 184.5
Start: Washington, DC (Georgetown neighborhood)
End: Cumberland, MD
Dog friendly: Yes, on 6ft or shorter leash
Bike friendly: Yes
Permit needed: For special events only; reservations required for drive-in campsites. Entrance fee at Great Falls Tavern Visitor Center; all other access points are free.
States covered: DC, VA, MD, WV

Key Bridge in Washington, DC, over the Potomac River.

is now overgrown, but the towpath, which ran alongside the canal and was used by mules, vehicles or even people to pull boats upstream, has been renovated for pleasure-seekers. Downstream was an easy float, while upstream required poles and mules.

Largely flat and well-maintained by volunteers, the dirt towpath attracts walkers and cyclists who enjoy its tree-shaded length and occasional views of the winding Potomac. The surrounding bluffs and forests are flush with wildlife – you may even be able to spot a bald eagle – and full of well-marked trails that cater to hikers of all abilities. Campsites dot the trail at regular intervals, as do historic small towns that grew up alongside the canal. A few of the canal's 74 locks are still in operation, and many of the homes of the former lockkeepers are still there as well: six of them are available as vacation rentals through the National Park Service.

The C&O Canal crosses through Virginia, Maryland and West Virginia, and the best way to see the entire length is by bike. For those who don't have time for a nearly 200-mile trek, it's easy to dip in and out of the canal towpath for a less expansive adventure. You can park at one of the seven visitors centers for an afternoon hike or pick a section for a day or overnight cycle tour; exercise caution during the summer's hottest days. Wherever your journey on the C&O Canal takes you, don't forget that the towpath is pack in, pack out, with no trash receptacles along the trail.

Each section of this national historical park has its own charms. The Eastern portion of the towpath is the busiest, thanks to both its dramatic sights and its proximity to Washington, DC. Mather Gorge, Great Falls and the Billy Goat Trail are all around mile 14 of the towpath, making for an easy day trip by bicycle from Georgetown's mile 0. This is also one of the best places along the C&O towpath to experience a working lock in the way that original users of the canal would have done: riding in a boat pulled by a mule.

The 60 miles between Hancock, Maryland, and Harpers Ferry, West Virginia, contain some of the most beautiful scenery. The towpath here is very flat and shaded by trees, and the canal is forest-like, quiet and still. This stretch also takes you through a few charming small towns and is home to interesting historical diversions. Take a 2-mile detour from the towpath at Shepherdstown, West Virginia, to Sharpsburg, Maryland, for a tour of Antietam battlefield, where 23,000 soldiers were killed or wounded in one day, the Civil War's bloodiest.

The stretch from Hancock to mile 184 in Cumberland, Maryland, has the greatest elevation change, presenting more of a challenge to cyclists than the rest of the towpath. This canal section was the greatest challenge to engineers too: the highlight of this section, the 3118ft Paw Paw Tunnel, cost almost $600,000 (in 1840s dollars) to build over the course of more than a decade. In fact, the canal was meant to go all the way to Pittsburgh on the Ohio River until the Appalachian Mountains proved too daunting a barrier. As you walk through the tunnel's eerie blackness, with your steps echoing along the six million handmade bricks used to construct it, it's easy to feel the enormity of the engineering task. The Cumberland Visitor Center here has displays on the importance of river trade along the Eastern Seaboard.

Highlights

Because this was a canal towpath, it's almost completely flat, making the C&O a wonderfully accessible way to experience the lush scenery of the Potomac watershed, with a few scenic stand-outs and historical features.

BILLY GOAT TRAIL
The three sections of the Billy Goat Trail total 8 miles and offer views of Mather Gorge and Great Falls. It's less a traditional hike than a rock-hopping adventure.

GEORGETOWN
The portion of the towpath that runs through Georgetown in DC feels more like a city park, following extensive renovations to the locks here.

GREAT FALLS
The most dramatic falls on the Potomac, Great Falls near DC shows the river's power from an accessible boardwalk overlook.

PAW PAW TUNNEL
More than six million bricks were used to construct this 3118ft engineering marvel, completed in 1850. Bring a flashlight to explore its depths.

APPALACHIAN TRAIL
Three miles of the 2190-mile Appalachian Trail run along the C&O Canal, including at Harpers Ferry, West Virginia. The trail here leads to a beautiful view of the Potomac from Weverton Cliff.

11
Colorado Trail

Spanning six national forests and six wilderness areas, and touching eight mountain ranges, the Colorado Trail encompasses all that is glorious about the wilds of Colorado.

➦ Kennebec Pass, at about 11,000 feet elevation, on the Colorado Trail. Right: Restored steam train of Durango & Silverton.

A thru-hike isn't for everyone. Preparation and planning aside, the sheer amount of time it can take is limiting for most. But the Colorado Trail offers hikers an opportunity to start and finish a thru-hike in about six weeks – you may not even have to quit your job to take this journey. Can't do it in one piece? Section hikes cover the same glorious territory, though they're best done with a second car waiting at your endpoint.

Here's the reason you might want to move this trail up your list of options: Colorado isn't like anywhere else. It isn't that other places are less beautiful or even more beautiful. It's just that Colorado is different, and this hike penetrates some of the most incredible backcountry the state offers. Denver and the surrounding plains are considered high desert. And it's so flat you'd wonder if the mountains are just a rumor, except that you can see them, like the spine of a giant sleeping dinosaur, piercing the sky and creating an ever-present, perfect backdrop for every photo. From the start of the trail, the task before you seems overly dramatic. How can you go from perfectly flat to scaling 14,000ft peaks in the span of just a few days? It's hard, but it's worth it.

The start of the hike, through the sandy-red high desert, is hot and dusty. The red rock formations loom like lost ruins in the underbrush. At some point you'll stop to put on another layer of clothing and turn around to see how far you've come. This is the first of the gasp-inducing moments that you'll experience for the next few weeks. Hopefully you'll get the opportunity to watch a storm brewing over the plains, or you'll get up early to watch dawn blossom over the seemingly endless Great Plains.

Sleep here...

The Colorado hut system makes for great sleeping options in the backcountry (the 10th Mountain Division Huts are a trail favorite), and a bonus Colorado Trail Friends Yurt adds character. Another delight of the Colorado Trail is the many communities it passes through where you can enjoy creature comforts along the way. When sleeping out on the trail, be sure to secure your food from bears per official guidance.

Hostel Fish, Denver
Don't blow your budget on the fanciest lodging at the start of your trip. Instead, try Denver's squeaky-clean Hostel Fish. It's modern, comfortable and filled with outdoors lovers.

Liar's Lodge B&B, Buena Vista
Reserve ahead and treat yourself to a night at this B&B in Buena Vista. The Arkansas River will sing you to sleep, and breakfast on the terrace will revive you for the next leg of your journey. To the west, Mt Princeton (14,197ft) and Collegiate Peaks provide a dramatic backdrop.

Apple Orchard Inn, Durango
Ease back into civilization at Durango's Apple Orchard Inn. The daily breakfasts are amazing, the beds cozy, and the surrounding gardens soothing. Ask for a room with a spa tub; you'll want it after your hike.

Toolbox

When to go
July and August are the best months to hike the Colorado Trail. Before mid-June the trail's higher elevations are still snow-covered, and after September the snow starts again. Thunderstorms often strike in the afternoons; start hiking early so you can be at a sheltered spot when the rain hits.

Getting there
The trailhead in Waterton Canyon is 40 miles southwest of Denver; find someone to drop you at the trailhead parking lot. Denver is well connected by air and is also a stop on Amtrak's California Zephyr line.

Practicalities
Length in miles: 485
Start: Waterton Canyon, southwest of Denver
End: Durango
Dog friendly: Yes, except a small section at the start
Bike friendly: Yes
Permit needed: Yes; wilderness permits required for certain areas can be picked up along the way
States covered: Colorado

➜ Mountain goat climbing
down from Mt Massive.

Being higher than the wide-open spaces feels like flying, but keep walking because it just gets better.

Mustering the strength to climb into the cold is challenging – and worth the effort. The high country is where Colorado truly shares its gifts. Initially you will venture through meadows surrounded by pines in central Colorado's well-named Lost Creek Wilderness. These miles are quiet and relaxing, possibly filled with sightings of grazing wildlife, especially deer and elk. The elevation gain is steady and slow.

Soon you are in for thigh-busting ascents and amazing views. Passing near Breckenridge, Colorado, you will rise above 10,000ft and stay there. These high mountain valleys are dotted with alpine lakes surrounded by colorful wildflowers, while the peak of each mountain offers more views of miles and miles of craggy ranges. Be sure to catch your breath: the trail goes even higher.

Beyond Copper Mountain, you enter the Holy Cross Wilderness. Filled with alpine lakes and streams, the area has plenty of water and wildlife. It is also home to Mts Massive and Ebert, two of the tallest peaks along the trail, which you can summit if you choose. You will also skirt Leadville, the original mining boomtown of Colorado. It's a great place to stop for a beer and a refuel, as the locals welcome thru-hikers with just the right amount of rugged hospitality.

While Mts Massive and Ebert are two of the state's highest mountains, they are not the only tall mountains here. At this point you need to decide if you will do the traditional Collegiate East trail or the newer, slightly more challenging Collegiate West. The former will have you passing through pine and aspen forests and within spitting

distance of Salida – a must-stop on the trail. The picturesque little town is a favorite among river lovers and welcomes outdoorsy folks of all types. The Collegiate West trail is more challenging but takes you along exposed ridges of the Collegiate Peaks for miles upon miles of unparalleled views.

From here the trail drops into the Cochetopa Valley, offering another look at Colorado culture: cowboy culture. Ranches stretch end to end, peppered with cows enjoying the grasses while their minders herd them through the wide-open valleys. After these luxurious days in the valley, the trail finally hits the San Juan Mountains.

To most who go there, the San Juans are unlike any other mountains. There is something special about these craggy, wild southern peaks. Perhaps it's the intensely forested lower elevations, full of aspen trees and blooming wildflowers. Or perhaps it's the way the rocky spires and buttes rise so dramatically from the verdant valleys. This is where the trail tops out in elevation at 13,271ft, near Coney Summit.

Through the Weminuche Wilderness and along Indian Trail Ridge, the trail climbs up and drops down again relentlessly. But this section also claims some of the trail's most scenic sections. Suddenly you will find yourself in Durango, a quintessential Colorado mountain town filled with skiers and cyclists and river rats – people for whom the outdoors is not just a six-week adventure but a lifestyle.

Traveling from the bustling city in the high desert, over 14,000ft peaks and mile after mile of chilly summits, through endless wilderness and finally into the lush southern Colorado mountains, and seeing the state's many faces, you'll understand why Colorado just isn't like the rest.

Highlights

The Colorado Trail will blow your mind. As the Centennial State's signature trail winds 500 miles from Denver to Durango, it passes some drool-worthy natural scenery, as well as some quintessential Wild West towns.

SAN JUAN MOUNTAINS
Laced with wildflowers and cold mountain streams, the mostly protected San Juans are a perfect slice of untouched wilderness.

HOPE PASS ON THE COLLEGIATE WEST TRAIL
One of the best sections of the trail, Hope Pass is mostly above tree line, and the views of the Collegiate Peaks are unparalleled.

MT PRINCETON HOT SPRINGS
Tucked high in the mountains, these naturally fed pools are the perfect place to soak tired bodies. Book in advance for an overnight.

LEADVILLE
The highest incorporated city in the US, this now-tiny town is a throwback to all that is Western.

FOURTEENERS
There are multiple opportunities to scale Colorado's famed fourteeners, peaks exceeding 14,000ft, on the trail. Bag a few and touch a piece of the endless sky.

→ Mountain at Rogers Pass, Glacier National Park.

12.

Continental Divide National Scenic Trail

Rugged, wild and truly Western, traverse the literal spine of the country on this trail, which marks the line where water will eventually run to either the Atlantic or the Pacific Ocean.

This trail is hard; there is no doubt about that. As the third – along with the Appalachian and Pacific Crest Trails – in the Triple Crown of US thru-hikes, the Continental Divide National Scenic Trail (CDT) is the most rugged, the most technical and maybe the most rewarding. It is somewhere between 2800 and 3100 miles (depending on whom you ask), traverses five states and spends a decent amount of time above 10,000ft. Hikers on this trail are prepared for absolutely anything, from sweltering heat to pounding rain and deep snow.

Still, imagine wandering from the deserts of New Mexico through the incredible Colorado Rockies, into the vast Wyoming wilderness, and finally finding yourself among Montana's most stunning vistas. There is a catch, though: the trail is not quite finished.

The Continental Divide of the Americas stretches from the Bering Strait in the north to the Strait of Magellan in the south, demarcating the watersheds that drain into the Pacific Ocean from those that drain into the Atlantic. The divide is mostly mountainous from North America into South America, and traversing that would be a truly epic adventure.

As it is, the Continental Divide Trail Coalition has been working diligently since the trail was designated in 1978 to move sections in the US to more remote and nonmotorized trails. However, some sections still require the use of roadways to connect parts of the trail. Because of this, a lot of thru-hikers use alternate routes to avoid roads; others swerve to hit popular attractions. For now, there is a designated route, but putting your navigational skills to the test is part of what makes this hike so exciting.

Sleep here...

Heed the words of the Continental Divide Trail Coalition regarding camping permits, required for camping in Glacier National Park, Yellowstone National Park, Rocky Mountain National Park, and Colorado's Indian Peaks Wilderness. Some other Wilderness areas require free self-service permits, which can be filled out at the trailhead. When not camping, seek out the trail's Gateway Communities.

Murray Hotel, New Mexico
There isn't much in the terminus town and Gateway Community of Silver City, New Mexico, so book a room at this historical hotel. It isn't where you'll want to spend a vacation, but it's enough to start or end your trip.

Hotel Bristol, Colorado
Steamboat Springs, Colorado, is a great place to stop and get back into civilization for a few days. Stay at the Hotel Bristol near downtown. It's small but sophisticated and very comfortable.

Lake Lodge, Wyoming
In Wyoming, linger in Yellowstone for a few days to really appreciate the park. If you're looking for a real bed, try the Lake Lodge, the most peaceful of the three in-park hotels.

Belton Chalet, Montana
Near the entrance to Glacier National Park in Montana is Belton Chalet. While you are wrapping up your journey, overnight at this historical hotel for simple but beautiful comfort.

Toolbox

When to go
If you're planning a southbound (SOBO) trip, it's best to start in mid-June or early July. For a northbound (NOBO) route, start in mid-April to early May. Most hikers go NOBO and take about six months to complete.

Getting there
The Continental Divide Trail Coalition runs a shuttle from Lordsburg, New Mexico, to the southern terminus of the trail from late March to mid-May for NOBO hikes. Schedule your shuttle in advance. Lordsburg is about equidistant from the Tucson and El Paso airports.

Practicalities
Length in miles: 2800
Start: Crazy Cook Monument, NM
End: Glacier National Park, MT
Dog friendly: Yes, except in national parks
Bike friendly: Yes, in some places, but designed primarily for hikers and equestrians
Permit needed: Yes, for New Mexico State Trust Lands and Montana's Blackfeet Reservation; also for camping in national parks
States covered: NM, CO, WY, ID, MT

Autumn foliage close to the Continental Divide in Montana.

What began as a massive conservation effort has led to the creation of one of the more inclusive looks into the history of the American West. In New Mexico the CDT utilizes 1000-year-old Zuni–Acoma trade routes. These byways were developed by Native Americans between AD 850 and 900 to facilitate relationships between the Zuni and Acoma Pueblos. People traversed the lava fields for trade and ceremonial purposes, filling crevices with lava boulders to create bridges that are still used today.

In Colorado the journey through the 800 miles of the Rocky Mountains has hikers spending nearly 70 miles at or above 11,000ft, capping out on top of the majestic 14,270ft Grays Peak (see p108). Here in the alpine tundra, while trudging through the snow, you will marvel at how nature's most powerful forces are as terrifying as they are beautiful.

The remote Never Summer Wilderness bordering on Rocky Mountain National Park is filled with high alpine lakes that reflect the surrounding peaks on their mirror-still surfaces. The night sky here, free of the light, noise and air pollution of so many areas of the world, is filled with stars reaching down through the millennia. They are so close it's like sleeping in the Milky Way.

Continue into vast and raw Wyoming for nearly 550 miles filled with all the power that creates mountain ranges. Huge glaciers slowly shape the Absaroka Range while geysers erupt in Yellowstone National Park.

The CDT ventures through South Pass City, a former station on the Oregon Trail, where Samuel Clemens (later known as Mark Twain) passed through with his brother in 1861. The town was added to the National Register of Historic Places in 1970, and the still-extant evidence of homesteaders is a reminder of the harsh realities of the western expansion.

Just down the road, Atlantic City, Wyoming, with a population that hovers around 57, has recently been working to accommodate thru-hikers and their varying needs. Go to the Miner's Grubstake and Dredge Saloon, where the motto is 'suck 'em up and get the f out,' referring to a beer and a foot soak.

The CDT next enters Idaho for some 180 miles before its 800-mile journey through Big Sky Country. This is the trail of Native Americans who were forced from their homelands and chose to fight for their ancestral rights. Chief Joseph Pass is named for the leader who brought the Nez Perce north as they looked for allies in their struggle against the US Army (p192). It is also part of the story of Lewis and Clark (p152), who were part of the first official exploration of the western United States after the Louisiana Purchase. They first crossed the Continental Divide in present-day Montana.

Craggy and raw, the northern terminus of the trail in Glacier National Park is one of the most stunning vistas the US has to offer. The mountains here, cut by glacial melt, are sharper, and the mountain lakes are pristine. Follow the CDT as the Highline Trail contours across the face of the famous Garden Wall to Granite Park Chalet – one of two historic lodges only accessible by trail. The summer slopes are covered with alpine plants and wildflowers while the views are nothing short of stupendous. Take Highline to Fifty Mountain and then to the Waterton Valley Trail, and you'll reach the Canada border. It's a striking and well-earned contrast to the deserts of New Mexico.

Highlights

Running 3100 miles from Mexico to Canada through New Mexico, Colorado, Wyoming, Idaho and Montana, the CDT offers volcano hopping, route finding, altitude sickness and heat exhaustion, coupled with grizzly bears and rattlesnakes. It's a great adventure.

HOT SPRINGS
All along the trail you will find natural hot springs to soothe your tired feet. Strawberry Park near the gateway town of Steamboat Springs, Colorado, is particularly enticing.

GILA NATIONAL FOREST
The first officially designated wilderness area in the world, New Mexico's Gila is the definition of isolated and undiscovered. Check out the cliff dwellings of the Mogollon people.

YELLOWSTONE NATIONAL PARK
In Wyoming, plan extra time to explore all that Yellowstone has to offer, including geysers, wildlife and some of the country's most impressive views.

GLACIER NATIONAL PARK
One of the most astounding natural wonders in the US, Montana's Glacier is as pristine as it is dramatic.

ROCKY MOUNTAIN NATIONAL PARK
When you're passing near this Colorado park, it's well worth a stopover to listen to the elk bugling.

Resources

O1 Continental Divide Trail Coalition
continentaldividetrail.org
The coalition's website has plenty of information about the CDNST; it also sells books and maps produced by the organization. The most up-to-date and well-organized resource, it should be your first stop for all trail information.

O2 REI Co-op
www.rei.com/blog/travel/continental-divide-trail-backpacking-gear-list
The outdoor recreation retailer has a trail packing list and breaks down food and supplies you'll need to accomplish your goals.

O3 *The Continental Divide Trail* **by Barney Scout Mann (Rizzoli, 2018)**
Beautiful trail photos and maps for aspiring and armchair hikers.

Hike This...

The Continental Divide Trail encompasses some of the country's finest national parkland, from Glacier to Yellowstone and the Rocky Mountains. Hikers here are spoiled for their choice of day and section hikes.

▶ Hiking Rocky Mountain National Park. Opposite spread, from left: cactus blooming on the CDT in New Mexico. Medicine Grizzly Lake from the Triple Divide Pass Trail.

01
Rocky Mountain National Park

For some 30 miles the Continental Divide Trail loops through Colorado's Rocky Mountain National Park in a stretch perfect for a shorter experience. This trail explores the less-traveled wilderness of the park. The views of the divide are expansive, and the trail spends most of its time above the tree line. When the trail drops to lower elevations, it winds its way through aspen and pine forests. Undulating up and down, the trail skirts high alpine lakes dotting the valleys and tackles bald mountaintops high above. A river snakes its way through much of the area, cascading into the occasional waterfall and helping to create stretches of green meadows popular with deer, elk and moose.

Black bears also call Rocky Mountain National Park home, so a bear canister is necessary. These mostly harmless omnivores tend to avoid humans as much as possible, but practice vigilance and pack away your food and waste securely using approved techniques and devices.

02
Triple Divide Pass and Rising Wolf Mountain Loop

Spending much of the initial part of this hike in Montana's Glacier National Park in the shadow of Mad Wolf Mountain and Bad Marriage Mountain may sound a bit ominous, but the hike is through pleasant, rather verdant meadows. The peaks in the distance make for a stunning backdrop, and your chances of sighting wildlife are high, whether wolves or bears. But remember to be prepared to pay for that sightseeing with some climbs. As the elevation gains start burning your thighs a little, the views become even more phenomenal. The hike passes over the steep, vertigo-inducing slopes of Mt James, with wide-open views of Razoredge Mountain's sheer cliff faces and Medicine Grizzly Lake. Further beyond Mt James, the trail reaches its terminus at Triple Divide Pass between the peaks of Triple Divide, Mt James and Norris Mountain. It is here that water flowing from the various sides of the mountain eventually finds its way to one of three oceans – the Atlantic, Pacific and Arctic – forming what is known as a hydrologic apex.

03
Lone Star Geyser Hike

This Wyoming hike isn't technically on the Continental Divide, but if you are doing the thru-hike, it's worth diverting your Yellowstone route. After all, geysers are the name of the game here. On this trail you can catch an often overlooked geyser up close. Head to the Kepler Cascades parking area and take the 4.8-mile hike to Lone Star Geyser. The geyser itself has a 12ft cone and erupts fairly regularly every three hours. Its display lasts from 30 minutes to an hour, with several small eruptions before the major blast. In addition to the geyser, there are small pools and steam vents throughout the forest along the trail.

Alternately, check out the DeLacy Creek Trail. This 6.2-mile out-and-back route to Shoshone Lake is a great place to find some secret camping spots and hang out at the black-sand beaches along the shore. Shoshone Lake itself is the largest backcountry lake in the lower 48, and one-third of all of Yellowstone's backcountry use takes place along its shores.

13

Crawford Path National Recreation Trail

On the mighty 8.2-mile path on the slopes of Mt Washington, you'll spend much of the day above the tree line with sweeping views.

⬈ Mt Jefferson and Jefferson Ravine viewed from Mt Washington Auto Rd. Right: The Mt Washington Cog Railway through Bretton Woods.

It's an otherworldly landscape of gnarled krummholz (stunted, windblown trees near mountain tree lines), jumbles of giant granite, and rocky ledges. Dense clouds hover overhead. Rare and fragile alpine plants peek out from under their sheltering rocks. Soon these will disappear as you climb above the tree line, following cairns marking the way. It's a steep scramble, rock hopping and stone stepping, but the rewards are immense: expansive 360-degree views of New Hampshire's Presidential Range in the White Mountains. Up ahead are two pristine alpine lakes and, just beyond, the summit of Mt Washington, the highest peak in the Northeast.

The historic 8.2-mile Crawford Path, scaling the slopes of Mt Washington to its 6288ft summit, is considered the oldest continuously maintained footpath in the US. It's also one of the top hikes in New England, renowned for its open, sweeping views. The path crosses five mountains – Mts Pierce, Eisenhower, Franklin, Monroe and Washington – and makes up a portion of the Appalachian Trail (AT). From Mt Pierce to the summit of Mt Washington, you'll be walking in the footsteps of thousands of AT thru-hikers, who walk the 2190-mile National Scenic Trail from Georgia to Maine.

This area in the southern Presidentials had long been the stomping and hunting grounds for Native American groups, who likely bushwhacked footpaths through the dense forests. But it was Abel Crawford and his son Ethan Allen Crawford who recognized the benefits of a path to the summit of Mt Washington (Ethan had already guided groups up the mountain) and cut the first trail in 1819. The Crawford

Sleep here...

Covering one-quarter of New Hampshire (and part of Maine), the vast White Mountains area is a spectacular region of soaring peaks and lush valleys, and contains New England's most rugged mountains. Note, however, that this wondrous place is popular: six million visitors flock here annually to use its 1200 miles of hiking trails, 23 campgrounds and eight Nordic and alpine ski areas. Book ahead!

Crawford Notch Campground
Occupying 100 acres along the Saco River, the campground has 100 woodsy campsites, along with log cabins and yurts to rent. It's also pet friendly.

Lakes of the Clouds Hut
The spectacular, above-tree line hut, on Crawford Path near the Mt Washington summit, has coed bunk rooms, meal service (breakfast and dinner are included in the price) and sweeping mountain views.

AMC Highland Center at Crawford Notch
The center has shared and private rooms, free programs, a restaurant (breakfast and dinner are included with most stays) and close proximity to Crawford Path and other trails.

Omni Mount Washington Resort
For a pampering splurge, consider this historic, sprawling grand hotel from 1902 with indoor and outdoor pools, tennis courts, a spa, a golf course and myriad amenities and activities.

© MIHAI ANDRITOIU / Alamy Stock Photo; © Robert K. Olejniczak / Alamy Stock Photo

Toolbox

When to go
This is one of the most popular routes up Mt Washington. June, when summer hikers have yet to arrive, can be perfect. Fall is splendid. But it's all about timing around the fickle mountain weather. Take particular care with the weather and avoid winter unless you have specialized gear and extensive experience.

Getting there
The trail is in the White Mountain National Forest in northern New Hampshire, just off Rt 302. It's about a half hour from Jackson and close to the Highland Center of the Appalachian Mountain Club (AMC).

Practicalities
Length in miles: 8.2 one-way
Start: Trailhead at southeastern end of Mt Clinton Rd, just off Rt 302
End: Summit of Mt Washington
Dog friendly: Yes, on leash
Bike friendly: No
Permit needed: No
States covered: New Hampshire

➡ View from Mt Washington, New Hampshire.

Path marked the beginning of recreational hiking in the East and jump-started tourism in the region. Grand hotels, carriage roads and railroads would soon follow. The trail has been improved several times throughout its 200-year history, most recently in summer 2018, when massive repairs included replacing large portions with rocks flown in by helicopter from other parts of the Presidential Range.

A word of caution: much of this hike is spent above tree line, in one of the harshest mountain environments in the East, and several people have died on this path. The weather here is fickle and can turn nasty quickly. Consult forecasts but also be prepared to turn around and seek shelter fast. Start out early and plan for a full day. That said, prepare for a spectacularly scenic hike in the Whites.

The trail travels through three climate zones, gaining some 3130ft in elevation. You'll start with a moderate walk through a dense forest of beech and hemlock trees, following the banks of the Gibbs Brook. Shortly, at about mile 0.5, you'll see a spur path leading to Gibbs Falls; it's worth a quick stop to view the cascades. You've entered the Gibbs Brook Scenic Area, lush with undergrowth and a canopy of hardwoods. Lacy old man's beard lichen drips from low-hanging tree branches and coats the trunks. There are fields of ferns and carpets of thick moss as the trail crosses several small brooks, working its way up the valley. At mile 3.1, you'll have your first opportunity to bag a peak, taking the Webster Cliff Trail to the summit of 4312ft Mt Pierce. It's a short, moderate climb with views of Mt Washington – if the clouds stay away.

From here, the views continue to open up. Follow the cairns across ledges to Mt Eisenhower; the short Mt Eisenhower Loop will take you to the peak, with open vistas. Keep trudging up the shoulder of Mt Franklin, where a short footpath leads to the summit and views into the valley of Oakes Gulf, a vast glacial cirque. Up next is the Mt Monroe Loop; the mile or so flat track skirting the summit has open, jaw-dropping views of the Presidential Range and the Dry River Wilderness that are worth the extra mileage. You'll have a breather after this, as the trail descends to the AMC Lakes of the Clouds Hut. Hikers are always welcome to stop in at this backcountry hut, overlooking two alpine lakes. Take off your boots and enjoy a cup of hot chocolate and calorie-loaded cookies. Back on the path you'll pass the highest lake in the East and start your final ascent to the summit of Mt Washington. Considered the trail's most dangerous section, it is wide open as it climbs a rocky trough to the top.

One note: expect a crowd when you reach the top. Both the Mt Washington Auto Road and the vintage Mt Washington Cog Railway carry hundreds of visitors to the top daily during the summer and fall seasons. There's development here too, including the Sherman Adams Visitor Center, with a small museum, cafe and observation deck; the historic Tip-Top House, a former hotel; and radio transmitter facilities. No matter – you've made it. Mt Washington, home to the world's worst weather, is one of the windiest and cloudiest places on Earth. Put on your fleece (it can snow at the summit any month of the year), and when the clouds part, you may catch views from Canada clear to the Atlantic Ocean.

Highlights

Connected by scenic drives and rugged trails, these areas in the White Mountains are rightly popular for recreation: Mt Washington Valley to the east, Crawford Notch and Bretton Woods along US 302 in the center, and the Franconia Range to the west.

AMC LAKES OF THE CLOUDS HUT
Stop for a rest (and perhaps a cookie) at Lakes of the Clouds, the AMC's highest and most popular backcountry hut.

SUMMIT OF MT WASHINGTON
Stand at the summit of Mt Washington; at 6288ft, it's the highest peak in the Northeast and home to some of the world's worst weather.

MT MONROE LOOP
For more open views, take the Mt Monroe Loop, where you'll have a glorious look at the Presidential Range and Dry River Wilderness.

VIEWS OF THE PRESIDENTIALS
On the trail between Mts Pierce and Eisenhower, you'll break into the open, traversing ledges with views of the southern Presidential Range.

MT EISENHOWER LOOP
The scenic loop adds 0.2 miles and about 300ft in elevation, but the reward is a 360-degree mountain vista.

14

Cumberland Trail

View of the Cumberland Trail from the top of the ridge at Devil's Racetrack. Right: Rhododendron in the Smokies.

Following the ridges and gorges of East Tennessee's Cumberland Plateau for 300 miles, this trail is not quite finished, but it's already magnificent.

It's not every day that America gets a new epic hiking trail. Blazing a trail isn't about tramping through the woods with a machete and a loop of ribbon. It's about tedious negotiation with local authorities and private landowners, about hiring consultants to research the impacts on traffic and wildlife, and about holding endless public hearings to let neighbors air their views. Most people don't have the stomach for it.

Luckily, East Tennessee has a ferocious network of volunteers who've been toiling for years to string together a corridor stretching through 11 counties. They're almost done. More than 200 miles of trail is open to date. The remaining 100 or so miles are planned to be finished by late 2021. The Cumberland Trail will eventually be part of the Great Eastern Trail, a planned Alabama–New York footpath aiming to rival the Appalachian Trail.

The Cumberland Trail route goes from north to south along the remote eastern escarpment of the Cumberland Plateau. Divided into 12 segments, it has more than 50 trailheads; at the time of publication, some gaps remained between the sections.

You'll begin in the ancient mountains of the Cumberland Gap National Historical Park on the Kentucky border, an area that was once the gateway to the West for 19th-century frontier settlers. Wind along rocky ridges passing wild and whimsical geologic formations: a stone arch, pink-orange sandstone cliffs, two rock walls so big they've been nicknamed the 'Great Walls of China.' Stop to listen to the wind and gaze down at the emerald-carpeted Powell River valley below. You'll see beaver dams and white-tailed deer and maybe, if you're extra lucky, an elk. In spring the slopes

Sleep here...

The Cumberland Gap National Historical Park serves as a kind of bridge between Appalachia and the southern and western US, and lodging options are cozy and down-home. Chattanooga makes a great start or end point, with tons of appealing options. (Just be careful when searching for accommodation at the northern terminus that you don't get led astray by Maryland's own Cumberland Gap.)

 Trail Camping
Many sections of the trail have state-run campsites with running water and bathrooms. Some also allow backcountry camping in designated spots, with advance reservation. Be mindful of bears and hunters.

 Olde Mill Inn Bed & Breakfast, Cumberland Gap
This quaint spot, with a working 19th-century mill, is in Cumberland Gap, a few miles from the park where the trail begins. The town is like a historical postcard; it's well worth a stroll.

Arrowhead Resort, Stinging Fork Falls
Stinging Fork Falls is near Spring City and Watts Bar Lake, a popular recreation spot with a handful of unpretentious seasonal resorts. This family-friendly spot has a restaurant and boat rentals.

Crash Pad Hostel, Chattanooga
In a funky pink house, this hostel in Chattanooga is beloved by the many hikers, rock climbers and river runners who flock to the city. You might even meet a future hiking buddy here.

Toolbox

 **When to go**
The trail can be hiked in any season, though winters are quite cold. Spring means colorful wildflowers, while fall is a visual feast of russet and burnt sienna. Summers are warm but pleasant enough due to the altitude and breezes.

 Getting there
The northern terminus is in Cumberland Gap National Historical Park on the Tennessee–Kentucky border. The nearest airport is 90 miles away in Knoxville, Tennessee. The southern terminus is just outside Chattanooga, Tennessee, which has a midsize airport.

 Practicalities
Length in miles: 300+ (when complete)
Start: Cumberland Gap National Historical Park
End: Signal Mountain
Dog friendly: Yes
Bike friendly: No
Permit needed: No
States covered: Tennessee

→ The Cumberland Gap at sunrise from the Pinnacle Overlook at the Cumberland Gap National Historical Park

bloom with trilliums, blue violets and star chickweed. In fall the tree canopy bursts into flaming oranges and reds.

Now you're moving south into the New River segment and some of Tennessee's most rugged and isolated territory. You'll ascend steep ridges lined with hemlock and mountain laurel, follow creek beds and wade waist-high through grass in alpine meadows. This is former coal country, a part of America that has been depopulated as miners and their families moved on. Traces remain: ghost towns concealed in the crooks of distant valleys, scars from strip mining on mountaintops, logging roads overgrown with flowers – even occasional chunks of coal amid the rocks. Lead from surface mining makes some of the water sources unsafe to drink.

The trail becomes steeper as it traverses the Cumberland Mountains in the strenuous Bird Mountain segment. This is the site of the infamous Barkley Marathons, an annual ultramarathon so insanely difficult that sometimes no one finishes. You'll understand why as you pick your way up the rocky switchbacks in Frozen Head State Park.

The Obed Wild and Scenic River segment is just that. Highlights include the 1930s iron bridge over the Emory River. Does your cell phone keep telling you it's 1pm, then 2pm, then 1pm again? You're straddling Eastern and Central time zones, and likely picking up signals from towers on either side. Ascend and descend the steep sides of the river gorge, looking for herons and belted kingfishers in summer, and perhaps even an otter or two. If a swimming hole beckons, well, go for it.

Further south you'll hit Stinging Fork Falls, a 35ft beauty that in full force looks like a giant bridal veil. The Lower Piney River has more waterfalls, but its coolest feature is a 100ft suspension bridge across the Piney River: Instagram gold. The Laurel-Snow segment will have you crisscrossing creeks as you move through the gorges of Walden Ridge. There are more waterfalls in the area – Laurel Falls is 80ft high. This segment follows the path of an old coal railroad, another vestige of the area's mining past. At Henderson Creek, hold on tight to cross the 150ft bridge over foamy water.

The Three Gorges segment snakes through the gorges carved by the Soddy, Possum and Rock Creeks. You'll slip your way over mossy rocks and use ladders and bridges to make tricky crossings. Pause at overlooks to watch hawks circling above the sandstone cliffs. The Little Soddy Historic Mining Area has several eerie abandoned mines and a nifty suspension bridge.

In the trail's southernmost segment, you'll travel into the Tennessee River Gorge. Here the Signal and Edwards Points section is the trail's southern terminus. Climb out of the gorge and onto the plateau rim, gazing down at the wide, shining Tennessee River below. Don't miss Mushroom Rock, a 20ft-high sandstone pedestal that will make you feel like Alice in Wonderland standing below a giant toadstool. Eventually you'll emerge onto the road, finally back to familiar civilization.

As a brand-new trail, the Cumberland doesn't yet have the culture and traditions of the Appalachian or the Pacific Crest. That may come with time as the Great Eastern Trail gains fans and new stretches of trail that allow it to connect existing National Scenic Trail routes. For now, savor being one of the first people to tackle this raw, thrilling stretch of the great state of Tennessee.

Highlights

The Cumberland Trail connects two national parks as well as passing through a National Wild & Scenic River area. Designated the Justin P Wilson Cumberland Trail State Park in 1996, it's now the second largest Tennessee state park.

JULIA FALLS OVERLOOK
Near Signal Point at the trail's southern tip, this is one of the most jaw-dropping views over the primeval green hills of the Tennessee River Gorge.

BLACK MOUNTAIN
Pass boulders the size of houses and squeeze through a narrow rock passage carved with stairs as you ascend the mountain for panoramic views over Grassy Cove.

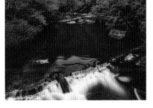

WILDLIFE
The more remote parts of the trail teem with animals, from bobcats to cottontail rabbits to foxes to hawks. Be careful of black bears, snakes and... skunks.

OBED WILD & SCENIC RIVER
White water foaming furiously, sandstone cliffs stretching above the trees, spooky old train tunnels and vintage bridges: this river is what adventure's all about.

BRIDGES
Who doesn't love a good bridge? The trail's tireless volunteers have built several delightful ones, including a 94ft suspension bridge above Big Soddy Creek.

15.

Derby Wharf National Recreation Trail

The history of Salem, Massachusetts, goes way beyond witches. This half-mile recreational trail offers an intriguing look at the Age of Sail and the unimaginable riches it brought to these shores.

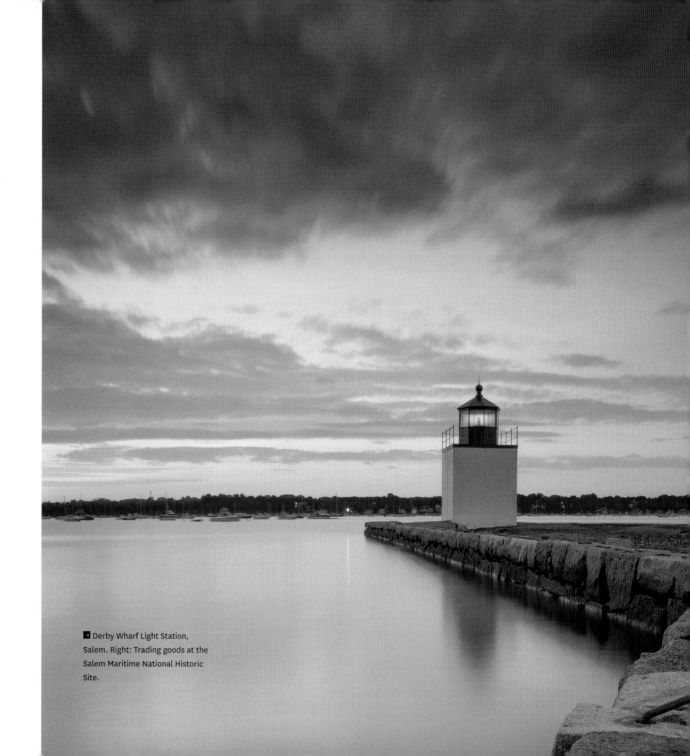

Derby Wharf Light Station, Salem. Right: Trading goods at the Salem Maritime National Historic Site.

The first thing you think of when you hear 'Salem' is likely witchcraft or, if you're a lover of literature, novelist Nathaniel Hawthorne. And, yes, you can visit several witch-themed attractions and the House of the Seven Gables during your visit. But this city of 43,000, located north of Boston, has another claim to fame: in the early 1800s, Salem was the wealthiest city per capita in the US.

From the 18th century and into the 19th, following the American Revolution, ships sailed from Salem to Asia, Africa, Polynesia, South America, Spain and Russia, and returned laden with exotic goods to be sold back home. The bounty included silks, porcelain, tea, coffee, cotton, rum, sugar, ivory, pepper (used at the time to preserve meats as well as for seasoning) and some curious items. Bills of sale at Waite & Peirce, a former merchant's shop, list water buffalo hides, tortoise shells, and dragon's blood. Trade with slave-based economies in British ports around the Atlantic brought vast wealth to this small New England seaport. Some wealthy families in Salem were slaveholders themselves.

The 50 wharves along Salem Harbor were the center of the action, home to customhouses, scales, warehouses, stores, shipbuilding structures and a lighthouse. Amazingly, some of these still exist today. They're part of the Salem Maritime National Historic Site – the country's first – established in 1938. In total this comprises 9 acres of land and 12 historic structures along Salem's waterfront, along with a downtown visitors center. Elements of the site include the Custom House and Public Stores, Scale House, Hawkes House,

Sleep here...

The entire coast of Massachusetts claims a rich history, but no part offers more recreational, cultural and dining diversions than the North Shore. Trade and fishing have brought wealthy residents, sumptuous houses and great collections of art and artifacts to the area. Campers, RVers and those who prefer to rough it can check out city-managed Winter Island Park outside Salem, with its own stop on the trolley.

The Merchant
The Federal-style building, designed by architect Samuel McIntire, hosted George Washington in 1789. Today the boutique hotel offers six rooms and suites, with modern amenities like iPads and Apple TV.

Salem Waterfront Hotel & Suites
Traveling with kids? This hotel will win 'em over with a heated indoor pool. The 86-room, nautically decorated hotel has an on-site seafood restaurant with patio dining and free parking.

Hawthorne Hotel
A Salem landmark from 1925, the 89-room Hawthorne Hotel is a local gathering place. The pet-friendly property offers a popular restaurant and tavern, plus an adjacent, 1807 Federal-style guesthouse with historic details.

Morning Glory Bed & Breakfast
Prefer the intimacy of a B&B? This c 1808 Federal-style home has two guest rooms and a 3rd-floor suite; it's across from the House of the Seven Gables.

Toolbox

When to go
The trail is open year-round, but hours are extended during summer. Guided tours generally run from June through October. The gravel surface of the wharf is slippery when covered in ice and snow, and the wharf can be windy, so use caution in winter.

Getting there
Derby Wharf is off Derby St in downtown Salem. The nearest major airport is Boston Logan, about 20 miles south. Salem is reachable from Boston via MBTA commuter rail (35 minutes); a short walk gets you to Derby Wharf. From mid-May through October, the Salem Ferry operates between Boston and Salem (55 minutes).

Practicalities
Length in miles: 0.38
Start: Derby St, across from the Custom House
End: Derby Wharf Light Station
Dog friendly: Yes, on leash
Bike friendly: Yes
Permit needed: No
State covered: Massachusetts

The wharves are among remnants of the shipping industry that once thrived in Salem.

Derby House, Waite & Peirce, Pedrick Store House, a lighthouse, three wharves and a replica tall ship, the *Friendship of Salem*.

Start your visit at the regional visitors center at 2 New Liberty St (park your car here rather than at Derby Wharf, where parking is scarce). A 27-minute video offers a solid introduction to Essex County. Pick up a copy of the Salem city guide; a map with a red Heritage Trail line will lead you to Derby Wharf. In real life, the line is faded or nonexistent in spots, but it's a short jaunt.

Derby Wharf is one of three remaining wharves on Salem Harbor that date back to the 1700s. In its heyday Derby Wharf had nearly 20 structures on it; now there are two, Pedrick Store House (1770), moved from Marblehead, and the *Friendship of Salem*. Tourists snacking on candy from Ye Olde Pepper Companie (America's oldest candy store, c 1804) amble along the wharf and in and out of the park's historic sites. Rangers – some dressed in period costume – conjure up the colorful, chaotic scene here during the Age of Sail, when ships arrived from faraway ports and locals scrambled to unload cargo, register ships, weigh goods and make repairs. Some ships were built directly on these wharves and launched into the harbor.

The replica *Friendship of Salem*, an East Indiaman tall ship, recently returned from dry dock in nearby Gloucester, where it underwent a $1.5 million restoration. Work on the vessel continues. When it's fully restored, the three wooden masts will reach the height of a 10-story building, and the rigging will include some 17 miles of line (rope). Step aboard the ship's 100ft main deck and consider what it was like to be one of the crew of 12 sailors who lived

belowdecks. With thin sleeping mats and little ventilation, this was no luxury cruise. The original *Friendship* was built in 1797. It entered the harbor at Derby Wharf seven years later and made 15 voyages to China and Sumatra before being captured by the British in the War of 1812. The ship's ultimate fate is unknown.

At the end of Derby Wharf is 12ft-square Derby Wharf Light Station, the only surviving original structure on the wharf. One of four lighthouses that aid mariners in navigating Salem Sound, the c 1871 light station is 20ft high to the top of its cupola. Originally the light was powered by an oil lamp, which illuminated a Fresnel lens. Still operating today, Derby Wharf Light Station is now solar-powered. It transmits a red flash every six seconds.

Since the actual trail isn't long, plan to explore the other buildings that make up the Salem Maritime National Historic Site. Should you need an energy boost, pop into Ye Olde Pepper Companie at 122 Derby St and try one of their signature Gibralters, a type of candy. Yes, even a visit to a candy store counts as a history lesson in Salem!

What's unique about this trail is its location: it feels like a living history museum in the heart of a city. And it's free (if you don't count parking fees and candy). As visitor Jarrett Kelley of Lexington, Massachusetts, put it, 'Let the accused witches rest in peace, and come see where and how the nation began.' And for those who'd like to look into those witches some more, the nearby 4.3-mile Danvers Rail Trail passes by the Rebecca Nurse Homestead, which features a reproduction of the Salem Village Meetinghouse and exhibits on the Salem Witch Trials, which cost Rebecca Nurse her life in 1692.

Highlights

Salem was among America's wealthiest ports during the 19th century, and its association with the witch trials have obscured Salem's true claim to fame: its glory days as a center for clipper-ship trade with the Far East.

SCALE HOUSE
Just behind the Custom House, the tiny brick Scale House (built in 1829) is filled with giant wooden contraptions designed to weigh ships' cargoes.

CUSTOM HOUSE
Marked by a gilded eagle, the 200-year-old, three-story brick Custom House is an imposing sight. Writer Nathaniel Hawthorne once served as a surveyor here.

NARBONNE HOUSE
The clapboard, one-room, 1675 Narbonne House, formerly occupied by a tanner, a weaver and a seamstress, offers a look at the daily life of residents.

DERBY HOUSE
The stately brick 1762 Derby House reveals the lifestyle of Salem's wealthiest merchants. Captain Richard Derby Sr, who built Derby Wharf, presented the home to his son as a gift.

PUBLIC STORES
Catch a whiff of spice in the air at the Public Stores, where cargo was held until duties were paid. An exhibit displays a variety of luxury items that entered the port in the 1820s.

16

East Coast Greenway

→ The US Naval Academy Chapel dome, Annapolis, Maryland.

This 3000-mile potpourri of shared-use pathways parallels the Eastern Seaboard from Key West, Florida, to Calais, Maine, as a more urbanized alternative to the Appalachian Trail.

One remarkable quality of the East Coast Greenway (ECG) is its ability to hide in plain sight. Increasingly well-signed across 450 communities in 15 states (plus Washington, DC) and located within 5 miles of 25 million people, its pathways are hardly camouflaged. In fact, at an average cost of $1 million to build each new mile, the ECG is perhaps the most ambitious infrastructure project in the country. As its stature grows, certain segments are expected to see as many as 50 million visitors a year, which would make the ECG far and away the most visited park in the US.

For now, though, the East Coast Greenway somehow flies under the radar: a free-to-use, 3000-mile trail from the southernmost tip of the US at Key West, Florida, to the town of Calais on the US–Canada border in Maine. Designed for commuting and recreational hikers, runners, bikers, skaters, dog walkers, wheelchair users, horseback riders and nature lovers, the ECG aims to offer 100% continuous car-free comfort by joining together dozens of existing municipal, county and state-owned trails through the construction of new connecting, traffic-free segments. As of today, approximately 35% of its course is off-limits to motorized vehicles, with more paths added every year; the rest detours along regular roads, streets, bridges and sidewalks.

Whether off-road or on, the ECG is more than a fantastically complex building project. It's a living, expanding embodiment of the complex beauty of American life – natural and manmade, urban and rural – scaled for both local and national use, and for all ages and inclinations. On the ECG, you're just as

Sleep here...

Whatever your preference – dense cities with hotel offerings to match, charming and historic seaside towns, or camping from the most basic tent site to the most luxe yurt – the 3000 miles of the East Coast Greenway have you covered. The ECG website even has sample trips with lodging recommendations. Pick your region of preference, and get planning.

Huntington Beach State Park Campground, South Carolina
For self-sufficient hikers, campgrounds abound along the ECG, especially in parks. This seaside retreat in Murrells Inlet, South Carolina, is a standout with a long list of nature-based activities, including alligator watching.

Sandy Pines Campground, Maine
Off the Maine ECG as it passes Kennebunk, the Sandy Pines Campground in Kennebunkport offers creatively designed glamping retreats in everything from Conestoga wagons to Airstreams, domes and wheeled cabins.

Historic Inns of Annapolis, Maryland
Traversing America's original colonies, the ECG brushes shoulders with history. Landmark hotels help bring that to life, like this collection of 18th-century residences in Maryland once frequented by Declaration of Independence signers.

1 Hotel Brooklyn Bridge, New York
In keeping with the ECG spirit, eco-hotels bring a bit of nature into the city. This LEED Gold building houses what is arguably New York's greenest hotel, built and operated with sustainability in mind.

© Sean Pavone / Alamy Stock Photo; © Still Bill / Shutterstock

Toolbox

When to go
Given the length of the East Coast Greenway (ECG), its hiking season varies by region. In general May through October are optimal – drier and warmer, though it can get very hot. The more temperate autumn months are especially delightful and, once foliage changes, colorful.

Getting there
The greatest challenge to accessing the ECG is choosing among the many points of entry. Running through the heart of cities like Miami, Savannah, Charleston, Raleigh, Richmond, Washington, DC, Baltimore, Philadelphia, New York, Boston and Portland, it's easy to find.

Practicalities
Length in miles: 3000
Start: Key West, FL
End: Calais, ME
Dog friendly: Yes
Bike friendly: Yes
Permit needed: No
States covered: FL, GA, SC, NC, VA, DC, MD, DE, PA, NJ, NY, CT, RI, MA, NH, ME

Brooklyn's Dumbo waterfront is part of the ECG.

likely to meet a group of retirees watching birds from the gravel trail through Maine's largest saltwater marsh at Scarborough as you are to see a family or a huddle of teenagers strolling the paved paths of the Cross-Triangle Greenway between Durham and Raleigh in North Carolina. Or you may spot a solo, long-distance hiker keeping pace toward her next rest stop. For the most part, everyone has sly, friendly smiles for everyone else, as if they share a special secret: the ECG.

This backs up the belief of the founding nonprofit, East Coast Greenway Alliance, that the ECG is really a massive investment in public health, environmental sustainability, economic development and civic engagement. The more communities have outdoor activity–focused opportunities available to them, the better off people are – exercising more, driving less, meeting more neighbors, appreciating and protecting nature, seeing tourism growth and supporting efforts to build it in a responsible way.

It also helps explain the obvious differences between the ECG and the Appalachian Trail, the famous north–south, long-distance path that the ECG shadows. Whereas the Appalachian Trail is a hikers-only wilderness route that does its best to discreetly snake through parks and preserves, the ECG imposes no limits on its nonmotorized users, nor does it divert around large cities. Instead, it dives straight into and across the likes of Miami, Savannah, Charleston, Raleigh, Richmond, Washington, DC, Baltimore, Philadelphia, New York, Hartford, Providence, Boston and Portland.

The direct transit through metropolitan areas gives the ECG some of its unique appeal. Unlike the wilderness camping and against-the-elements struggles that define the Appalachian Trail, the ECG is the kind of trail experience that beginner and intermediate hikers might be more inclined to undertake, especially over longer distances: full of variety, less rugged and remote. It dips regularly into population centers with food markets, restaurants, ample accommodation, and festivals and cultural attractions that celebrate the particular character of each place along the way.

As committed to opening pedestrian-friendly portals both into and from urban hubs as the ECG is, it also points to small rural communities and out-of-the-way, undervalued parkland. In many locations, when not following gently graded rail trails bisecting woodlands on hard-packed earth, the greenway favors passage through a gratifying mix of leafy villages and one-street towns. It also has lengthy traverses of fields and forests dotted with working farms, and waterfronts alive with maritime life.

Wayfinding along the ECG is refreshingly straightforward. Excellent signage has been added along much of the trail, with the rest scheduled to be completed by the end of 2020. The East Coast Greenway Alliance hosts a detailed web-based map, as well as clear instructions for how to download data for offline use with a mobile app. Turn-by-turn cue sheets can be printed too. The alliance additionally serves as the central advocacy and coordinating organization for turning the vision of the ECG into reality, a process that can take 10 years for each segment to get from route identification to ribbon-cutting!

Still a work in progress, the ECG is worth every stride, all the more so now before it becomes an open secret.

Highlights

With 450 municipalities and 15 states, this ambitious bike/walk trail winds through urban areas, suburban communities and rural districts. Its path down the Eastern Seaboard makes it a true sampling of everything the East Coast has to offer.

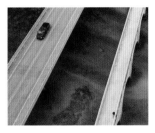

CROSS-TRIANGLE GREENWAY
The ECG's most complete urban trail, this 40-mile protected greenway between Durham and Raleigh in North Carolina passes through city parks, museums and woods.

FLORIDA KEYS OVERSEAS HERITAGE TRAIL
Hikers tackle shorter segments of a 106-mile paved, flat corridor between Key Largo and Key West that is known for its two dozen bridges and vast expanses of water.

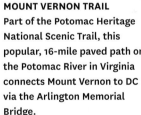

MOUNT VERNON TRAIL
Part of the Potomac Heritage National Scenic Trail, this popular, 16-mile paved path on the Potomac River in Virginia connects Mount Vernon to DC via the Arlington Memorial Bridge.

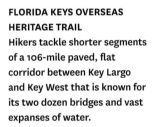

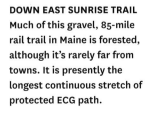

DOWN EAST SUNRISE TRAIL
Much of this gravel, 85-mile rail trail in Maine is forested, although it's rarely far from towns. It is presently the longest continuous stretch of protected ECG path.

HUDSON RIVER GREENWAY
The 12.4 miles of this protected path in New York City hug the west side of Manhattan along the Hudson River from Battery Park to the George Washington Bridge.

Apalachicola in Florida.

17

Florida National Scenic Trail

The 1100-mile trail wends its way through Florida's wild and extravagant landscapes, from cypress swamps to dry prairies, ferny forests and powdery sand beaches.

Think of the Florida Trail as a snake. It glides gracefully across the state's watery landscapes – blackwater rivers the color of over-brewed tea, freshwater marshes tangled with pickerelweed, old-growth bald cypress swamps with snowy-white orchids blooming in the murk. Flicking its gleaming tail, the snake/trail winds through ecosystems bearing names as lovely as poems – pine savannas, wetland hammocks, sawgrass prairies, cypress domes. Its body curves along the length of the state, from the southern tip of the peninsula to the far northwestern reach of the Panhandle, where it curls up to sleep in the warm white sand.

Snakes themselves are just some of the many animals you'll share space with in the steaming primeval wilderness of the Florida Trail. The state is heaven for serpents – cottonmouths and copperheads, coachwhips and southern black racers, redbellies and diamondbacks. Then there's the rest of the reptile parade: tiny darting skinks, sleepy scrub lizards, spotted turtles and red-bellied cooters, lumbering crocodiles and, of course, the granddaddy beast of them all, the American alligator, all wicked teeth and gleaming eyes. Not to mention bears and foxes and otters and boars and birds of all kinds. Humans, however, are often few and far between.

The hike starts, appropriately, in a swamp. The Big Cypress doesn't ease you in. Nope, this is nearly 40 miles of slogging through knee-deep water, the mud threatening to suck the shoes right off your feet. Forget pitching a tent; you'll want to hang a hammock from tree to tree. You'll rock to sleep to the whine of mosquitoes and the splashes of night animals slipping

Sleep here...

The Florida Trail offers an escape from the world of resorts most associate with the state, and to get the full effect, stay in cabins and campgrounds. Undeveloped campgrounds are just that (undeveloped), while most public campgrounds have toilets, showers and drinking water. Reserve state park sites in advance (yes, you need to!) by calling 800-326-3521 or visiting www.reserveamerica.com.

 Florida Trail Camping
There are designated campsites along the length of the trail; backcountry camping is also common. Using designated campsites is a must during hunting season, which coincides with thru-hiking season.

 Big Cypress RV Resort & Campground, Clewiston
The Seminole-owned campground in Clewiston has all the amenities you could desire after emerging from the Big Cypress swamp slog, including a heated pool, laundry facilities and a cafe.

 Suwannee River Cabins
Rent a cabin along the Suwannee River at Stephen Foster Folk Culture Center State Park, a park honoring the composer of Florida's state song, or at the Suwannee River State Park, about 30 miles away.

 Shell Island Fish Camp, St Marks
The family-run lodge in the fishing village of St Marks is a popular Panhandle stop for weary hikers. It has motel rooms and rental cabins, and burgers and beer are nearby.

Toolbox

 When to go
Florida weather fluctuates between warm and extremely hot. Late October through April is best for hiking, as it's cooler and less stormy. Thru-hikers should start in the south in early January and end by April.

 Getting there
The southern trailhead is at Big Cypress National Preserve, 45 miles west of Miami and 35 miles southeast of Naples. The northern trailhead is in Pensacola Beach, 13 miles south of Pensacola International Airport. There is no year-round public transportation to the trailheads, though there is a beach trolley to Pensacola during summer.

Practicalities
Length in miles: approximately 1100
Start: Big Cypress National Preserve
End: Fort Pickens, Pensacola Beach
Dog friendly: No, except Apalachicola, Ocala and Osceola National Forests
Bike friendly: No
Permit needed: For some sections
States covered: Florida

→ Entering the Big Cypress Seminole Reservation, Florida Everglades. Left: Shrimp boat in a waterway near the Apalachicola marina.

SEMINOLE INDIAN RESERVATION

NO TRESPASSING. NO CAMPING. HUNTING OR FISHING. NO DUMPING.

SPEED LIMITS STRICTLY ENFORCED

VIOLATORS WILL BE PROSECUTED BY SEMINOLE POLICE DEPARTMENT

US DEPARTMENT OF INTERIOR BUREAU OF INDIAN AFFAIRS

→ The dunes at Pensacola Beach, Gulf Islands National Seashore.

through the water below. Creepy? A little. Cool? Absolutely. Oh, and you'll definitely see alligators. But don't worry too much; you're probably too big for them to bother with.

North of the swamp you'll need a permit to hike through the Big Cypress Seminole Reservation, the largest of six reservations owned by Florida's Seminole tribe. It's mostly ranchland and farmland; to the north you'll be walking through the agricultural fields that were once part of the 'sea of grass' that is the Everglades. Now they're drained, dry and crisscrossed with levees.

A bit further north are the shores of Lake Okeechobee, Florida's largest lake. Unlike in the swamp, you get to go around the water, not through it. Walk the paved dike encircling the lake, built to prevent flooding of low-lying South Florida. Okeechobee's shallow waters look pretty but are gravely polluted because of runoff from the surrounding sugar plantations.

You'll go east or west around Orlando (hello, Mickey!) before hitting the Ocala National Forest. The 72-mile Ocala section was the first part of the Florida Trail, blazed in 1966. It's a dreamy landscape of sand hills, scrubland and freshwater marshes. Though rivers and lakes cut through the forest, most of the trail here is high and dry, giving you a chance to air out your boots. You may hear the rumble of bombs being dropped at the Navy's Pinecastle Bombing Range, a reminder that the ills of civilization are not far away.

Heading into North Florida, the deep shade of longleaf pines provides relief from the heat. The Osceola National Forest was the site of Florida's biggest Civil War battle; later it was a hot spot for logging and turpentine distilling. The area around

the Suwannee River is challenging terrain, with deep valleys, jagged sinkholes and sometimes-flooded sections of trail.

The section of the state curving toward the Panhandle is known as the 'Big Bend.' You'll walk about 50 miles along rural roads between the Suwannee and Aucilla Rivers before plunging into dense, almost claustrophobic thickets of bent cypress, black gum, water oak and palmetto. This is a Swiss cheese–like karst landscape with rivers that disappear into the earth, only to reappear later; water-filled sinkholes; and gaping cave mouths overhung with moss.

Rounding the bend onto the Gulf of Mexico and St Marks National Wildlife Refuge, you're now officially in the Panhandle. The salt marshes and maritime forests of the refuge are a winter habitat for millions of migratory birds and home to several rare species, including the red-cockaded woodpecker. Enjoy the open views of the Gulf because soon you'll be mucking through the trail's boggy Apalachicola section. Keep your eyes open for carnivorous pitcher plants, which trap and digest insects inside their cupped leaves.

You'll need an advance permit to walk through Eglin Air Force Base, which will deliver you to your final destination: the 32-mile seashore section of the trail. Though hiking through fine sand with a heavy pack is not easy, you'll be amply rewarded with breezes and sea views. The trail ends at the historic 19th-century Fort Pickens on Santa Rosa Island, with a beach as lovely as you'll find the world over: Pensacola Beach, 8 miles of pristine shoreline on this 40-mile long barrier island, part of Gulf Islands National Seashore. Take off your pack and wade into the water to experience bliss, as only Florida can deliver it.

Highlights

The Florida Trail runs north from the swamps of Big Cypress National Preserve, around Lake Okeechobee; through the Ocala National Forest, and then west to the Gulf Islands National Seashore. All these are filled with great hikes, and there's history on the path too.

AH-TAH-THI-KI MUSEUM
This Smithsonian-affiliated museum in Clewiston offers exhibits on Seminole history and culture, with artifacts like beadwork and clothing, and has occasional cultural events with music and dancing.

JUNIPER PRAIRIE WILDERNESS
The scrub forests, marshes and sawgrass seas in this part of Ocala National Forest are some of the loveliest and most iconic Floridian landscapes along the trail.

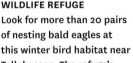

ST MARKS NATIONAL WILDLIFE REFUGE
Look for more than 20 pairs of nesting bald eagles at this winter bird habitat near Tallahassee. The refuge's lighthouse dates to 1831.

FORT PICKENS
The trail's northern terminus, this 1834 fort in Pensacola Beach has seen Civil War battles, held the Apache leader Geronimo as a prisoner and served as a U-boat lookout in WWII.

AUCILLA SINKS
The many limestone sinkholes around the Aucilla River have names like Chocolate, Mosquito Slap and Long Suffering. It's a landscape like no other.

Resources

01 Florida Trail Association (FTA)
www.floridatrail.org
The FTA's website is full of useful info, including current section closures.

02 Thru-Hike Florida
www.thruhikeflorida.com
This privately maintained website offers excellent planning and logistical details for wannabe thru-hikers.

03 Florida Hikes
floridahikes.com
This website created by a hiking guidebook writer includes thorough descriptions of various trail sections and sells trail guidebooks.

04 *The Yearling*
Marjorie Kinnan Rawlings' classic 1938 novel tells the story of a Florida boy who adopts a pet fawn, set near Ocala National Forest.

Hike this...

One thing Florida hikers never have to worry about is elevation gain. But the rewards might surprise those used to hikes measured in altitude gain. Try these paths through national forest and stands of palm.

 Tate's Hell State Forest. Opposite spread, from left: View of Ocala National Forest; alligator at Big Cypress National Preserve.

01
Sopchoppy River

An hour's drive from Tallahassee brings you to this 4-mile section of trail in the Apalachicola National Forest, the largest of Florida's three national forests. You'll follow the coffee-colored river from the trailhead at Oak Park Bridge to FR 329, ascending and descending along sand bluffs and limestone outcrops. Bony white cypress knees jut from the black water, its mirrorlike surface reflecting the gnarled gum trees above. Birds land on sandbanks, while the occasional snake slithers its way along the wet ground. You'll diverge from the river to meander through titi swamp, a habitat native to the southeastern US that is named for the black and white titi trees it nurtures. Cross the delightfully named Monkey Creek Bridge before following the river again. In spring the air is fragrant with the azaleas that bloom thickly along the banks. It's eerie in the most wonderful way, though it can be dangerous in high water; turn back if water flows across the trail.

02
Hopkins Prairie

In the Ocala National Forest, this 9.5-mile one-way hike takes you into the heart of open (no shade) grassland that is Hopkins Prairie. This is prime territory for sandhill cranes, who amble gracefully through the shallow waters. The prairie, see, is actually a wetland, dotted with small ponds. It's all fringed by saw palmettos and ringed by pines. Watch out for alligators – seriously. Oh, and bears too. Just off the trail is the Hopkins Prairie Campground, a little piece of sandy oak–shaded heaven hung with curtains of Spanish moss. When the prairie is wet, it cools the wind blowing onto the campsites: natural air-conditioning!

A spur trail leads to the unincorporated community of Salt Springs; the trail parking lot is about 30 miles from the city of Ocala. For thru-hikers, there is also a designated backpacking campsite located at Hopkins Prairie, open October 1–June 1, the proper backcountry season in steamy subtropical Florida; it's one of the only shaded spots here in the grassland.

03
Cathedral of Palms

The high point of this 5.5-mile loop hike is a stand of native sabal (cabbage) palms – the 'cathedral' – so tall and thick they let in only slivers of sunlight. Start from the Spring Creek Hwy trailhead at Shell Point Rd and Vickers Dr. Meander beneath dense canopies of oak and magnolia until you reach it, looking out for otters and wild pigs.

Expect to get your feet soaked by spillover from the cypress swamp adjacent to the trail, unless you're hiking at an absolutely dry time of year. While it's not a difficult hike per se, navigating marshy ground can be a challenge; be sure to don proper footwear. Afterward, take a turn on the spur trail toward Shepherd Spring. Emerging from the forest like a strange blue eye, its water is clear enough that you can see schools of garfish swimming far below; don't go for a dip yourself, however. This hike is in the St Marks National Wildlife Refuge, on the eastern end of the Panhandle, an easy half-hour drive from Tallahassee.

The Old State House. Right: A trail marker on the Freedom Trail.

18

The Freedom Trail

Take a time-travel trek to the American Revolution on this 2.5-mile urban walking trail featuring 16 of Boston's most iconic historic sites.

Follow the redbrick road – or red-painted stripe, in some places – that links 16 of Boston's (and the country's) most cherished landmarks. Against the backdrop of a modern city, these sites pop into focus and illuminate the drama of America's fight for independence. The Freedom Trail is no walled-off historic park: these 17th-, 18th-, and 19th-century sites are woven into the rich fabric of Boston's vibrant downtown. Here, an ancient cemetery is home to Paul Revere's grave; there, a plaque marks the Boston Massacre. (And over there, alas, is a fast-food joint. This is a modern city, after all!) Preserved and dedicated by the people of Boston in 1951, the Freedom Trail is one of the city's classic experiences, and a designated National Recreation Trail.

How to best discover the Freedom Trail? It's possible to 'do' this walk in an hour or so if you trot from site to site, snap a few photos, and spend a minimal amount of time at each stop. Ideally, though, set aside a day to explore this unique collection of parks, burial grounds, churches, museums, meetinghouses, historic markers – and one ship. Venture inside the sites that capture your interest, and feel the power of their history (and perhaps sense a passing ghost or two.)

Make your first stop the Freedom Trail information booth at Boston Common (139 Tremont St) to pick up a map and brochure or purchase an audio tour. The Freedom Trail Foundation offers MP3 audio downloads. To dig a little deeper, join a guided tour. The National Park Service offers free, guided tours seasonally, and the Freedom Trail Foundation offers public tours for a fee. The latter are hard to miss, as guides wear Colonial-period costumes. On one of our

Sleep here...

Many B&Bs and inns are housed in historic or architecturally significant buildings, but in recent years, Boston has become a hotspot for small and stylish boutique hotels. The most convenient neighborhoods to the trail are Downtown Boston, the North End and Bunker Hill, but public transport is plentiful and means you can stay anywhere.

Revolution Hotel
The 163-room Revolution Hotel, in Boston's South End, offers stylish, wallet-friendly digs. Options include king and queen rooms, and triple and quad bunk-style rooms for guests traveling in groups. Some rooms have shared bathrooms.

Godfrey Hotel Boston
Just a half mile from the Freedom Trail, the Godfrey Hotel Boston has crisply tailored guest rooms (think Frette linens) and an on-site restaurant, Ruka, specializing in Peruvian-Japanese cuisine.

Boxer Boston
Near the Freedom Trail and Boston's North End, the Boxer Boston hotel, set in a flatiron building from 1904, offers 80 rooms done up in industrial-chic style. The hotel's restaurant, Finch, serves American-style cuisine.

The Whitney
A former 1909 nurse's dorm at Massachusetts General Hospital on Beacon Hill has been transformed into this spiffy, 66-room luxury boutique hotel. The modern Italian restaurant, Peregrine, is open for breakfast, brunch, lunch and dinner.

Toolbox

When to go
More than four million people walk this trail every year. In summer and fall, expect crowds at popular sites like the Paul Revere House and Old North Church. Guided tours are offered year-round.

Getting there
The Freedom Trail is in the heart of downtown Boston. The nearest major airport is Boston Logan, about 5 miles from Boston Common, where most people begin the walk. Boston Common is right by the Park St subway stop on the MBTA, the city's public transit system.

Practicalities
Length in miles: 2.5
Start: Boston Common, downtown Boston, MA
End: Bunker Hill Monument, Charlestown neighborhood, MA
Dog friendly: Exteriors, yes; interiors, no
Bike friendly: Yes
Permit needed: No
States covered: Massachusetts

→ The USS *Constitution*.

tours, a vest-and-breeches-wearing guide backed into a fellow decked out as Benjamin Franklin, who was leading a different history tour. Only in Boston! A tour allows you to ask questions on the way, and a guide will also point out oddities that aren't officially on the Freedom Trail, like Boston's 10ft-wide 'narrowest house' across from Copp's Hill Burying Ground.

At the trail's start, the pealing bells of the Park Street Church punctuate the lively scene of the Boston Common; this church is where 'America (My Country 'Tis of Thee)' was first sung in 1831. Today the oldest park in America is filled with office workers munching sandwiches and toddlers chasing squirrels, but the Common has a storied past. In the 1600s it was a common grazing ground for locals' sheep and cattle. Later, the pastoral plot morphed into a training field for militia, and then a British Army camp during the occupation of Boston. Those accused of piracy and witchcraft once hung from the Common's trees, and assorted criminals were pilloried here. Happier scenes followed, as the Common became a center of public oratory; Martin Luther King, Jr and Gloria Steinem are among the notable speakers. Pope John Paul II said Mass on this spot in 1979. Today the Common is the city's backyard, with its wading pond (turned ice-skating pond in winter), concerts and alfresco Shakespeare performances.

Across the Common, the golden dome of the Massachusetts State House is a major attention-getter. Designed by noted architect Charles Bulfinch and completed in 1798, the 'new' State House didn't always have a shiny topper. The golden dome was originally covered with wooden shingles and, later, overlaid with copper by Paul Revere. The 23-karat gold leaf was added in 1874.

A short walk away, the Granary Burying Ground is the final resting place of A-listers like John Hancock (marked with a lavish obelisk), Paul Revere, Samuel Adams and Benjamin Franklin's parents. Although there are only 2345 markers, an estimated 5000 people are buried here, with many families sharing the same headstone.

The interior of the stone King's Chapel, completed in 1754, is considered the finest example of Georgian architecture in North America. The church houses the oldest continuously used American pulpit, and the belfry holds an 1816 Paul Revere–crafted bell that still calls people to worship. Among those buried in the cemetery are John Winthrop, Massachusetts' first governor, and Mary Chilton, the first woman to step off the *Mayflower*.

After a few more stops on the trail, you'll enter Boston's North End. Over time this neighborhood has been home to waves of immigrants, most recently Italians. Pick up a cannoli at Mike's Pastry or Modern Pastry (both worthy) en route to the Old North Church. Henry Wadsworth Longfellow's poem 'Paul Revere's Ride' immortalized this 1723 church. On the night of April 18, 1775, two signal lanterns were hung in its steeple to alert Patriots outside the city that the British were heading to Lexington and Concord by river, launching the American Revolution.

Walk over the bridge to Charlestown for a couple of key sites: the USS *Constitution* (aka 'Old Ironsides,' though it's made of wood) and Bunker Hill Monument, commemorating the Battle of Bunker Hill. A 221ft granite obelisk marks the spot where Colonial forces prevailed against the British Army on June 17, 1775. This is the end of the trail, but let's hope you've got energy to spare: a climb up the monument's 294 steps reveals stellar views.

Highlights

Trace the locations of the events that earned this town its status as the 'Cradle of Liberty' by walking the trail, getting the best introduction to revolutionary Boston's colonial past.

PAUL REVERE HOUSE
Dating to about 1680, this is the only Freedom Trail site that is a former home. Revere and his family lived here when he made his famous ride on April 18–19, 1775.

BOSTON COMMON
America's oldest public parkland began as a common grazing ground for sheep and cattle. As the setting for events from public hangings to papal masses, Boston's backyard has quite the past.

OLD SOUTH MEETING HOUSE
Five thousand angry colonists gathered here on December 16, 1773, to protest a tax on tea, sparking the revolution. The congregation was also connected to African American poet Phillis Wheatley.

USS *CONSTITUTION* MUSEUM
Discover the stories of America's ship of state, the 1797 *USS Constitution*, at this free museum in the Charlestown Navy Yard. It is still a commissioned US Navy warship.

OLD NORTH CHURCH
Boston's oldest church, built in 1723, played a pivotal role in the American Revolution. Visitors can tour the chapel, bell-ringing chamber and crypt.

Sandia Peak, New Mexico.
Right: Mountain biker in the
Sandia Mountains.

19.

The Grand Enchantment Trail

A wild backcountry trekking route, this trail connects over 700 miles of diverse terrain in the Southwest, from mountains, canyons and deserts to historical places of interest.

The Grand Enchantment Trail (GET) is not for the faint of heart. This 770-mile-long backcountry route crosses the wild and dramatic landscapes distinct to Arizona and New Mexico – from the high-altitude forest of the Sky Island mountains to the Continental Divide and the biologically diverse Chihuahuan and Sonoran Deserts. This series of open country trails, sometimes overlapping with the AZT and CDT, is the key to the hidden corners of the Southwest.

Developed in 2003, the GET leverages existing trails, dirt roads, public lands and cross-country hiking routes to create an unusually natural wilderness path mostly untouched by people. Here, hikers can connect with some of Earth's greatest works of art. Solitude, serenity and majestic scenery are what make this trail deserving of its name. It is neither the shortest nor the most direct route, but rather offers optimal exposure to the greatest sights of these two states. Although it remains an undesignated wilderness recreational trail, the GET awes and draws adventurers, naturalists and seasoned hikers from across the country.

Elevation ranges from 1750ft to 10,700ft, in combination with the trail's ruggedness and the conventional challenges of long-distance hiking, ensure an ambitious hike from end to end. What the GET demands in strength and grit, it delivers tenfold in rewards; deep gasps from climbing high are exchanged for wide eyes gazing at juniper-studded canyons and the blue sky animated by cotton clouds.

The journey begins in Arizona's Superstition Mountains, a natural treasure marked by volcanic rock, picturesque canyons and panoramic views of the

Sleep here...

Unlike the regular amenities of most National Scenic Trails (even if those amenities are just huts), this unsanctioned trail lets you figure it out on your own, from backcountry camping to resupply stops in the small towns en route. Lightly trafficked, its solitude means nights under the open sky with no sound but nature around you. To navigate between food cache boxes, water sources and town stops, strong compass skills are required.

Backcountry Camping
There are no backcountry shelters or huts along this route, so pack accordingly (tarp, tent and foam pad recommended) and be prepared to camp under the stars.

Ojo Caliente Resort & Spa
Treat yourself at this New Mexico resort southwest of Taos, a historic adobe-style hotel and bathhouse with access to the local springs. It was long a sacred Apache oasis, its soothing hot springs bringing health to Native Americans for centuries.

Capilla Peak Campground
The campground is a popular stop for thru-hikers in New Mexico's Cibola National Forest in the Manzano Mountains. It's first come, first served. Call a ranger for info at 505-346-3900.

Towns Along the Way
Rest and resupply in nearby Superior, Mammoth, Safford, and Clifton (Arizona), and in Glenwood, Gila Hot Springs, Monticello, Magdalena, Mountainair, and Tijeras (New Mexico). Stop at Klondyke, Arizona, to resupply before entering the Santa Teresa Wilderness.

Toolbox

When to go
Be wary of climatic extremes on this rugged route, and avoid summer and winter. Opt for a spring trek for longer days, desert flowers in bloom and plentiful water sources. Fall brings bright foliage, colder temperatures and limited access to water.

Getting there
Both termini are close to international airports and near large urban areas. Embark from the First Water trailhead in Tonto National Forest, 45 miles east of Phoenix, Arizona; or head 16 miles northeast of Albuquerque, New Mexico, to the Tramway trailhead.

Practicalities
Length in miles: 770
Start: First Water trailhead, Tonto National Forest, AZ
End: Tramway trailhead, Cibola National Forest, NM
Dog friendly: No, due to water availability and potential wildlife hazards in the backcountry
Bike friendly: Not recommended
Permit needed: Required for the Aravaipa Canyon Wilderness
States covered: Arizona, New Mexico

Sonoran Desert. Revel in the great beauty of these vast lands; the remarkable flora and fauna are sure to capture the hearts of even the most experienced hikers. Weavers Needle – a fang-shaped rock formation – and the 700-year-old Salado cliff dwellings are not to be missed.

White Canyon Wilderness welcomes with steep volcanic peaks, rows of saguaro cacti and sedimentary cliffs that display thousands of years of erosion history. Pass the Gila River, pausing to take in the views of the Santa Catalina Mountains in the distance – best seen when painted red by a setting sun. The San Pedro River, a rare oasis in these desert mountains, offers calm, cool waters and a serene stop before you reach Hwy 77 in Arizona.

Enter the Galiuro Mountains and find the 1000ft-high walls of Aravaipa Canyon, with Aravaipa Creek a guiding compass through miles of lush landscapes into the Santa Teresa Wilderness. This extremely rugged cross-country terrain requires the utmost effort. Quiet trails deliver pure solitude; a traverse through Holdout Canyon, known for its granite domes, leaves hikers to stand in wonder before continuing the climb to the Pinaleño Mountains. Riggs Lake is a peaceful pause; Webb Peak – the tallest of the Sky Island ranges at 10,000ft – offers panoramic views of the Rincon, Huachuca, Chiricahua and Mogollon Mountains shortly thereafter. Spend some time here; this is one of the greatest moments along the GET.

Old roads, remote paths and a former trade route lead hikers into the Gila Mountains to find canyons carved by the Bonita Creek. Bellmeyer Saddle, open grassy lands 6000ft above sea level, calls to climbers for a break and a bite. Sweet solitude lingers in this high-desert

mountain. Look for bighorn sheep, white-nosed coatis and ancient pictographs in Eagle Creek's canyon and along the Painted Bluff Trail.

March through the Blue Range's mountainous landscape, down the banks of the Blue River and to the Mogollon Mountains, not far from a ghost town rich with mining history and the famous Catwalk National Recreation Trail. What were bridges (the Catwalk) used to transport water for mining are now rebuilt in a history buff's paradise. From the Gila Wilderness, over Mogollon Baldy – at 10,774ft the tallest peak on the GET, with breathtaking views – through the wildflower meadows of the Gila River, to the Gila Cliff Dwellings National Monument (built in the 13th century) and along the Continental Divide, New Mexico enchants and delights. Its rolling grasslands and aspen trees, lit afire during autumn, offer miles upon miles of serenity. Pause at secluded Ojo Caliente to experience a respite from the GET's challenging backcountry travel.

Through the San Mateo Mountains, into the Cibola National Forest and past the resting place of the infamous outlaw Apache Kid, this strenuous trek across steep ridges and cross-country tracks is one to remember. The Grand Enchantment Trail unfurls itself in final moments marked by forested roads, riverside woods and the labyrinthine San Lorenzo Canyon. Expect sandstone arroyos, spring pools and a forested plateau in the Chihuahuan Desert. Traverse the Manzano Crest Trail along the edge of a limestone 'reef' above the Rio Grande valley. Climb Sandia Crest, the final obstacle, to take in the natural glory conquered on this truly grand, enchanting trail.

Highlights

Not a thru-hiker? The GET is parsed into 39 segments, allowing hikers of all types to experience this great route. Try some of the below options, and check the official trail website for more pointers, necessary as there are no trail blazes.

PICKETPOST TRAILHEAD
Experience Sonoran Desert charm by driving to Picketpost trailhead for a 4-mile out-and-back up Picketpost Mountain, west of Superior, Arizona.

TRAMWAY TRAIL
This 5-mile hike outside Albuquerque, New Mexico, treks through wildflower meadows, connecting with La Luz Trail before climbing up the Sandia Mountains.

GILA CLIFF DWELLINGS
Visit New Mexico's Gila Cliff Dwellings National Monument, near Silver City, for a peek into the past. A short walk is required to enter the ancient caves and dwelling rooms with pictographs.

ARAVAIPA CANYON WILDERNESS
North of Mammoth, Arizona, find the West trailhead of this wilderness area and see all this grand canyon has to offer on the 12.25 miles to the East trailhead. Permit needed.

BLACK MESA LOOP
Embark on a 9-mile scenic loop from the First Water trailhead to Second Water trailhead and the Black Mesa Trail in the Superstition Mountains near Phoenix.

20

Grays Peak National Recreation Trail

Heading straight up into the crystal-blue Colorado sky high above the tree line, this National Recreation Trail will literally take your breath away, and the views from 14,000ft are nothing short of sublime.

Alpine meadow and stream on the way up to Grays Peak in Colorado. Right: Rock marking the summit on Grays Peak.

There are 96 peaks in the US over 14,000ft – and 54 of them are in Colorado (second-place Alaska has 29). Climbing fourteeners, in local parlance, has become a rite of passage for Coloradans and is often a source of conversation on par with older generations' 'fishing stories.' People are so proud of their fourteener accomplishments that they make it a point to climb as many as they can in a summer, keeping exhaustive track and proudly displaying their summits via social media as often as possible. Some hikers might even have a poster with handy little spaces to stamp red when a peak has been 'bagged' (when you make it to the top).

The first recorded ascent of Grays Peak was in 1861 by the botanist Charles C Parry. In a sign of respect, Parry named the mountain after one of his mentors, the botanist Asa Gray. Parry spent many years in the area measuring peaks and identifying and classifying species of plants.

Grays Peak is one of the most accessible opportunities to climb into the sky, but being accessible does not mean it isn't a challenge. At 14,278ft Grays is the 10th-highest summit in the state and the highest point along the Continental Divide in Colorado. The hike to the top from the trailhead is only about 4 miles, but the 3040ft elevation gain means it is a steep, rigorous climb. The trail is also well-known, well-used and not particularly treacherous, making it popular. Those squeamish about heights won't find that the climb triggers their fear, and there will be company along the way.

Start from the Grays Peak trailhead on Stevens Gulch Rd, a gravelly 3-mile stretch which is best traversed by 4WD (you can reach it from exit 221 of I-70). The beginning of the trail meanders through an

Sleep here...

Colorado provides a vast array of accommodation options: from pitching a tent under a starlit sky to budget motels and B&Bs, adobe inns and historical hotels to spas and dude ranches. Camping is the cheapest, and in many ways the most enjoyable, approach to a Colorado vacation. Car campers can take advantage of hundreds of private and public campgrounds and RV parks. The best resource is www.recreation.gov.

Guanella Pass Campground
Camping at the Guanella Pass Campground south of Georgetown is a great option if you want to stay close to the trailhead. There are 18 sites available, and you will need to make a reservation during summer high season.

Loge Camps
In nearby Breckenridge, Loge Camps has everything you need for a mountain adventure. With both hotel and hostel rooms, it has a variety of options for all budgets. Bike and other gear rentals are on site.

Fireside Inn
For a little more comfort but a still budget-friendly price, try this Breckenridge inn. The charming B&B boasts a barrel hot tub, movie nights and a snuggly resident pooch. It's just a quick walk from town.

Crawford Hotel
If you're looking for something a little more upscale, try the Crawford Hotel in Denver. Luxurious and art-filled, this hotel in Union Station is as charming as it is comfortable. Service is impeccable, and the deep claw-foot tub is perfect for a post-hike soak.

© Brandon Grenier / Alamy Stock Photo ; © Brandon Grenier / Alamy Stock Photo

Toolbox

When to go
Hiking in high altitudes should only be done in the summer months, unless you are an expert. The best time to go is July through September; start early in the morning so you are down the mountain before afternoon thunderstorms strike.

Getting there
The only way to go is to drive, unless you arrive as part of a thru-hike on the Colorado Trail. From Denver, take I-70 west about an hour to Georgetown. Take exit 221 and follow Steven's Gulch Road for 3 miles to the trailhead. This is a popular hike, so arrive early to secure parking.

Practicalities
Length in miles: 8.6 round trip, including Torreys Peak
Start: Grays and Torreys Peak trailhead at Stevens Gulch Rd, outside Georgetown, CO
End: Same
Dog friendly: Yes, on leash
Bike friendly: Yes
Permit needed: No
States covered: Colorado

→ Grays and Torreys Peaks in Colorado.

alpine basin bisected by a cold mountain stream and dotted with high-altitude wildflowers. This part of the hike is fairly level, with only slight elevation gain. Soon the well-trodden trail morphs into slow and steady switchbacks, quickly rising above tree line into the alpine tundra. Wildflowers get smaller but no less stunning, and the views just get better and better.

While the axiom that it is the journey and not the destination that is important is widely accepted as sage wisdom, when climbing fourteeners, it is the destination that far outstrips the journey in every way. Climbing to over 14,000ft often leaves the lungs screaming and the muscles feeling as if they were injected with lead. Never is gravity more powerful than when you are attempting to defy it. There are joys along the way; mountain goats can be highly diverting, and appreciating the persistence of the tiny wildflowers is always inspiring. Still, when your head starts to swim and your fingers start to tingle, it becomes challenging to focus on anything but putting one foot in front of the other.

So for a few miles it is just that, one foot and then another, using nothing but willpower and muscle power some of us never knew we had. And then it's done, and suddenly the world opens up and the earth never looked so beautiful.

The views alone will steal whatever breath is left in your lungs. For endless miles in every direction, the Rocky Mountains pierce the sky, one after the other in ranges that stretch to an impossibly distant horizon. The cold wind is certainly persistent, but the sun is fierce and warm, wrapping you in its rays and welcoming you to this land above.

From this vantage point, well above most

of the rest of the world, there is nothing to mar the smell of crisp, clean air. There is nothing to make a noise, except the wind gusting over the mountaintops. The feeling of elation coursing through every part of your body is partially due to a goal accomplished and partially because you have found one small secret place that the human world just can't touch. While there will be other people on the mountain with you, it is with the same awe and reverence that they will be relishing their accomplishment and contemplating all that is larger and more powerful than any human force could ever be.

While this mountain is easily climbed relative to many of the others in the state, it is important to be safe. Go in July or August for the least amount of snow and ice, and start early in the morning, 6am at the latest. In the afternoon, thunderstorms strike, bringing lightning, rain and even ice and snow. Go slowly, particularly if you aren't used to the altitude, and give yourself time to adjust. Altitude sickness can strike even the most fit among us.

If you've gotten to the top and are struck by the stunner next to you, why not try to climb it too? Colorado locals often don't separate Grays from its sister peak Torreys, and always refer to them as Grays and Torreys. To bag two peaks in one day, you'll need to descend to 13,707ft in the saddle of the two peaks before you climb up to the 14,274ft summit of Torreys Peak, 4.6 miles into your hike and less than a mile from the summit of Grays Peak. If you relish the sensation of clambering along the Continental Divide Trail, you may have unwittingly gotten your first addicting taste of hiking's Triple Crown, the start of an even more unforgettable journey.

Highlights

Fourteeners come with myriad attractions. But besides the mountains, the historic town and former silver mining camp Georgetown is one of the first mountain towns outside Denver that slope-bound skiers encounter while driving west along I-70.

GUANELLA PASS BREWING COMPANY
Nothing beats a cold beer at the end of a really challenging hike. This Georgetown brewery is a Colorado tradition, with great views.

TORREYS PEAK
If you're up for it, you can actually bag two fourteeners on this hike. Sister peak Torreys adds a few miles, but it's worth it for the bragging rights.

MOUNTAIN GOATS
With gleaming white fur that blends with the patchy snow on the steep switchbacks, these epic climbers bring a sense of awe when you glimpse them on the hike.

WILDFLOWERS
Delicate, brave and vibrant wildflowers dot the heights here. Look for the blue alpine forget-me-not and the stunning yellow of old-man-of-the-mountain.

BAGGING A FOURTEENER
Summiting fourteeners allows you to get about as naturally high as you possibly can with a day pack and good footwear. The rush from the accomplishment is totally worth the climb.

→ Delicate Arch in Arches
National Park in Moab,
near the Hayduke Trail.

21

Hayduke Trail

More crazy idea than actual marked trail, this epic trek through the red rock scenery of the desert Southwest is for hardcore explorers.

Hayduke Trail

The Hayduke Trail is an outrageous, rambling, renegade outlaw of a trail. Routed exclusively and deliberately on public land, it wanders for an epic 800 miles through the lonely red rock canyons, mesas and mountain wilderness of the desert Southwest, passing through a literal A to Z (Arches to Zion) of life-list national parks – Arches, Canyonlands, Capitol Reef, Bryce Canyon, Grand Canyon and Zion – as well as Grand Staircase–Escalante National Monument, Glen Canyon National Recreation Area and a dozen other wilderness areas. At its heart the Hayduke is an ambitious celebration of the American Southwest.

This is not an ordinary trail. For a start, it's not really a trail at all. You won't see a Hayduke Trail sign anywhere. Nor is it an official route, but rather a suggested collection of trails happy to hide subversively under the radar, known only to those mad enough to consider it. It is perversely circuitous. Its start and end points are only about 300 miles apart by road, yet the trail meanders for a masochistic 800 miles, deliberately snaking and detouring to lead you away from the man-made world and deep into the canyons and gullies of the Colorado Plateau.

As you'd imagine for such a long trail, the landscapes are immensely varied, from narrow slot canyons, sculptured smooth by wind and water, to high wind-whipped mesas and snowcapped mountains. From a high point of 11,419ft on frosty Mt Ellen in Utah's Henry Mountains, the trail drops to a low of around 2000ft on the sweltering floor of Arizona's Grand Canyon. In between, hikers must be prepared to wade through soft sand and silty rivers, hop over slick rock and ankle-twisting canyon

Sleep here...

Anyone setting out on the Hayduke Trail is comfortable sleeping on a bedroll, but occasional stays in a real bed on the way are a well-earned treat. Accommodation ranges from end-of-the-world motels to historic national park lodges. In the backcountry you'll need to research camping restrictions, as these vary considerably.

Wild Camping
The Hayduke deliberately avoids civilization, so you'll spend the bulk of the trail camping on sandstone ridges or in sandy valleys. The key is to ensure a reliable water supply.

Zion Lodge, Utah
In Zion National Park, this lodge's coveted location surrounded by red rock walls in the middle of Zion Canyon makes for a modest splurge at the end point of the trail.

El Tovar Lodge, Arizona
Albert Einstein and Teddy Roosevelt are among those who have stayed in this genteel 1905 wooden lodge on the South Rim of Grand Canyon National Park.

Phantom Ranch, Arizona
Dorm-style bunk beds in cozy cabins await at the bottom of the Grand Canyon, with meals, beer and wine available; supplies are brought in by mule.

Toolbox

When to go
The spring months between March and May bring pleasant temperatures and the most reliable water sources, making this the best time. September to December is a good time for fall foliage and crisp days. Summer months have extreme desert heat and very limited water.

Getting there
The popular trailhead of Klondike Bluffs in Arches National Park is just a few miles' hike from Moab's Canyonlands Field Airport in Utah, or get a lift from Moab on BLM Rd 142. The major airport closest to Zion is in Las Vegas, Nevada, a three-hour drive away.

Practicalities
Length in miles: 812
Start: Klondike Bluffs trailhead, Arches National Park, UT
End: Weeping Rock, Zion National Park, UT
Dog friendly: No
Bike friendly: No
Permit needed: Yes, but details vary park to park; research ahead of time
States covered: Utah, Arizona

➡ Arches National Park. Left: Jacob Hamblin Arch, Grand Staircase–Escalante National Monument.

➜ Alstrom Point overlooking Lake Powell.

boulders, and slog down the occasional dirt road. Red sand will fill your shoes, clog your Velcro and break your zips (and occasionally your heart). Every day you will suck in purifying desert air. Occasionally, ancient petroglyphs from another age will stop you in your tracks.

Every mention of the Hayduke comes with a long list of warnings. The lack of water, strong desert sun and physical remoteness all bring inherent dangers. You will need to carry lots of water and cache more in remote locations, a logistical puzzle that makes the Hayduke feel more like an expedition than a hike. Navigation skills and experience with GPS are essential in the disorienting canyonlands. Throw in cacti, scorpions, rattlesnakes, flash floods and quicksand – yes, quicksand – and you soon realize that this is one intimidating trail. More people have summited Everest than have completed the Hayduke. As the official website declares, in bold red type: 'You must be a very experienced desert backpacker in peak physical condition before attempting any section of the Hayduke Trail!' Consider yourself warned.

The few dozen thru-hikers who attempt the route each year figure on between two and three months for the trail's 14 sections, though any one of these sections could make for a fabulous weeklong adventure. Bolted on to the main route are dozens of alternate routes and wonderful side trips.

It's the scope of the route that is most astonishing. From Arches National Park and the outdoorsy town of Moab, the trail has a remote section to Canyonlands National Park, followed by a trek through waterless Dark Canyon and across the Colorado River into Glen Canyon National Recreation Area. For the next few days of hiking, place-

names like Dirty Devil River, Poison Springs and Tarantula Mesa offer an idea of the kind of terrain the trail crosses.

Desert yields to the snowy Henry Mountains; then it's back down to Swap Canyon and Capitol Reef National Park. The Escalante River offers an intriguing potential packrafting section, before a further week of scrambling takes you into Bryce Canyon National Park. The Hayduke then heads south through epic Grand Staircase–Escalante National Monument to enter one of the route's highlights, the Paria Canyon–Vermilion Cliffs Wilderness Area on the Utah–Arizona border. Another unmissable section is the astonishing weeklong trek through the Grand Canyon, before a two-week homestretch ends in Utah's Zion National Park.

The concept of the trail was conceived by co-creators Mike Coronella and Joe Mitchell in the late 1990s, and it was named after George Washington Hayduke III, the fictional antihero of Edward Abbey's 1975 novel *The Monkey Wrench Gang*. The novel follows the Vietnam vet and his motley gang of eco-warriors and political saboteurs as they take radical, violent steps to protect the desert from the encroaching threats of dams, roads and mines.

Hayduke is in many ways a perfect symbol for the rebellious, untamed nature of the trail, which the creators say was born out of a fierce love of the desert and a desire to shield it from the threats of development, mining and grazing. As the Trump-era revocation of protected status in parts of Utah's Bears Ears and Grand Staircase–Escalante National Monuments makes clear, the spirit of the Hayduke Trail remains as relevant as ever.

Highlights

Utah and Arizona harbor some of the most extraordinary landforms on Earth, and let visitors travel through geological time, from the eroded arches and 60-million-year-old rocks of Bryce Canyon to the two-billion-year-old Grand Canyon schist.

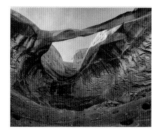

PARIA CANYON–VERMILION CLIFFS WILDERNESS AREA
Section 14, the last, explores some of the Southwest's most amazing slot canyons, including 15-mile-long Buckskin Gulch and Paria Canyon.

ARCHES NATIONAL PARK
An easy start in Utah passes iconic sandstone arches, and encourages hikers to choose the trail of their preference. Edward Abbey worked here for three seasons as a ranger.

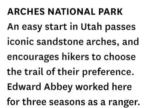

CAPITOL REEF NATIONAL PARK
The switchbacking Burr Trail and sinuous Lower Muley Twist Canyon walls are two highlights of sections 5 and 6 through the striking rock formations of Capitol Reef.

GRAND CANYON NATIONAL PARK
Hike under the radar and under the rim of the famous canyon, with spectacular views and lots of up and down over four sections and almost 200 miles.

CANYONLANDS NATIONAL PARK
Sections 2 and 3 traverse this Utah park's remote southeastern Needles district through Salt Creek, with its archaeological sites and pictograph of the All American Man.

Resources

O1 Hayduke Trail
www.hayduketrail.org
The closest thing to an
official trail website has
links to several excellent
trail blogs.

O2 *The Hayduke Trail: A*
Guide to the Backcountry
Hiking Trail on the
Colorado Plateau
Dating from 2005, this
route guide was written
by the trail's cofounders,
Joe Mitchell and Mike
Coronella.

O3 *The Monkey*
Wrench Gang
Edward Abbey's 1975
comic novel featuring
the eponymous George
Hayduke is a must. Also
bring Abbey's classic *Desert*
Solitaire.

⬆ Juniper snag in Big Spring
Canyon in Canyonlands National
Park. Left: The Weeping Rock in
Zion National Park.

Hike this...

Are you an experienced desert hiker in peak physical condition, but have less than enough time for a thru-hike? Then you may want to bite off smaller portions. Each national park requires a permit; backcountry trails are rugged and require some wayfinding.

➡ A backpacker on the Hayduke Trail, Grand Staircase–Escalante National Monument.

01
Arches National Park

Get a feel for the Hayduke's mix of trails, dirt roads and detours on its initial two days through Arches National Park. Starting at the northwestern edge of the park at Klondike Bluffs, visit Tower Arch and the sandstone towers of the Marching Men. The 'official' route follows a dirt road down Salt Valley, a collapsed former salt dome, and then hugs the park's western boundary. A popular alternative is to cut east to Dark Angel tower and popular Devils Garden, with its iconic arches. Then overnight at Devils Garden Campground if you are foresighted enough to have a reservation. The trail then follows Courthouse Wash to meet the Colorado River just outside Moab town. Be careful not to disturb cryptobiotic soil crusts when hiking off-trail. One of the desert's most fascinating features is also one of its least visible and most fragile: living crusts that cover and protect desert soils, gluing sand particles together and preventing erosion. This thin crust is easily destroyed by human footsteps.

02
Bryce Canyon: Under-the-Rim Trail

This 23-mile, two- or three-day trek offers a taste of the Hayduke to mere mortals unable to budget three months of travel or deal with water caches (but comfortable with outdoorsmanship and wayfinding, as this is no simple stroll). The Under-the-Rim is the park's primary backcountry trail, running almost the entire length of beautiful Bryce Canyon. From Bryce Point you cross the drainages of Yellow Creek and then Swamp Canyon and Agua Canyon, passing under elaborately eroded hoodoos and salmon-pink canyon walls.

As you make the final climb and huff up to the fabulous views of Rainbow Point, consider that this entire hike represents just 3% of the Hayduke's total length. For more of the park's best views, add on an extra day at the beginning and day hike around Peek-a-Boo Loop Trail. Check all trail closures before you head out and be aware that it's a risky route. A backcountry permit is required.

03
Grand Canyon Traverse

One popular short trek that follows the Hayduke is a south–north traverse of the Grand Canyon, taking two or three days (thru-hikers generally take one). From the South Rim, take the popular Bright Angel Trail or South Kaibab Trail down to twin suspension bridges over the Colorado River and spend a night at Bright Angel Campground in the sultry canyon depths. From here it's a relentless 5760ft climb over 14 miles to pop out on the North Rim, with the option of a night at Cottonwood Campground along the way. For a remoter, wilder add-on, take the unmaintained Nankoweap Trail on the North Rim, descend to the north bank of the Colorado, cross on a raft and then hike downstream via Escalante and Tonto Trails to Grand Canyon Village. This takes an additional six or seven days, commensurate skill and a taste for adventure. Mostly waterless with steep drops, eleven-mile Nankoweap Trail is the Grand Canyon's most dangerous trail; it can also be done as out-and-back.

22.
Ice Age National Scenic Trail

Take a walking tour through the geologic history of Wisconsin on this 1200-mile trail featuring varied landscapes that glaciers left behind 15,000 years ago.

Don't let the name scare you away. This thousand-mile historic trail in Wisconsin was carved by nature's glacial forces. Every step takes you back millions of years, when ice up to two miles thick sculpted the landscape. Devotees of the Ice Age National Scenic Trail (IAT for short) are called 'thousand-miler wannabes,' unless they have actually hiked the whole 1200-mile stretch, in which case they are simply 'thousand milers.' From your couch or your barstool, before you've hiked the trail yourself, you might call these people weird. But that's before you hit the IAT yourself.

The Ice Age National Scenic Trail has a little bit of everything Wisconsin has to offer. There are spectacular water views and beautiful dark forests that are, in the words of singer-songwriter Gordon Lightfoot, 'too silent to be real,' but then there are rows of rusted-out cars and old couches lining some of the segments that go through private property. Thousand-miler wannabes can hike the whole thing: pristine park, run-down backyards and all. It's suitable for avid hikers, but not necessarily required that trekkers be advanced. For the rest of us, there are the highlights. And with 1200 miles of trail, there are plenty of highlights.

An Act of Congress officially designated the IAT a National Scenic Trail in 1980. But, as the name 'Ice Age' suggests, it has been with us much longer. Fifteen thousand years ago, glaciers covered much of Wisconsin. The glaciers acted as massive, slow-moving conveyor belts, bringing rocks and earth down from Canada and then leaving them behind as the great sheets of ice melted. The IAT roughly follows the terminal moraine of the glacier across

➡ Sandhill crane at Kettle Moraine State Forest. Left: Ice Age Trail, Devil's Lake State Park.

Sleep here...

Forty B&Bs, inns and hostels consider themselves 'Friends of the Ice Age Trail' and are located on or near the route. You may even get a shuttle to the trailhead out of these establishments! Official campsites can be reserved in advance, but where primitive camping is allowed on the northern portion of the trail, no permit is needed. Dispersed camping areas (DCAs) are also available for thru-hikers, again with no reservation.

White Lace Inn
This charming B&B in Sturgeon Bay is a great home base to access both the eastern terminus of the IAT and Door County, a popular tourist destination year-round. A made-from-scratch breakfast is included.

Delafield Hotel
Ideally situated for those looking to explore the Kettle Moraine State Forest (with notable IAT segment Lapham Peak), this upscale hotel in Delafield offers big-city sophistication and dining.

Camping the IAT
Primitive camping is allowed in the trail's northern sections, as long as it is not in a state park (which requires a fee) or on any private property that the trail occasionally cuts through. Sites must be at least 200ft from water and 200ft from the trail. Dispersed camping areas are also available in 19 spots en route.

Backpacking Shelters
Trailside shelters with fire rings, pit toilets and Adirondack-style shelters can be reserved in advance in parts of the Kettle Moraine State Forest and the Chippewa Moraine State Recreation Area.

Toolbox

When to go
The Ice Age Trail (IAT) is a trail for all seasons. Conditions vary by segment, so it's a good idea to check with trail groups on Facebook or to look at www.iceagetrail.org.

Getting there
You're never far from the Ice Age Trail when you're in Wisconsin. The trail snakes its way through the state, which means a trailhead is always only a few hours away by car. Flying into Madison, Milwaukee or Green Bay will get you on the trail soon.

Practicalities
Length in miles: 1200
Start: Potawatomi State Park, Door County, Eastern WI
End: Interstate State Park on the St Croix River, Western WI
Dog friendly: Yes, but leashes required
Bike friendly: Yes, in many sections
Permit needed: Fees required to access trail via state parks, but no permits required
States covered: Wisconsin

Wisconsin. The terminal moraine is as far as the glacier got, and there are many features that let you know you're standing on the edge of the Ice Age. What looks like a ridiculous place for a huge rock is really just an erratic, a boulder the glacier took along for a ride thousands of years ago. What appears to be a big crater is a kettle pond, formed by a block of stagnant ice pressed into the earth. What the glaciers left behind in Wisconsin has become the stuff of legend, drawing geologists here from across the globe to study one of the world's finest examples of how continental glaciation formed the earth…and drawing hikers, of course.

It's hard to feel particularly important on the IAT even if you don't know its age and provenance. Life goes on all around you – from the 12in snapping turtle making its way uphill, to the mother deer staring at you, all but willing you not to find her hidden fawn nearby. Mayapples bloom, the smell of honeysuckle enchants; yet it would all still happen even if you weren't there.

Of course, not everyone will feel so reverent. The beleaguered Harrison Hills segment in the middle of the state is a sad reminder of that, with logging wiping out half a mountain of trees and ATV trails, along with very loud ATVs, blasting across the IAT's course. Nearby Grandfather Falls, however, as you pick your away along the river rocks, helps you feel much more peaceful and connected with nature. You only need to get past the hydroelectric plant. With an average of 105 people for every square mile in the state, the IAT shows how geology weaves through the suburbs and small towns, not just parks.

Practically anywhere you go on the IAT, except when boardwalks do the work for you, you will need to watch your step. Roots and rocks creep up from the blazed trail and will trip you up if you get distracted by the scenery around you. As beautiful and grand as the landscape is, you've got to admit that the glaciers didn't leave things any too tidy. The IAT also expects hikers to treat the private property on the route respectfully; owners gracefully allow the trail passage via 'handshake agreement,' but hikers must keep to the trail itself and be good trail representatives.

More affluent areas of Wisconsin near the trail have better bets for day hiking. Devil's Lake, Sturgeon Bay and Lapham Peak are great for this. Lapham Peak is maintained like a country club, but the climb to the observation tower will remind you that even on this segment, you don't have it too easy. If you access the peak via the Kettle Moraine Scenic Drive, look forward to following a ribbon of road undulating up and down the hills and through charming towns.

Point Beach is thrilling for its proximity to Lake Michigan as well as the route to get there, which passes the infamous Avery's Auto Salvage, depicted in the Netflix documentary series *Making a Murderer*. A state forest, it has six miles of Lake Michigan frontage and offers camping.

There are both literal and metaphorical ups and downs along the Ice Age Trail, but every segment will change you, inch by inch, step by step. Whether you realize you are braver and stronger than you thought, discover you're particularly grateful for a hiking companion, or resolve to explore just one mile more, you'll come away improved. It's the work of the trail, which, after all, is itself the product of miniature changes over a long, long time.

Highlights

From the shores of Lake Michigan to one of the tributaries of the mighty Mississippi River, the trail winds, turns and curves its way through forest, grasslands and rocky outcroppings. This trail gives you an up close look at the formation of the land.

POINT BEACH

This segment is the only part of the trail that runs along the shore of Lake Michigan, near Two Rivers. A black-sand beach, sand dunes and a lighthouse complete the experience.

THRILLING TOPOGRAPHY

Here's a chance to learn new vocabulary! Rare are the dull moments on the Ice Age Trail: kettles, swales, eskers, erratics and moraines keep the scenery interesting and your feet guessing.

PLOVER RIVER

This is spectacular on snowshoes in winter but also a steady favorite year-round. Boardwalks make it an easy hike to help avoid ever-present mud; in spring, trilliums abound.

LAPHAM PEAK

Less than 30 minutes from Milwaukee, this well-kept part of the IAT has wide cross-country ski trails and mountain bike paths. In season, find mayapples, morels and wild asparagus.

PRAIRIE PINES BULK FOODS

A bright spot for resupply on your hike, this Mennonite-run country store in Gleason has every sundry in the book.

The stairs within the wooded area on the Kettle Moraine leading up to the Parnell Observation Tower.

Resources

O1 Ice Age National Scenic Trail
www.nps.gov/iatr
The National Park Service website for this NST has information and helpful links.

O2 Ice Age Trail Alliance
www.iceagetrail.org
The alliance's mission is to 'create, support and protect' the IAT. Their volunteers are largely responsible for the trail's upkeep. They publish a newsletter, Mammoth Tails, and the indispensable *Ice Age Trail Guidebook*, which breaks down the huge hike into user-friendly sections.

O3 *After the Ice Age: The Return of Life to Glaciated North America*
A well-regarded 1992 book on the ice age by EC Pielou.

Hike this...

As the Ice Age Trail runs along some quiet country roads and through private property over its route, many hikers prefer to experience it via section hike, selecting the most rewarding natural settings for their outing. These are some of the top options.

→ Dells of the Eau Claire River Park. Opposite page from left: Devil's Lake State Natural Area; Sturgeon Bay.

01
Sturgeon Bay, Door County

The journey of (more than) a thousand miles starts – or ends! – here. The Sturgeon Bay segment is the eastern terminus of the Ice Age Trail, set in picturesque Door County, a charming 75-mile peninsula sandwiched between Lake Michigan and Green Bay that attracts more than two million visitors each year. The segment is 13.5 miles long, starting in Potawatomi State Park and ending in Maplewood, Wisconsin. If bogs and trekking through town aren't for you, a better bet is to connect with one of the state park trails that will loop you back to your car or campsite. The trail begins with a photo op at the old ski hill overlook and winds through a thinned-out forest with wild raspberry bushes, trilliums, dogtooth lilies and beech trees. The biggest payoff is when the trail opens up to Sturgeon Bay. The Niagara Escarpment's slices of limestone give way to the bay and create rock stairs that lead to the water. The trail goes on through the town of Sturgeon Bay itself.

02
Devil's Lake State Park, Sauk County

An easy favorite of thousand-miler wannabes is this 13.7-mile segment of the Ice Age Trail through Devil's Lake State Park, Wisconsin's largest state park. Glacier-created Devil's Lake is set within the Baraboo Range, whose different kinds of topography, including bluffs and hills to climb, make it a solidly intermediate hike. One of the best features of this segment is its rock formations, such as the famous Devil's Doorway, a gravity-defying formation overlooking the lake. Due to its distinctive bluffs, the park also boasts some of the Midwest's best rock climbing and bouldering.

Just off the trail are replica effigy mounds; the originals were created between 900 and 1200 years ago by Native Americans known as the Effigy Mound Builders. The views from the 500ft quartzite bluffs overlooking the lake are spectacular at any time of year. There are many other trails in Devil's Lake State Park, so keep your eyes open for the signature yellow blazes of the IAT.

03
Dells of the Eau Claire, Marathon County

Beautiful in summer, brilliant in fall and a little dangerous in winter are the Dells of the Eau Claire in north central Wisconsin. The Ice Age trail passes through a Marathon County park on its banks for 2.6 lovely miles, especially beautiful in fall foliage. Note that it's not close to Wisconsin Dells or the city Eau Claire. The segment is named for the Eau Claire River, which formed the terraced outcroppings of rock known as dells. Water cascades over these rocks in countless waterfalls of various sizes. Some of the oldest exposed bedrock made of rhyolite along the trail can be found here; its estimated age is 1.8 billion years old.

It's an easy walk with drama not just from the terrain but also from the locals, whether they're posing in wedding photograph sessions or basking on the rocks in summer. During the spring thaw, water rushes through with frightening urgency. The river has deadly undercurrents, so stay on marked trails and do not trust its calm surface.

Stand up paddleboarding on the headwaters of the Middle Fork of the Salmon River, Idaho. Right: View of the East Centennial Mountains in eastern Idaho, part of the Greater Yellowstone area.

23

Idaho Centennial Trail

Stretched 900 miles lengthwise to showcase Idaho's history and wilderness, this trail is a rough gem of canyons, sawtooth mountains, cedars and pioneering persistence.

For those who love the solitude of unadulterated wilderness, the whim of nature's variables, and improvisation in the moment the 900-mile Idaho Centennial Trail (ICT) from Nevada to Canada has yet to be walked the same way twice. Trail angels, the companionship of festive thru-hikers, signposts – even the actual trail – are luxuries not easily found on the ICT. But in the words of the two Idaho men, Roger Williams and Syd Tate, who conceived the trail and walked its maiden voyage in 1986, the ICT offers a 'tremendous, once-in-a-lifetime experience' through diverse and varied geography.

Passing through both private and public land, it traverses the best of Idaho: six national forests and three federally designated wilderness areas. Here you'll step through desert sagebrush cut by basalt canyons in southern Idaho. As you walk sun-drenched under wide-open skies, watch your step for rattlers. If you're lucky, witness a sea of periwinkle-blossomed camas rippling in the prairie at the foot of your first mountain climb. If you're not lucky, you may find yourself scrambling sawtooth peaks still with their winter snowpack or suffering the frigid bite of a rushing stream blocking your way. Oh, and you'll need robust maps and a compass, as well as GPS.

Beginning at the southern trailhead by the Nevada border in June, a very fast pace will see you reach Canada after 50 days; at a slower 90 days, the snows will start to close in. Continuing on from the starting high desert canyonlands, the well-trodden paths along the boater's paradise of the Wild and Scenic Salmon River are a heady delight. Push deeper still into the Frank Church–River of No Return Wilderness (affectionately nicknamed 'the Frank'), past

Sleep here...

You'll find modern hotels in booming Boise, while Ketchum retains its classic mountain-west charm. Popular tourist destinations like Coeur d'Alene have reliable accommodations, but with National Forest covering half of Idaho a tent will provide the most options. Permission to camp on private land must be obtained from the owner, but the wilderness is full of choice spots for camping.

Redfish Lake Lodge & Campground
Find rustic comfort at this family-friendly place with access to the ICT and Sawtooth Range splendor via Stanley. A general store, restaurant and swimming beach sweeten the deal. Reservations are required well in advance.

Whitewater Ranch
This backcountry guest ranch on the Salmon River is powered by hydroelectricity. The ranch contracts with rafting companies, but thru-hikers can coordinate package resupply and accommodations – real luxuries in the Frank.

Lunch Peak Lookout
The remodeled, simply outfitted fire lookout perched above Lake Pend Oreille is available by reservation. Indian and Sheep Creek Forest Service stations are still operational and stocked with emergency supplies: worth noting.

Sawtooth Lodge
One mile off the trail in Grandjean, this former hunting lodge has cabins, campsites – and most importantly, hot meals and hot springs. Grandjean Campground is a less ritzy option directly off the ICT, first come, first served only.

Toolbox

When to go
Hiking south to north in mid-June is one option. It is a downhill start and avoids heavy snow in mountain sections. Going north to south can work with a mid-July start, but extends fire season overlap. In either direction, cache water in the desert to be safe.

Getting there
The southern terminus is south of Murphy Hot Springs along a primitive road (with spotty signage) to the Idaho–Nevada border. The northern terminus of Upper Priest Falls, less than a mile from the Canadian border, is accessible from FS Rd 312/1013 in Idaho's panhandle.

Practicalities
Length in miles: ~900
Start: Idaho–Nevada border near Murphy Hot Springs
End: Upper Priest Falls, ID
Dog friendly: Yes (leashing required in some areas), but not advised for thru-hiking
Bike friendly: In theory; parallel routes for bikers skirt wilderness areas, but southern and northern sections offer reliable terrain for riding.
Permit required: No
States covered: Idaho

Alpenglow on the Montana–Idaho Divide from Blodgett Lake.

historic ranches, fire lookouts, and Thunder Mountain, site of the last American gold rush. Feel the pioneering spirit in you.

In the Selway-Bitterroot Wilderness of northeastern Idaho, choose your own adventure through overgrowth and blowdowns. In this tangled stretch of wolf country, you will develop an appreciation for any evidence of humanity. Know there is a highway at Wilderness Gateway. But it is still a long walk out, and if you take it, you will miss a refreshing, peaceful walk along the canyon of Kelly Creek as well as the windswept ridgeline between Idaho and Montana.

Some of the best gems are saved for last as you descend into the lushly forested lakes region of the panhandle, dwarfed beneath a canopy of ancient cedars. At the trail's northern terminus, the gentle cascade of Upper Priest Falls finally beckons you to sit. Time to put this unique experience into perspective.

Since the dedication of the ICT as the official state trail in 1990, only 20 or so individuals have completed it in one fell swoop (including one legendary end-to-end mule ride). Without one sole organization coordinating maintenance and communication efforts, the ICT remains an untamed wild card of thru-hikes, with an emphasis on wild. Dan Noakes, who completed it in 2018, noted, 'You want to do it because it's hard, but you don't want to do it because it's hard.' For ultrarunners Andrija Barker and Taylor Neal, an abandoned attempt in 2016 left them 'bloodied, bruised and craving a steak.' When early snows detoured their trek to roads instead of trail, hikers Raj and Kathy Vaughn say the ICT taught them to say yes to whatever the story was becoming rather than resist it. Though hikers are motivated by unique intentions, the individual narratives of ICTers are pinned together with the same thesis: Idaho wilderness isn't for conquering, but it sure is something special to experience.

Unlike the groomed and populated trails of the Appalachian Trail or Pacific Crest Trail, the ICT demands constant improvisation and self-reliance. It is an intoxicating breath of sagebrush after a desert rain, followed by log-humps over gnarly, roaring snowmelt. It is jagged, unforgiving boulder fields. It is also the welcoming green X of a backcountry airstrip and gracious hosts with their own wilderness stories to tell. It may be wildfires, hours attempting to hitchhike to the next resupply, loneliness or questioning your choices as you lock eyes with a moose. That is the allure of the Idaho Centennial Trail. Which of its mercurial moods will show up for your trek, and will you be able to morph appropriately for the occasion?

As in a good fable, the ICT's moral is that patience, effort and reward are intertwined. The relationship of humans to wild lands can be tenuous but is not impossible. Sit beneath the shade of the lovingly tended English walnut tree, a wedding gift to Frances Zaunmiller Wisner on her homestead property (Campbell's Ferry) in the Frank, and feel the roots of that place in your bones. Know that Lewis and Clark ran into the same snowy predicament on Lolo Pass, and, like you, they were grateful for the Nimiipuu (Nez Perce) who navigated the mountains before them. Walk along the precipice that divides Idaho and Montana. Look east, and you'll see sheer granite dropping into alpine basins. Look west, and Idaho's northern greenery rolls into the horizon. While thru-hikers may lose the trail at points along the way, on their path through the state they gain much more.

Highlights

More than 60% of Idaho is public land, and with 3.9 million acres of wilderness, it's the third-wildest state in the union. The ICT is the ideal way to get close to that wild side, from national forests to untamed rivers.

KELLY CREEK
This creek in Clearwater National Forest is famed for fly-fishing and backcountry tranquility. The rough travel in (hiking or driving) is offset by easy walking alongside emerald waters.

UPPER PRIEST LAKE
Two miles north of Priest Lake and just south of the Canadian border, this pedestrian-only area at the trail's northern terminus preserves the pristine, quiet intimacy with nature ICTers expect.

THE FRANK
The more than 2.3-million-acre Frank Church–River of No Return Wilderness is the largest contiguous wilderness in the Lower 48, with 425 miles of world-class rafting.

ATLANTA
The small community of locals, artists-in-refuge and outdoor enthusiasts on the edge of the Sawtooth Wilderness at the Middle Fork of the Boise River brims with character.

ROSS PEAK
In the Boise Mountains near the Sawtooth Range, Ross Peak is the highest point on the trail at over 9000ft.

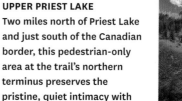

Eagle River Nature
Center in Alaska

24

Iditarod National Historic Trail

Alaska's only national historic trail, this route crosses a lineup of Alaska's best hits and vast swaths of wilderness, familiar from the storied annual race.

Iditarod Trail

The Iditarod National Historic Trail is one of Alaska's most famous routes, thanks to the 1000-mile dogsled race of the same name. The trail and the race commemorate the hurried delivery of diphtheria vaccine in late January 1925, when the life-saving vaccine was rushed to Nome by dogsled in a frantic push to save lives. The vaccine arrived by boat in Seward, traveled by train to Nenana and then was taken to Nome by 20 teams of dogs in a six-day relay. Today the trail traverses the same route, though a section of the actual race from Ophir to Kaltag alternates each year between a northern (on even years) and a southern route (on odd years). Encompassing most things typically associated with Alaska, the trail covers rugged, isolated swaths of wilderness, pops into Alaska Native villages and sweeps through valleys and over mountain passes.

Though the route is most famous because of the vaccine run, local tribes had used the network of trails for travel and trade long before surveyors mapped the Seward to Nome route in 1908, driven by the Iditarod gold rush. Until the advent of cars, planes and snowmobiles, dogsled was the main mode of transport during Alaska's winters, and indeed much of the gold from the 1908 rush was taken out by dogsled. It's this history that the Iditarod National Historic Trail, established in 1978, commemorates. The state's boggy tundra, as well as its swamps and rivers, can be hazards in summer but are easily traversed once they freeze. In summer, rivers are the most passable route, but in winter, travel by dogsled (or snowshoe) is more straightforward.

The official sled race trail crosses

➡ View along the Iditarod Trail at Turnagain Arm.

Sleep here...

Highly-trafficked Anchorage, Seward and Nome all offer good sleeping options for visitors. Small towns are more limited. There are 10 public safety cabins along the trail, mainly accessible only in winter by dogsled, snowshoe, snow machine or river float. The southernmost is the National Register of Historic Places–listed Rohn Roadhouse Safety Cabin near Rainy Pass, a race checkpoint. Or check out public-use cabins.

Camping Along the Trail
Along the trail's backcountry sections in south central Alaska, you can camp anywhere that's flat enough. The Turnagain Pass Trail segment is a good option for primitive camping.

Public Cabins and Yurts
On the popular Crow Pass section of the trail, public-use cabins and yurts are highly sought after. Book ahead online about six months in advance for weekends and midsummer weekdays. Safety cabins along the National Historic Trail, by contrast, are unreservable and meant to bolster public safety for winter travelers.

Alyeska Resort, Girdwood
Encircled by mighty peaks brimming with glaciers, Girdwood is a laid-back antidote to the bustle of Anchorage. Home to the luxurious Alyeska Ski Resort, it offers access to the Iditarod Trail via the Winner Creek Trail.

Dredge No.7 Inn, Nome
Nome's gold-rush-era buildings have been lost to fire or weather conditions, but the Dredge 7 Inn is run by a mining family connected to Alaskan history. In winter during the race, rooms in Nome will fill.

Toolbox

When to go
March is the race month, and winter is the time to explore the northern sections by snowshoe, sled and more. Much of the trail is swampy and impassable in summer, except for sections in south central Alaska, which are instead off-limits in winter due to avalanche risks. In late winter, brave cyclists on fat-tire bikes will take on the trail to Nome. Snowpack is less predictable nowadays; check conditions in advance.

Getting there
The trail system starts in Seward on the road system. Since only a few sections are interesting to a casual summer visitor, your best bet is to explore in Seward and around Anchorage. Nome and the bush are accessible by plane.

Practicalities
Length in miles: 1000–2300 (race trail length versus total system)
Start: Seward, AK
End: Nome, AK
Dog friendly: Yes
Bike friendly: Yes; some sections
Permit needed: No
States covered: Alaska

Nome, Alaska.

1000 miles from its kickoff in Willow (the new restart after the Anchorage ceremonial start once lack of snow made Wasilla impractical), but the trail system comprises more than 2300 miles after its start in Seward. Much of the trail is accessible only during winter, but there are sections of it you can explore in summer, most of them between Seward and Eagle Rivers in south central Alaska. Once the trail heads north from Eagle River, it is undeveloped and marked by swampy lowlands. Travel in these parts is possible only in winter. In contrast, the lower sections are generally accessible only in summer due to high avalanche danger. These sections are gorgeous, mountainous hikes that showcase some of south central Alaska's best wilderness.

Due to the historical and cultural significance of the trail, as well as the recreational opportunities it offers, plans are in the works to complete the 120-mile Southern Trek over the next few years. The trek would connect Seward and Eagle Rivers in a cohesive stretch, although for now it's not feasible to hike the trail in sections longer than 20–30 miles at a go.

The trail to Nome begins as a paved bike path along the waterfront in Seward at mile 0, where you're treated to views of mountains crashing right into the sea. A busy, scenic public campground is sandwiched between the path and the ocean. Pick the trail up again off Nash Road, a few miles north of town, along a brushy section to Bear Lake. Once you reach the lake, the trail peters out into the wilderness.

The next best place to pick it up is at the Johnson Pass trailhead, at mile 32.5 of Seward Hwy. Here you can hike a scenic 23

miles to a trailhead at mile 64, surrounded by mountains the entire time. You'll pass alpine lakes and ponds, meadows full of wildflowers, and rushing streams and waterfalls along this gorgeous section.

Continue north by road along the Seward Hwy to Girdwood, where you can walk a section called the Lower Iditarod Trail for 6 miles along Crow Creek Rd. Even better, take the Winner Creek Trail from the Alyeska Resort. Pull yourself across a gorge on a hand tram and follow the trail through moss-carpeted spruce forest to meet the Iditarod Trail. The trail continues at the Crow Pass trailhead. This section, which ends in Eagle River and Chugach State Park outside Anchorage, is one of the area's most popular and gorgeous trails. Give yourself a minimum of two days to hike it, and make sure you know how to cross the icy Eagle River at mile 12. On the Girdwood side you'll have a steep 3-mile climb up to Crow Pass, passing old mine tailings and catching a glimpse of the dramatic Raven Glacier. From the pass, the trail descends 9 miles to Eagle River, past Thunder Gorge (you'll hear it before you see it) and mountain-lined meadows. After you ford the river, the trail stays mostly flat as it follows the water's course 12 miles to the Eagle River Nature Center.

After Eagle River there aren't many summer hiking options on the Iditarod Trail, but winter sports fans can hit sections of the trail, especially by plane. In winter the month-long Iditarod Trail Invitational ultramarathon sees hardy beings race 350 or 1000 miles on bike, skis or on foot, but for most, these regions are inaccessible. The middle and northern sections of the trail are in the bush, beyond the reaches of the road system.

Highlights

Ready for beautiful alpine hikes with gold-mining relics, alpine lakes and Dall sheep on the slopes? What about seeing the shores of the Bering Strait, the snow-speckled expanses of bleak tundra, and getting the chance to cheer on teams finishing a grueling race?

IDITAROD TRAIL SLED DOG RACE
Watch teams of mushers cruise through downtown Anchorage at the ceremonial start or take a bush plane to a race checkpoint for the full experience.

WASILLA
The Iditarod Trail Sled Dog Race Museum on Knik Rd has free admission and offers exhibits on mushing that pull from years of racing history.

MANLEY HOT SPRINGS
In recent years the second checkpoint of the race, the well-kept town of Manley Hot Springs near the Tanana River is a hotbed of high-level dog mushing.

NOME
Catch the Iditarod finish in March, complete with triumphal pine arch, news cameras and diehard fans, or follow the trail along the Bering Sea.

SPENCER GLACIER WHISTLE STOP
Ride the Alaska Railroad from Girdwood to Spencer Glacier along the original Iditarod Trail route. You'll be off the road system for the day.

Resources

O1 Iditarod Trail Sled Dog Race *iditarod.com* The official site for the famous race is geared to spectators, with trail info including maps and checkpoints.

O2 Iditarod National Historic Trail Alliance *www.iditarod100.org* The site covers the history of the trail and has an excellent PDF visitors guide.

O3 The Cruelest Miles Gay Salisbury describes the infamous race to Nome in page-turning detail.

O4 *Welcome to the Goddamn Ice Cube* Blair Braverman wrote this 2016 memoir about learning to mush before her successful 2019 Iditarod.

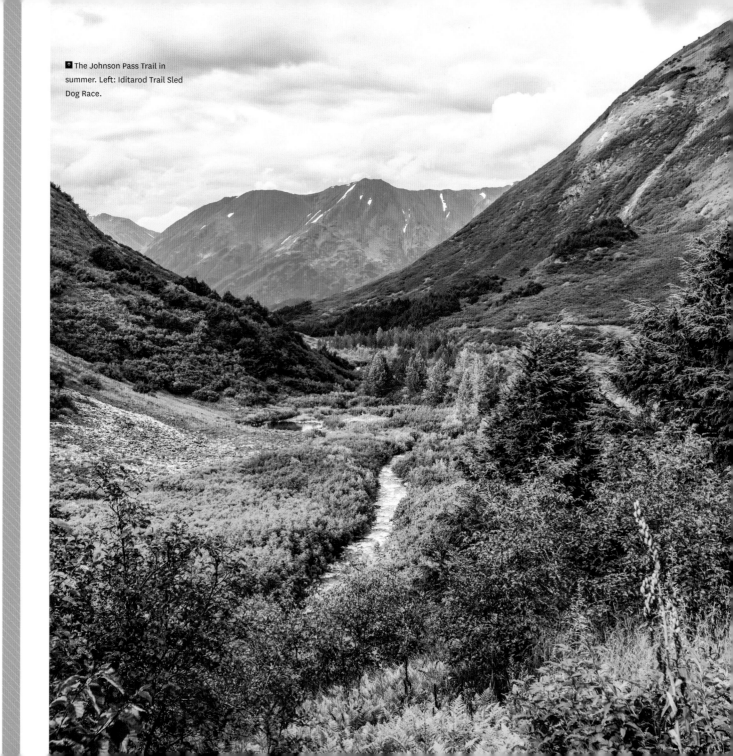

The Johnson Pass Trail in summer. Left: Iditarod Trail Sled Dog Race.

Hike this...

If you're unlikely to race your own sled on the trail or take a plane into the bush, these options near the beginning and end of the Iditarod National Historic Trail are a wonderful way to sample its unique flavor.

➔ Nome, the end of the trail.

01
Crow Pass

This section of trail from Girdwood to Eagle River, locally called Crow Pass for its highest point, is the most popular hiking section of the Iditarod National Historic Trail in south central Alaska. With a steep, rocky climb to the pass, stream crossings (go ahead and get your shoes wet, but better be wearing waterproof boots), glacier views, wildflowers and a thundering gorge all within the first half, it's easy to see why hikers love it. You'll need to ford a waist-deep (sternum-deep for some folks) glacial river so cold that chunks of ice from the glacier upstream often whiz by on the current.

The second half follows Eagle River as it rushes through a steep, mountainous valley. There are plenty of campsites as well as public-use yurts and cabins, so long as you reserve in advance. In Chugach State Park, hike to Crow Pass, marveling at Raven Glacier and fording Eagle River along the way. The trail is off-limits in winter, and requires warm gear even in summer.

02
Johnson Pass

A 23-mile multi-use stretch of subalpine rivers, lakes, meadows, forests, flowers and wildlife offers excellent mountain biking and takes recreational users from mile 64 to mile 32.5 of Seward Hwy. This segment in Chugach National Forest between Seward and Anchorage is deservedly popular, and if you want to experience the Iditarod Trail by bike in summer, this is generally agreed upon as the terrain to take on.

Many experienced cyclists can cover the distance in a short day, but give yourself a solid seven or eight hours, as the trail is technical and steep in places, gaining and losing close to 3000ft of elevation. It's best in mid-June, as by midsummer it can be too overgrown to be enjoyable; snow can linger at elevation until mid-June, however. Watch for bears and moose and carry emergency gear. Don't forget to look up: the mountains are calling you. Hikers will find a few steep sections and designated backcountry campsites, typically with bear-resistant food lockers.

03
Nome Beach

Perched on the tip of the Seward Peninsula along the Bering Sea and near the Arctic Circle, the town of Nome was founded during the 1899–1909 Nome Gold Rush as a base for hopeful miners. No longer a boomtown, its raucous energy lives on at the finish of the Iditarod Trail Sled Dog Race, when thousands of spectators descend on the town of 4000 to cheer on finishing mushers. You can still pan for gold along Nome's rocky beaches, and a few people have permits to dredge in the area (including under the sea). Nome offers a quirky combination of modern conveniences in a remote region. It's far, far removed from the road system, meaning you must travel by plane to reach it if you're not riding along with a sled dog team.

Teams arrive into Nome via the coast, coming from Cape Nome along the windswept, treeless shore. It's one of the best places to walk the Iditarod National Historic Trail outside of south central Alaska. You can also drive the gravel trail to the Solomon River in summer.

25

John Muir Trail

Often dubbed 'America's most beautiful trail,' the magnificent John Muir Trail leads hikers – at least those who can get a permit – through the mountain splendor of California's high Sierra Nevada.

For most visitors the granite towers and waterfalls of Yosemite National Park are the scenic highlight of their trip through California's national parks. For hikers on the John Muir Trail (JMT), they are just the starting point. From the Yosemite Valley the trail climbs right into the granite heart of the high Sierra Nevada, passing turquoise lakes and remote peaks while traversing the Ansel Adams and John Muir Wildernesses and Sequoia and Kings Canyon National Parks. Most people who finish the trail regard it as one of the world's finest hikes, through what is quite possibly America's finest mountain scenery.

A glance at an elevation profile of the JMT shows prospective hikers exactly what they are in for. It's a jagged sawtooth that crosses 10 major passes to gain a total of nearly 46,000ft of elevation – that's one and a half times the height of Mt Everest. As you head south, the elevation increases, the crowds thin and the landscape gets ever wilder as the trail crosses remote sections of Kings Canyon National Park. Finally, the hike culminates at the summit of Mt Whitney, a literal high point and the tallest mountain in the contiguous US at 14,505ft. It's a crescendo in this incredible symphony of the wild.

The trail is named, of course, in honor of John Muir, the naturalist, environmentalist and cofounder of the Sierra Club who was the driving force behind the creation of Yosemite National Park in 1872. Muir spent decades wandering the high Sierra Nevada and wrote volumes rhapsodizing about its wild beauty, leading many to consider him the de facto patron saint of the American wilderness. Construction of the John Muir Trail was completed in 1938 on what would

➡ The climb on John Muir Trail. Left: John Muir Trail and the Pacific Crest Trail in the Sierra Nevada.

Sleep here...

If you've got your JMT wilderness permit sorted out from either Yosemite or Inyo National Forest (depending on your starting point), that's most of your worries solved. The hardest part of this trail can be getting permission to hike it. After that, most of your nights will be spent backcountry camping, with carefully planned, and widely known, resupply stops along the way.

Wild Camping
There is no accommodation on the actual trail, but you'll find no shortage of stunning wilderness camp spots. You need to be totally self-sufficient. No campfires are allowed above 10,000ft.

Muir Trail Ranch
This wilderness guest ranch halfway along the trail has been hosting guests since 1940 and offers cabins and a resupply service. A three-night minimum stay applies between June and September.

Red's Meadow Resort
A thru-hiker's refuge just a half mile off the trail near mile 57, Red's has a restaurant, store, showers and resupply service. Accommodation ranges from bunk beds to motel rooms or cabins.

Vermilion Valley Resort (VVR)
Thru-hikers are welcomed at the seasonal VVR with a free cold beer and two nights' free camping, making it worth the short detour and boat shuttle. It's off mile 97, and resupply is possible.

Toolbox

When to go
July to early October is the only feasible time period for this hike, though the start date depends on the amount of winter snowpack. September is perhaps the best month, after the worst of the mosquitoes but before the first winter snowfall.

Getting there
Park your vehicle at southern Whitney Portal and take Eastern Sierra Transit from Lone Pine to Mammoth Lakes, then take the Yosemite Area Regional Transportation System (YARTS) to Yosemite. Reno–Tahoe International Airport in Nevada has public transportation to Yosemite via Mammoth Lakes, and San Francisco International Airport connects via the Amtrak station at Merced.

Practicalities
Length in miles: 211
Start: Happy Isles trailhead, Yosemite National Park, CA
End: Mt Whitney summit (Whitney Portal), CA
Dog friendly: No
Bike friendly: No
Permit needed: Yes
States covered: California

have been Muir's 100th birthday. How's that for a present?

Exploring the Sierras may be easier now than in Muir's day, but the JMT is still a major undertaking that requires meticulous planning. It's a long walk: some ultralight backpackers may rush the trail in 11 days (the unsupported speed record is an insane 3½ days), but most hikers take a solid three weeks. This means prearranging resupply drops en route and being prepared to be totally self-sufficient for up to 10 days. Food supplies need to be measured to the ounce, and all of it needs to be carried in an approved bear canister, just in case. Nights can be cold as well, and require appropriate gear.

Disappointingly for modern-day Muirs intent on experiencing the wilderness alone, the JMT no longer offers much in the way of mountain solitude. Over 3600 thru-hikers tackle the trail each summer, three-quarters of them heading south. Add in plenty of day hikers in the more easily accessed northern sections and a stream of northbound Pacific Crest Trail thru-hikers (the PCT and JMT share a trail for 170 miles), and you will probably end up passing another human being roughly every 30 minutes. Expect to make plenty of trail friends, but you'll also face stiff competition bagging the choicest lakeshore campsites in many popular basins. There's a reason that this is one of the most-Instagrammed trails in the world.

Popularity inevitably brings a permit quota and with it the thru-hiker's greatest potential challenge. An online lottery system limits the number of trekkers who can exit the Yosemite Wilderness over Donohue Pass at the start of the hike to just 45 people a day. To put it more starkly, 97% of JMT permit applications are unsuccessful. Send in your permit request exactly 168 days (aka 24 weeks) before your proposed start date and don't hold your breath. Permits to start from the southern terminus of Whitney Portal and Inyo National Forest are reserved online at www.recreation.gov via lottery.

If you are lucky enough to secure this Willy Wonka–like golden permit, what can you look forward to? Translucent streams, green forests and lush meadows lead to superb primitive campsites on the shores of endless alpine lakes, surrounded by slabs of granite that resemble bleached bones. The last pines cede to basins of rock and tarns, and switchbacking climbs to high passes reward with views of echoing lines of 13,000ft and 14,000ft peaks. The trail is a breathtaking roller coaster of high mountain scenery, but it is surprisingly well maintained and easy to follow. Only one man-made structure mars the wilderness – the stone John Muir Hut built by the Sierra Club in 1930 atop 11,955ft John Muir Pass.

Perhaps the most profound moments on the trail are in the silences and early morning reflections before dawn, or as the alpenglow lingers on the granite walls after dusk. Time slows on the trail, allowing you to truly appreciate Muir's spiritual connection with the wilderness. The wonders of the Sierra Nevada are humbling but also hold the power to restore, heal and reinvigorate, which is one reason so many thru-hikers are attracted to the range's long-distance trails. In the words of the great man himself:

'Keep close to Nature's heart...and break clear away, once in a while, and climb a mountain or spend a week in the woods. Wash your spirit clean.'

Highlights

Is anything on the John Muir Trail not a highlight? Situated within the stunning Sierra Nevada mountain range in California, it takes in the scenic highlights of three national parks and more besides.

FORESTER PASS
At 13,153ft, the highest pass on the JMT (and highest point on the PCT) offers incredible views over Kings Canyon and Sequoia National Parks.

HALF DOME
Start your JMT with a bang (and an early start) on the iconic day hike up to Half Dome in Yosemite; permits are decided by lottery.

DEVILS POSTPILE
The most fascinating attraction in Reds Meadow is the surreal volcanic formation of Devils Postpile National Monument. These 60ft-tall basalt columns of frozen lava form a dramatic cliff where the JMT and PCT diverge.

THOUSAND ISLAND LAKE
Part of the Ansel Adams Wilderness and one of the most picturesque camping spots on the JMT, the lake offers classic dawn views of Banner Peak.

MT WHITNEY
The epic summit climb to the highest peak in the Lower 48 states is also possible as a classic day hike, assuming you can get the permit.

Vernal Fall on the John Muir and Mist Trails.

Resources

O1 Pacific Crest Trail Association

www.pcta.org

The JMT follows the PCT for over 170 miles, and the latter's official trail association has dedicated JMT planning info.

O2 *John Muir Trail: The Essential Guide to Hiking America's Most Famous Trail*

The best trail guide, with a southbound print version and a northbound ebook, is from author Elizabeth Wenk and Wilderness Press.

O3 *Journeys in the Wilderness*

Get inspired with a classic selection of John Muir's writings, including two full books and several curated chapters from his best works.

⬆ The morning light hits Banner Peak behind Thousand Island Lake in the Ansel Adams Wilderness. Left: The John Muir Trail in Tuolumne Meadows.

Hike this...

Whether you can't get a permit for the John Muir Trail or you simply don't have three weeks to spare to complete a thru-hike, don't despair. There are great section hike options, including 100 daily Mt Whitney summit permits.

➜ A hiker on the John Muir Trail.

01
Tuolumne Meadows to Devils Postpile

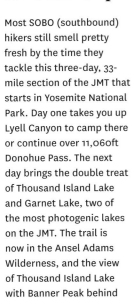

Most SOBO (southbound) hikers still smell pretty fresh by the time they tackle this three-day, 33-mile section of the JMT that starts in Yosemite National Park. Day one takes you up Lyell Canyon to camp there or continue over 11,060ft Donohue Pass. The next day brings the double treat of Thousand Island Lake and Garnet Lake, two of the most photogenic lakes on the JMT. The trail is now in the Ansel Adams Wilderness, and the view of Thousand Island Lake with Banner Peak behind ranks as one of Adams' classic photos. Descend from here past Shadow and Rosalie Lakes to reenter the world at Devils Postpile National Monument and an overnight at Reds Meadow Resort. End with a shuttle to Mammoth Ski Resort and the YARTS bus back to Yosemite, and thank Muir for his advocacy work that ensured we could keep Tuolumne Meadows safe from development over the ages – or, heaven forbid, from the hydroelectric dam that destroyed Hetch Hetchy.

02
Rae Lakes Loop

To get a taste of the trail's remote southern section, try this four- or five-day, 41-mile backpack loop through Kings Canyon National Park. Park at the Road's End parking lot and hike up past Mist Falls to the upper Paradise Valley. Day two joins the JMT near Woods Creek Bridge and follows the Sierra crest south past Dollar Lake and views of Fin Dome to the three Rae Lakes, on one of the most scenic sections of the entire JMT. Budget time for this magnificent spot. The loop's second half takes you over 11,998ft Glen Pass (possibly over snow) before you descend into the Bubbs Creek drainage, arriving back in time for a celebratory dinner at Kings Canyon's Cedar Grove Lodge. Check the state of bridges with the park service when applying for permits. The applications for a wilderness permit here are accepted starting March 1, and must be sent in at least two weeks ahead of your hike. They must be picked up at the Road's End ranger station beyond Cedar Grove.

03
Mt Whitney

The mystique of Mt Whitney (14,505ft) captures the imagination, and conquering its hulking bulk becomes a sort of obsession for many. It's a superstrenuous, really, really long walk that'll wear out even experienced mountaineers, but it doesn't require technical skills if attempted in summer or early fall. Earlier or later in the season, you'll likely need an ice axe and crampons. Be sure your head torch is working for the predawn ascent of Mt Whitney. As you follow the line of hikers' lights bobbing in the darkness, you'll soon reach Trail Crest Junction, where most thru-hikers dump their heavy packs for an ultralight summit bid.

Time the 2-mile switchbacks right and you'll reach the hut atop Mt Whitney just as dawn bursts orange light over the Sierras. The thrill of standing on the highest spot in the Lower 48 is one to savor. From the summit it's a brutal descent back to the junction and down to Whitney Portal, a 9-mile section of trail that isn't even included in the official JMT total mileage.

2.6

Juan Bautista de Anza National Historic Trail

Travel from the desert to the sea by following the path of a Spanish expedition that shaped California history, including the establishment of San Francisco and San Jose.

↪ Mission San Antonio de Padua in Monterey County, California. Right: Spring wildflowers in Anza-Borrego Desert State Park, California.

A year before America declared its independence, on September 28, 1775, a group of around 240 Mexican settlers assembled near modern-day Hermosillo, Mexico, and began a journey that covered some 1200 miles over six months. The ultimate goal of the group, led by Juan Bautista de Anza, was to establish a settlement at San Francisco, a location previously identified, but not settled, by Gaspar de Portolá.

The present-day trail, which includes only the portion of the historic trek on US territory (though that is most of it), passes through what are now the states of Arizona and California. At the time of the 1775 expedition, this area was all New Spain. The motivation of the expedition was to strengthen Spain's claims by populating this remote part of the empire. Spain was concerned not with deterring envious Americans, who wouldn't become a threat until the next century, but instead with the British (in Canada) and Russians whose ships were venturing south along the California coast.

Walking or driving all or even sections of the historic trail is a reminder that the English settlements of Jamestown and Plymouth Colony are only one strand of the colonization of the US. Other efforts were also taking place in the southwestern part of the country, a history that is often forgotten – especially by Americans who didn't go to grade school in a state in one of the once-Spanish areas.

The trail passes through desert landscapes and stretches of the central California coast that appear largely untouched since the days of that expedition. Some of the missions that

Sleep here...

Stays at the trail's San Francisco terminus will be a question of choosing from an embarrassment of riches, and there are some historic spots through California, but not as much so on the other end of this trail. Because there is an auto route along the trail, however, it's possible to choose your mileage based on where you'd like to sleep for the night. The trail website (www.anzahistorictrail.org) is a great resource.

 Camping in Picacho Peak State Park, Arizona
Beneath the 1500ft-tall Picacho Peak, a landmark in southern Arizona, travelers can camp overlooking the route where the Anza expedition made its way through the Santa Cruz River valley.

 The Palms Hotel, California
Built in 1958 in a mid-century modern style, this hotel in Borrego Springs has only ten rooms and two casitas. It was a favorite of Hollywood celebrities: Marilyn Monroe, Clark Gable and other stars slept here.

 Hotel Californian, California
The new Hotel Californian in Santa Barbara is a luxe retreat with tiles, stucco and glass lanterns in the Spanish Colonial Revival style – a fantasy vision of the days of New Spain.

 The Lodge at the Presidio, California
Anza selected the site for San Francisco's Presidio, now part of the Golden Gate National Recreation Area. Sleep in one of the former military base's buildings, near the Golden Gate Bridge and the bay.

Toolbox

 When to go
While the northern portion of this trail might be bearable in summer's heat, spring and fall are ideal everywhere along its length. It is most stunning in spring when wildflowers bloom and California's hills are still green.

Getting there
It is easy to reach the northern end of the trail, urban center San Francisco. The southern end, near the Arizona–Mexico border, is an hour by car from Tucson or around three hours from Phoenix.

 Practicalities
Length in miles: 1200
Start: Rio Rico, AZ
End: San Francisco, CA
Dog friendly: Yes, in portions
Bike friendly: Yes, in portions
Permit needed: Some campgrounds
States covered: Arizona, California

Font's Point, Anza–Borrego
Desert State Park, California.

sheltered those original settlers still stand along the trail. On March 2, 1776, the expedition was welcomed by the Mission San Luis Obispo with the ringing of bells and the singing of the *Te Deum*. You might not receive quite the same reception, but the mission, built in 1772, is open to the public every day of the year.

Other parts of the trail are remarkable for how far these once-remote settlements have come. Frontier outposts have grown into booming cities. Where once there may have been a small presidio and a mission housing a few friars and Native American converts, now there are metropolises ringed with freeways. A number of California's most important cities, like San Francisco and San Jose, were established by Anza's expedition.

The settlers led by Anza were not the first people to arrive in this part of the world. They had been preceded by Franciscan missionaries and Spanish troops by 10 or 20 years. And hundreds, in some places thousands, of years before the Spanish, various Native American peoples had been living in parts of Arizona and California on or near the trail. In Arizona, sites along the way like the Casa Grande Ruins National Monument in Coolidge ('Great House' in English, or 'Sivan Vah'Ki' in O'odham), a gathering place for more than six centuries, and Huhugam Heritage Center in Chandler, with exhibits that cover the Akimel O'otham and Pee Posh peoples, are introductions to those who lived here long before Juan Bautista de Anza.

The remarkable Sonoran Desert covers some 100,000 sq miles of Southern California and Arizona as well as most of the Mexican states of Baja California and Sonora. It's the North American desert with the greatest biodiversity – 60 mammal, 350 bird and 2000 plant species have been identified here. The Sonoran Desert also has an unusual diversity of landscapes, from flat desert plains to peaks that approach altitudes of 10,000ft. At the summits, the plant life often resembles that of Canada more than that of the sunbaked lowlands below.

After passing through Anza-Borrego, California's largest state park, you'll make your way north along the state's coast. While San Diego, Los Angeles, Santa Barbara and many smaller suburbs and beach towns fill much of Southern California's coast, it doesn't take much effort to find hidden pockets of protected wilderness.

Once you're north of Santa Barbara, the stretches of untouched wilderness outnumber the areas that are developed. You'll find pine forests atop bluffs as well as coves with sea lions and seals sunning themselves. Some 1100 miles of the state's coast face the Pacific, but by some calculations the miles of coastline jump to more than 3000 once you factor in all the bays and inlets. Foremost among them is San Francisco Bay, the goal of Anza's expedition and the glittering end of your journey as well. In Presidio Park, what started as a Spanish fort built by Ohlone conscripts in 1776 is now a treasure hunt of urban surprises. You can glimpse its past at the free Spanish-Moorish Officers' Club from the late 1700s. A 2014 renovation revealed gorgeous original adobe architecture, and the Heritage Gallery now on the premises shows the history of the Presidio, from Native American days to Juan Bautista de Anza's arrival to the present, along with temporary exhibitions.

Highlights

This journey is of interest not only to armchair historians, but also to desert and coast lovers. As it passes from the Sonoran Desert to Southern California and then up along the state's coast, the trail makes its way through a variety of environments.

ANZA-BORREGO DESERT STATE PARK
This California state park includes two sections of the expedition's route that have been precisely identified: you can literally follow in the footsteps of the settlers.

SAGUARO NATIONAL PARK
This park near Tucson, Arizona, is the location of two camps used by the Anza expedition. Hikes here offer unparalleled views of the surrounding desert.

SEARS POINT PETROGLYPHS
Near the Gila River in Arizona, Sears Point was on the route of the Anza expedition; its history also includes petroglyphs dating back to AD 500.

MONTEREY
Monterey was already Alta California's capital when Anza visited. The settlers rested here and you should too, visiting its aquarium, Cannery Row and Spanish Colonial sites.

MISSION SAN GABRIEL
Most of California's missions were established after the Anza expedition. Mission San Gabriel, the state's oldest mission, is a rare surviving building where the settlers stayed.

27

Kaupō Trail

In 9 short, steep miles, tour Maui from top to bottom, literally, descending from the summit area of shield volcano Haleakalā all the way down to the southern coast.

→ The rugged Kīpahulu coast of Maui. Right: Haleakalā National Park sunrise.

When you step onto the trail atop Haleakalā on the Hawaiian island of Maui, you are entering a world linked with the spirits of the past, the realm of the gods, natural wonders and the stories of those who have come before. The story of the demigod Maui, who lassoed the sun from the mountaintop to slow its daily traverse to allow people time to complete their daily chores, is but one of many legends associated with Haleakalā.

The Kaupō area and its surroundings were once highly populated, and for centuries Hawaiians climbed up through the erosion crater that comprises Kaupō Gap to build ahu (altars), heiau (places of worship) and temporary rock shelters. The mountain is sacred to Hawaiians, as evidenced by the many archaeological sites, as well as by the gatherings and ceremonies that still take place here, with cultural practitioners visiting to chant, hula or make offerings. According to kūpuna, Hawaiian elders who have ancestral ties to the mountain, its ancient name is Alaheleakalā: the Road to Get to the Sun.

The first recorded trek up the mountain was made by three missionaries in 1828. This was followed in 1841 by the US Exploring Expedition and in 1881 by members of the US Geological Survey. After Western contact, the human activity on the mountain changed. Before joining the newly formed US National Parks system in 1916 as part of what was then Hawai'i National Park, Haleakalā was used for cattle ranching and horseback tours for hearty travelers. The current park headquarters visitors center is in the 'rest house' that was built on the rim of the crater for the comfort of travelers.

Sleep here...

No camping is allowed on Kaupo Ranch property, so most hikers spend the night at the Palikū campground and then get an early start. The 'village' of Kaupō is a long way from anywhere, with light traffic. If you have to walk the final stretch, it's 8 miles east to the Kīpahulu campground by 'Ohe'o Gulch. A good town base near the park is heavenly, sleepy Hāna.

Camping in Haleakalā National Park
There are two park campgrounds along the trail: Hōlua, 3.7 miles from Halemau'u trailhead; and Palikū, 10.3 miles from the trailhead. If you want to do the Kaupō Trail in two days, it's best to stay at Palikū, which is about halfway. Campsite permits are free and available daily at the Park Headquarters Visitor Center until 3pm.

Kīpahulu Campground
At sea level off the Hāna Highway, this drive-up campsite is first come, first served, with stays of up to three nights allowed.

Hāna's Tradewind Cottages
Tucked on the lush grounds of a tropical flower farm, these two cottages are extremely private and offer great value. The cozy two-bedroom Tradewind Cottage and spotless one-bedroom Hāna Cabana are nestled in greenery.

Hamoa Bay House & Bungalow
Close to Hāna, these two beautifully designed and very private cottages (one bedroom and two bedrooms) are a wonderful retreat near Hamoa Beach.

Toolbox

When to go
Haleakalā can be visited at any time of year, with the one constant being the changeability of the weather. Summer months are more stable. No matter when you go, it's wise to be prepared for anything, including snow, hail, rain and flash floods.

Getting there
You can drive to the mountaintop and walk down to Kaupō, or take Hāna Hwy 360 to Kaupō and walk up the mountain. For the first option, drive to the top and park at the Halemau'u trailhead. Overnight parking permits are required and can be obtained from the Headquarters Visitor Center. Kahului Airport is the main hub on Maui.

Practicalities
Length in miles: 19.3
Start: Halemau'u trailhead, Haleakalā National Park
End: Kaupō Gap
Dog friendly: No
Bike friendly: No
Permit needed: Free camping permits can be obtained at the Park Headquarters Visitor Center up to a day in advance.
States covered: Hawai'i

Panoramic landscape view of Haleakalā volcano, Maui.

Some of the secrets of pre-contact human activity on the mountain have been unlocked by the discovery of archaeological sites on the mountain. In her book *Born in Paradise*, Armine von Tempski, who with her siblings discovered one such site while on a cattle drive with their father, Louis, manager of Haleakalā Ranch, relates: 'Smooth water-washed boulders...were piled high in rectangular platforms, like small temples.'

Another site discovered by archaeologists Kenneth P Emory and Robert T Aitken contained upward of 150 rectangular rock formations, identified as sleeping shelters, indicating that large groups made the trek through the crater and across the mountain, perhaps as a military operation. Indeed, the route through the crater provided a direct passage between West Maui and Kaupō, Kīpahulu and Hana. It was thought that Kamehameha I (1758–1819), Hawai'i Island's high chief and unifier of the islands, might have come through this pass when he conquered Maui.

Due to the isolation of the islands, many of the flowering plants, insects and birds were once endemic to Hawai'i and specifically adapted to individual microclimates and ecosystems. These delicately balanced natural systems became threatened by human activities that included the introduction of goats and cattle. Through the efforts of the National Park Service, community volunteers and conservation groups, 'exclosures' have been erected and threatened native species have reemerged. Not all of the path is actively maintained however, meaning some wayfinding knowledge and willingness to hunt for the trail, which becomes a rough 4WD path on Kaupo Ranch, is useful.

As you descend through the gap to sea level, you will be traveling through various biozones. Beginning at the moonscape of the upper zone on the Halemau'u Trail, you will soon find yourself walking among the stunning silversword – an otherworldly-looking endemic plant with a 6- to 7ft flower stock emerging from a silver cluster of leaves – as well as native alpine plants. You will also encounter a thriving population of nene, the Hawaiian native goose and state bird.

The Palikū campground and cabins, the recommended overnight camping area and halfway point, are nestled in a meadow surrounded by forest, with a backdrop of cathedral-like cliffs. If you are camping, come equipped with warm clothing because the weather is changeable and tends to be rainy, windy and foggy at night.

As you descend, you will get a panoramic view of the ocean and biozones laid out before you like gigantic steps. Until Western contact, the slopes of Haleakalā were covered with koa, sandalwood and 'ōhi'a; below Palikū you will find these natives thriving in restored forests. Your ankles and knees may be feeling the strain by now. When you reach Kaupō, you will be in lush tropical forest and an historically significant area with an active ahupua'a (land district) community. Please be aware that you are walking through a neighborhood. Turning right will get you to the Kaupō Store, opened in 1925, a welcome respite – and a cold drink. A left turn (and eight more miles) will take you to Kīpahulu and the pools of 'Ohe'o Gulch, a series of gorgeous waterfalls and pools with a nearby campsite.

Highlights

The most extreme of Haleakalā's hikes, Kaupō Trail descends more than 6100ft before exiting into a forest where feral pigs snuffle about. It captures Maui's (dormant) volcanic heights and its lushness.

BIRDING
Besides the nene, the park bird species include golden plovers, chukars, petrels (once nearly extinct), Maui creepers, 'apapane, 'i'iwi, honeycreepers and the Maui parrotbill.

SILVERSWORD LOOP
Take a short side trip along the .3 mile Silversword Loop, 4.6 miles from Halemau'u trailhead. Stroll through clusters of silversword, one of the world's rarest plants.

'OHE'O GULCH POOLS
You will see why these pools in the Kīpahulu section of Haleakalā National Park were a favorite of Hawaiian royalty. They are a great place to relax after the strenuous Kaupō hike.

NENE GOOSE
The state bird, these native Hawaiian geese were almost extinct but are now plentiful in the park and always curious about human visitors.

STARGAZING
Watch the sun drop below the horizon from the Palikū campground, then scan the skies to study the cosmos.

28

Lewis & Clark National Historic Trail

Cross the nation from the Great Plains to the Pacific Ocean in the footsteps of the great explorers Meriwether Lewis and William Clark.

The Missouri River flowing through the Missouri Headwaters State Park in Three Forks. Right: Northwest Montana.

As Meriwether Lewis hauled himself to the top of the forested Lemhi Pass, he could scarcely contain his anticipation. After 16 months of hard travel, he was finally atop the Continental Divide, at the very edge of the US territory he had been sent to explore. As he left the last of the Missouri River tributaries, he paused to drink from waters that he hoped would take him all the way to his ultimate destination, the Pacific Ocean. It was, quite literally, a watershed moment.

It was in 1804 that President Thomas Jefferson asked Meriwether Lewis and William Clark to assemble an expedition – the Corps of Discovery – to explore the American West. The nation had just bought an immense swath of land from France, the Louisiana Purchase, suddenly doubling the size of the US. Jefferson wanted the Corps to explore the newly purchased lands and, most importantly, find a water route to the Pacific Ocean. Lewis and Clark's ensuing 2½-year voyage to the Pacific and back, across a largely uncharted continent, ranks as America's greatest feat of exploration

Perhaps for this reason, a modern re-creation of the journey along the 4900-mile Lewis & Clark National Historic Trail feels like an American pilgrimage. Pack your imagination and the epic road trip will take you to places where Lewis and Clark parleyed with peaceful (and hostile) tribes, built wooden forts, crossed mountain passes and, more than once, almost starved to death. The enormous herds of bison and the traditional Indian encampments that the duo described may be gone, but the trail still takes you past less-visited rural communities into the heart of America, where grizzlies still roam

Sleep here...

Accommodation on this transcontinental road trip can be as varied as the landscapes. Throughout the length of the trail, there are some truly memorable places where you can lay your head, from historic hotels to stunning mountain lodges. Steer away from generic highway motels at these historic sites brimming with atmosphere and the echoes of history.

Camping in Lewis & Clark Trail State Park, Washington
Pitch a tent where the Corps camped in spring 1806 on their way back east, between Pasco and Lolo Pass in Washington.

Camping in Cape Disappointment State Park, Washington
At this Washington park, tent and RV campsites and cozy yurts are just walking distance from the beach where the Corps finally reached the Pacific.

Grand Union Hotel, Montana
Opened in 1882, this hotel on the banks of the Missouri River in Montana's historic Fort Benton is full of period detail, making it a fine place to stay en route to Great Falls.

Sacajawea Hotel, Montana
Constructed in 1910 and revitalized on its centenary, this former railroad hotel in Three Forks, Montana, is on the National Register of Historic Places.

Toolbox

When to go
It's possible to explore the trail at any time, but winter brings some dangerous driving conditions and restricted opening hours. June to September are the most pleasant months for a road trip, though you'll find places noticeably quieter after Labor Day.

Getting there
St Louis Lambert International Airport is right at the beginning of the trail. Astoria on the Oregon–Washington border is 97 miles from Portland International Airport and 170 miles from Seattle-Tacoma International Airport.

Practicalities
Length in miles: 4900
Start: Pittsburgh, PA, or St Louis, MO
End: Astoria, OR
Dog friendly: Yes
Bike friendly: No
Permit needed: No
States covered: IA, ID, IL, IN, KS, KY, MO, MT, NE, ND, OH, OR, PA, SD, WA, WV

the wilderness in places. The trail today offers Americans a chance not only to celebrate the Corps' historic adventure but also to rediscover their own nation.

The first major decision of the trail is where to start. Lewis and Clark (aged 29 and 33, respectively) set off from Camp Dubois, outside St Louis, Missouri, on May 14, 1804, making this the most logical starting point, even if it is not the official starting point of the trail. Time your own departure around this date, and costumed locals in Hartford, Illinois, may even see you off with a reenactment of the event.

As the Corps hauled their boats up the Missouri River through the Great Plains, they inevitably started to butt up against powerful Native American tribes. The land the explorers were traversing may have been unknown to Americans (two-thirds of whom then lived within 50 miles of the Atlantic Ocean), but over 50 distinct tribes called the land home. At what is now Council Bluffs in Iowa, Lewis and Clark held the first fateful meeting between representatives of the US and western tribes, a historic spot and a chance to consider the legacy of the expedition from a Native American perspective.

With winter fast approaching, Lewis and Clark decided to hunker down near the earth lodge villages of the Mandan and Hidatsa people. They also built Fort Mandan, a location the modern trail still passes on its journey through North Dakota. This proved to be an important decision, not only because the Mandan helped them survive the -45°F winter, but also because it was nearby that they met the pregnant Shoshone teenager Sacagawea (also spelled Sacajawea), who became crucial to the expedition's success.

And the explorers needed help: from here onward, the Corps was literally traveling off the map.

Neighboring Montana offers one of the most rewarding sections of the modern trail, one highlight being Great Falls, one of the toughest sections of the expedition. Here a series of cascades forced the Corps to drag their canoes and gear on a brutal 17-mile portage. The biggest physical challenge facing the expedition, however, was the crossing of the Rocky Mountains. For this they needed help and horses from the local Shoshone tribe. Sacagawea played a fateful role, recognizing the Shoshone tribal leader Cameahwait as her brother; she had been kidnapped years before by Hidatsa warriors. The trail takes you past the spot at Camp Fortunate where horses and guides were secured after an emotional reunion, and then follows a dirt road up to Lemhi Pass. You can stand on the very spot where Lewis crossed the Continental Divide for the first time. A few weeks later they crossed the watershed again, traversing the Bitterroot Mountains over Lolo Pass, today marked by a modest visitors center.

Once over the watershed, the Corps could again travel by river, heading down the Clearwater and Snake Rivers to join the Columbia at the site of today's Sacajawea State Park in Washington. A month later they reached the mouth of the Columbia, where the end point of the modern trail at Cape Disappointment offers visitors the same stunning Pacific Ocean views enjoyed by the Corps. This stunning stretch of coast is a fabulous finale and the place where most visitors end their epic trip. Lewis and Clark weren't as lucky; they still had to get themselves all the way back home.

Highlights

From mountain passes and watersheds to Native American encampments and views of the Pacific Ocean, travelers on this route will keep company with the ghosts of Lewis & Clark.

POMPEYS PILLAR
Clark carved his name on this sandstone butte outside Billings, Montana, on his way from the Pacific, naming it after Sacagawea's baby, Pomp.

LEWIS & CLARK PASS
Crossed by Lewis in Montana on his return journey, this is the only roadless pass left on the trail. Watch for grizzlies on the 3-mile return hike.

COLUMBIA GORGE DISCOVERY CENTER & MUSEUM
This great museum in The Dalles, Oregon, just off the Historic Columbia River Hwy, discusses the 30 tons of cargo the Corps dragged with them.

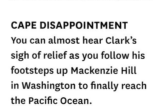

CAPE DISAPPOINTMENT
You can almost hear Clark's sigh of relief as you follow his footsteps up Mackenzie Hill in Washington to finally reach the Pacific Ocean.

LEWIS & CLARK NATIONAL HISTORIC TRAIL INTERPRETIVE CENTER
This museum in Great Falls, Montana, is perhaps the most engaging of the entire historic trail.

Resources

01 Lewis & Clark National Historic Trail
www.nps.gov/lecl
The official NPS website has interactive maps and details about historic sites.

02 *Traveling the Lewis and Clark Trail*
Julie Faneslow's 2007 guide to traveling the route could use an update, but it's still a fabulous resource.

03 *Undaunted Courage*
Historian Stephen Ambrose wrote this classic, immensely readable biography of Meriwether Lewis and the expedition.

04 *Lewis & Clark: The Journey of the Corps of Discovery*
Ken Burns' excellent 1997 PBS documentary of the Corps of Discovery is available on two DVDs.

The Pacific coastline looking south from Cape Disappointment State Park in Washington. Left: Boardwalk along hiking trail by Lewis and Clark River at Fort Clatsop.

Hike this...

Visitors aren't meant to attempt their own cross-country navigation except by car (the expedition mainly travelled by boat and on horseback, in any case); it's best to experience the route by driving between sites and seeing select portions of the explorers' path.

▶ Bronze statue of Meriwether Lewis and William Clark at the end of the Lewis & Clark Trail in Seaside, Oregon.

01
Long Beach Discovery Trail, Washington

The Lewis & Clark National Historical Park comprises 10 different sites clustered around the mouth of the Columbia River in Oregon and Washington, where the expedition spent approximately six months. Among the attractions is Discovery Trail in Washington's Long Beach Peninsula, starting from Ilwaco's waterfront. To the west, the beach here is separated from the town by a wide swath of dunes and dwarf pines and remains pretty wild along the 8.2-mile, only moderately trafficked, Lewis & Clark Discovery Trail. Most of the trail is paved, and there are interpretive signs. The culmination is a statue of Clark...and a statue of a 10ft sturgeon that he wrote about finding on the beach in his journal. Since this footpath traces Clark's hike from the initial Station Camp to the Pacific coast, it's appropriate.

South across the Columbia River in Oregon is a replica of the original Fort Clatsop, where the Corps spent a miserable winter from 1805 to 1806.

02
Sulphur Springs Trail, Montana

Start off the scenic Montana leg of the trail in Great Falls at the impressive Lewis & Clark Interpretive Center. After learning about the month-long portage effort, a 15-mile drive takes you to the Sulphur Springs trailhead at Morony Dam. A 3.6-mile round-trip hike along this remote stretch of the Missouri River in the Lewis & Clark National Forest leads to the eponymous Sulphur Springs; it was from here that Meriwether Lewis took the water that would supposedly help heal Sacagawea, suffering from an illness during the portage. The trail has interpretive signs and features an overlook at Portage Creek.

Thanks to the successful recovery of Sacagawea (and a successful portage, eventually), the Lewis and Clark expedition would go on to reach the Pacific Ocean, and on Lewis' return east he would cross the Continental Divide at what is now Lewis and Clark Pass near Great Falls, using what was then an old Native American pathway. It's another hiking option for your Montana leg of the trip.

03
La Framboise Island Loop, South Dakota

To get a sense of Lewis and Clark's journey through the Great Plains, follow the Missouri River through the Dakotas. An interpretive sign in Pierre, South Dakota, marks the spot where the Corps had a tense altercation with the powerful Teton Sioux at the confluence of the Bad River, a tributary of the Missouri River. It's now marked by the Bad River Encounter Site at Fischers Lilly Park in the city of Fort Pierre. At a bend on the Missouri River in between Fort Pierre and the state capital of Pierre, La Framboise Island has several hiking trails and plentiful wildlife. It's across from where the Lewis and Clark expedition spent four days in 1804 and was nearly derailed by the crew's offense.

Check water levels before you take the 4-mile loop of La Framboise; the Missouri often floods. As a next stop, with a new appreciation of the river's power, go to the Lewis and Clark Information Center in Chamberlain, to climb aboard a replica of the expedition's 55ft keelboat.

29

The Long Trail

The oldest named long-distance trail in the US runs the length of Vermont's Green Mountain spine from Massachusetts to the Canadian border.

Autumn in Vermont. Right: A hiker navigating the Long Trail on top of Mt Mansfield.

From the summit of Mt Mansfield, Vermont's highest peak, a stunningly lush landscape spreads out before you for miles in every direction. Far below, a patchwork of dairy farms and cornfields roll down to the shores of Lake Champlain, reflecting the pastoral vision of Vermont made popular by Ben & Jerry's. Farther up is a landscape equally verdant but less tamed, with endless waves of gentle green mountains stretching to the horizon; while here at the very top, ground-hugging plants laced amid the raw schist outcrops eke out an existence in near-arctic conditions. This view inspired the country's oldest named long-distance hiking trail, which rambles for 272 miles along the densely forested, glacier-scoured slopes that make up Vermont's Green Mountain spine.

The Long Trail was born in 1910 when two dozen outdoor enthusiasts gathered to form the state's Green Mountain Club, still going strong today; by 1930 the Long Trail had expanded to run the full length of the state. Along the way it became the inspiration and an early building block for the Appalachian Trail, which it pre-dates by over a decade. Indeed, the Appalchian Trail's route still overlaps with the Long Trail for 103 miles in southern Vermont.

Running from Vermont's southern border near Williamstown, Massachusetts, to the village of North Troy at the doorstep of Québec, the Long Trail traverses luxuriant deciduous forests, climbs through rugged rocky clefts and frost-pinched alpine tundra, and winds along riverbanks and lakeshores, dropping to elevations as low as 326ft above sea level and scaling the summits of Vermont's five 4000ft peaks: Mt Mansfield (4393ft), Killington Peak (4236ft), Camel's Hump (4081ft), Mt

Sleep here...

If you want an overnight stay near the trail but roughing it isn't your style, options abound in small villages along the trail. Closest to the trail itself is the Inn at Long Trail, a 1930s ski lodge at the junction of the Long Trail and US 4 outside Killington. Quite a bit fancier is the Mountain Top Inn, a resort whose trail network intersects the Long Trail near Chittenden. You'll find many other inns, B&Bs and mountain resorts within 10 miles of the trail.

Inn at Long Trail
Near the Long Trail's midpoint in Killington, the rustic inn with tree-trunk beams sits by US 4 and has an Irish pub, McGrath's, with live music on weekends.

Mountain Top Inn & Resort
For a luxurious break, head 2 miles off-trail to this 700-acre resort in Chittenden with fine dining, Vermont craft brews on tap, horseback riding, a spa, a heated pool and kayaking on its own lake.

Taylor Lodge
Built in 1926 near Underhill, the cozy enclosed shelter with picnic tables on its front porch is named for James P Taylor, who hatched the idea of the Long Trail in 1910.

Taft Lodge
The Long Trail's oldest and largest shelter, dating to 1920, enjoys a privileged position near the summit of Mt Mansfield, Vermont's highest mountain.

Toolbox

When to go
For the best weather and trail conditions, walk the Long Trail between June and mid-October. Nothing compares to the beauty of foliage season, centered around the first week of October. Avoid March through late May, the aptly named 'mud season.' Winter is also a difficult season; the trail blazes are white, blending with the snow, and blizzards are possible.

Getting there
The Long Trail runs the entire north–south length of Vermont and can be accessed via numerous roads crossing the Green Mountains from east to west. Vermont's only large airport is in Burlington, a 25-minute drive from the nearest trailhead at Jonesville.

Practicalities
Length in miles: 272
Start: Massachusetts–Vermont state line near Williamstown, MA
End: US–Canada border near North Troy, VT
Dog friendly: Yes
Bike friendly: No
Permit needed: No
States covered: Vermont

Vermont as seen from the top of Mt Mansfield near Stowe.

Ellen (4081ft) and Mt Abraham (4016ft). Unlike the Appalachian or the Pacific Crest Trails, this is a journey that can easily be completed in a month or less – long enough for a full immersion experience but short enough to fit realistically into a three-week vacation.

Hikers more accustomed to the grandeur of the American West – or even the neighboring granite peaks of New Hampshire's White Mountains – may scoff at the Green Mountains' diminutive stature and lament the relatively short amount of time spent above tree line, but these ancient mountains have their own kind of beauty. Here, rather than expecting amazing vistas at every turn, you learn to love the forest for the trees, especially in late September and early October when the colors of these northern woods are most spectacular: maples blazing crimson and gold, white-barked birches and red-spiked staghorn sumac juxtaposed against crisp blue autumn skies. Afterall, a little less than half of the trail is located inside the beautiful Green Mountain National Forest. When the trail does finally break above tree line, as on the slopes of Mt Mansfield, the long views across Vermont's undulating landscape come as a rare and welcome surprise.

The Long Trail is home to 70 rustic shelters offering protection from the elements and opportunities for camaraderie with fellow hikers. Spaced every 5 miles or so along the trail, they're all first come, first served and most are free. Simple three-walled lean-tos are the norm. Even the more elaborate shelters – known as 'lodges' in Long Trail parlance – don't get much fancier than four walls, a window or two and perhaps a panoramic front porch, a picnic table, a woodstove or the occasional on-site caretaker. It's imperative to bring a tent as shelters often fill up. And unlike mountain refuges in Europe or the AMC huts of New Hampshire's White Mountains, shelters on the Long Trail don't serve meals, so hikers need to carry their own camp stoves, fuel and food, and arrange for grocery runs or food drops at key highway crossings along the way.

Of course you don't have to commit to a full-on backpacking trip to enjoy the trail. Many people opt to day-hike small sections that take in highlights like Mt Mansfield or Camel's Hump, the former easily accessible by the gorgeous Sunset Ridge Trail from Underhill State Park, the latter reachable via similar spur trails from Huntington or Duxbury. Even a very short walk along the Long Trail can yield splendid scenic rewards.

Several Vermont state highways cross the trail, including Hwy 73 at Brandon Gap and Hwy 108 at Smugglers Notch. From the former, a 0.8-mile uphill jaunt leads to the Great Cliff of Mt Horrid, one of the state's prettiest fall foliage viewpoints. The latter, at Barnes Camp Visitor Center in Stowe, offers wheelchair and stroller access to a boardwalk traversing a montane wetland. Meanwhile, for those willing to brave dirt road driving, even remoter sections of the trail are easily accessible at places like Hazen's Notch, Mt Tabor and Lincoln Gap.

While the trail is wonderful for multiday excursions, it's also popular for day hikes. Regardless of hiking style, anyone who walks the whole Long Trail, whether in 14 days or over the course of a lifetime, qualifies for the coveted End-to-Ender certificate. Ask for it at the Green Mountain Club's headquarters in Waterbury Center.

Highlights

Often only 3ft wide, the trail traverses streams and forests, skirts ponds and weaves up and down mountains to bare summits. From up top, enjoy vistas with wave after wave of hillside gently rolling back to a sea of green dotted with occasional pasture.

GREAT CLIFF OF MT HORRID
From Brandon Gap, the Long Trail climbs north to this cliff top with awe-inspiring perspectives over beaver and moose country and waves of mountains beyond.

MT MANSFIELD
Climb Vermont's highest peak, Mt Mansfield (4393ft), for views that stretch from Montréal to Lake Champlain and down the length of the Green Mountains' spine.

CAMEL'S HUMP
Explore Vermont's most distinctively shaped peak, with its abrupt, exposed cliff face – the only major Green Mountain summit that hasn't been developed for skiing.

MT ABRAHAM
Good road access makes this one of Vermont's easiest 4000-footers to bag; join the Long Trail at Lincoln Gap and hike 2.6 miles north for beautiful views above the tree line.

WHITE ROCKS NATIONAL RECREATION AREA
Join the trail near Wallingford and hike to White Rocks Cliffs, where peregrine falcons share views west to the Taconic and Adirondack Mountains.

30

Maah Daah Hey Trail

Hike or bike America's heartland on this epic 144-mile single-track National Recreational Trail through the Wild West landscapes of North Dakota's badlands.

Mountain biking the Maah Daah Hey Trail. Right: Autumn cottonwood in Sully Creek State Park.

People don't find themselves in northwestern North Dakota by chance. It's pretty much a blank on the map for most outdoorsy types, who may be drawn to the Black Hills to the south or to the bigger mountains of neighboring Montana or Wyoming. If you do find yourself here, standing on a clay butte overlooking rolling prairie and eroded badlands, as hawks fly overhead and bison graze the billowing grass, you are likely here for one of two reasons: you are either lost, or you are tackling the Maah Daah Hey (MDH).

The Maah Daah Hey (meaning 'an area that has been around for a long time' in the Mandan language) connects the North and South Units of Theodore Roosevelt National Park via the Little Missouri National Grassland, through an area known as the Dakota Prairie Grassland. Dotted with mule deer, coyotes, skunks, porcupines and pronghorn, this is an archetypal American landscape. The herds of mustangs that roam the park are descendants of those belonging to Sitting Bull and his Sioux warriors. In places the rolling hills break open to reveal the sedimentary layers of a 70-million-year-old seabed.

The MDH is probably best known as one of the country's great mountain bike trails, offering the longest single-track ride in the nation. Around 70% of the trail's traffic is mountain bikes, followed by 25% on horseback; this leaves a hardy 5% on foot. But hikers have some tricks up their sleeves. Where mountain bikers have to detour around Theodore Roosevelt National Park, hikers can walk straight through it, allowing some great side trips and plenty of wildlife-watching opportunities. On horseback is also a great way to traverse this classic cowboy country; history buffs

Sleep here...

On the trail, you'll be sleeping each night at one of the Maah Daah Hey's nine fenced campgrounds, which include picnic tables, fire rings, hitching posts, potable water and even toilets. Best of all, sites are available year-round. Sites are spaced twenty miles apart, given that it's a popular mountain biking trail with greater mileage covered each day.

CCC Campground
No reservations are accepted at this US Forest Service site at the start of the trail, just south of the visitors center of the North Unit of Theodore Roosevelt National Park, next to the Little Missouri River.

Roosevelt Inn & Suites
Nothing fancy here, but it's the closest hotel to the northern start point of the trail, around 20 miles north in Watford City.

Rough Riders Hotel
The kitschy Middle American resort town of Medora offers the only real hotel accommodations in the area. If you've camped on the trail, you'll appreciate the creature comforts.

Sully Creek Campground
Just 2.5 miles south of Medora at the southern end of the main MDH, the state-run campground (reservations accepted) with showers is near the start of the Deuce section of the trail.

Toolbox

When to go
North Dakota has an extreme continental climate, with hot summers and extraordinarily cold winters. The months of May to September have the best temperatures, with May offering the lushest scenery.

Getting there
Fly to Bismarck Airport and make the 170-mile drive to the northern trailhead, or travel 137 miles to the southern junction town of Medora, where you can book local shuttles through Dakota Cyclery.

Practicalities
Length in miles: 144
Start: US Forest Service CCC Campground, 20 miles south of Watford City, ND
End: Burning Coal Vein Campground, 29 miles south of Medora, ND
Dog friendly: Yes, on leash, but strictly prohibited in the backcountry and not allowed on trail within Theodore Roosevelt National Park
Bike friendly: Yes, except on trail sections that lie within the national park
Permit needed: No
States covered: North Dakota

and adventurous spirits will find it hard to resist seeing these landscapes as Teddy Roosevelt himself did. The South Unit Visitor Center can provide info on planning a trip on horseback.

While in his twenties Theodore Roosevelt came hunting here and quickly formed a powerful connection with the land, still the Dakota Territory at the time. He ended up buying the Maltese Cross Ranch south of Medora that year and setting up his beloved Elkhorn Ranch the next. He hoped to find solace after the death of both his wife and mother in a matter of hours earlier in 1884. His time ranching cattle here would inform his attitude to conservation throughout his life and his presidency, during which he protected 230 million acres of federal land, creating 150 national forests and five national parks in the process. 'It was here,' Teddy Roosevelt said in 1903, 'that the romance of my life began.'

These days the gullies and buttes of the Dakota plains hide something else: oil. Not far from the MDH is the Bakken oil field, epicenter of a huge fracking boom that has brought money, an increase in crime and a Wild West vibe to parts of the state, as well as a billion-dollar state budget surplus. You may glance at the occasional nodding oil derrick from parts of the trail.

Getting to the start of the trail involves a bit of legwork. The Maah Daah Hey Trail is in the remotest corner of one of the least visited states in the country. Your friends can probably dig up a bad *Fargo*-inspired North Dakota accent (you betcha they can), but just try to find someone who's actually been there. It's only when you start driving through the country's fourth least densely

populated state that it dawns on you that you will probably have this landscape to yourself. And then you start to smile.

The main section of the trail starts near the North Unit of the national park and winds south for 96 miles through a crumpled landscape of yellow grasslands, eroded bluffs, clay buttes and wooded draws that remains largely unchanged since Roosevelt's time. Six campgrounds (with potable water), 16 to 22 miles apart, divide the main trail into five manageable sections. The trail is clearly marked by wooden trail posts branded with a turtle logo, a symbol borrowed from the Lakota Sioux.

Unlike the situation on some oversubscribed trails of the East and West Coasts, no permits are required for the MHD, and you won't find any lines or full campsites here. The motels are cheap and the highways are empty, giving you a freedom, flexibility and spontaneity that are hard to find on more popular national trails. With this emptiness comes the need for self-sufficiency and a certain resilience. Sudden afternoon thunderstorms, frequent high winds and persistent summer bugs make for a tough environment at times.

In recent years the Maah Daah Hey Trail Association has built another section of trail, known as the Deuce, extending south from Medora for a further 50 miles. This is one reason that the MDH was designated a National Recreation Trail in 2016.

Together this makes for an epic 144 miles of single track, linked by a total of 10 public campgrounds. Only a handful of people have biked or hiked this additional section of trail so far. Make the effort and you'll be inheriting the mantle of a long line of hardy North Dakota pioneers.

Highlights

The Maah Daah Hey Trail linking the park's North and South Units passes through a dauntingly rugged but awe-inspiringly scenic stretch of badlands. It's adventure as Teddy Roosevelt himself would have appreciated it.

ELKHORN RANCH
Walk with the ghosts of Teddy Roosevelt at the site of his former ranch, about halfway along the main trail by the Little Missouri River.

ICONIC WILDLIFE
Few visitors make for lots of wildlife, from shaggy bison and wild mustangs to coyotes, prairie dogs, wild turkeys and golden eagles.

PETRIFIED FOREST LOOP TRAIL
Theodore Roosevelt National Park's best day hike takes you along a section of the MDH to visit an ancient petrified forest in the South Unit.

DEVIL'S PASS
Take an exciting ride along a clay ridge that drops away 150ft on both sides, or visit on a 9-mile round-trip hike from Magpie Campground.

CHINA WALL
This dramatic, sheer sandstone wave can be hiked from Bennett Campground or by following the MDH between CCC Campground and Bennett Campground.

31

Mormon Pioneer National Historic Trail

This 1300-mile trail follows the journey of the 19th-century Mormons from persecution in Illinois to the promised land of the Salt Lake Valley.

A lush field and snow-covered peaks in Utah. Right: Bison grazes on grasslands near a rock on Antelope Island.

The story of the Mormon journey west is a captivating episode in American history. It's a story of persecution and survival, of suffering and miracles, of man versus pitiless nature. Above all, it's a tale of faith: in God, in fallible human leaders, in the promise of an unknown frontier.

But, if you're not a practicing Mormon, why would you want to drive more than a thousand miles to see sites sacred to the Church of Jesus Christ of Latter-Day Saints? Well, first, there's the scenery. The trail leads through some of the most glorious landscapes of the American West: the vast grass seas of the Nebraska prairies, the snowy Rockies reaching heavenward, the spruce-lined canyons of northern Utah. You'll see sandhill cranes gliding above the Platte River, catch grizzlies snuffling through the blue-black forests of Wyoming, gawk at bison stampeding over the sandy hills of Antelope Island in the Great Salt Lake.

Second, there's the history: not just Mormon history, but the complex, bittersweet story of America's westward expansion. Fort Laramie, Wyoming, perched on the wind-whipped northern Great Plains, saw pioneers bound for Utah, for Oregon, for the California Gold Rush. The town of Council Bluffs, Iowa, named by Lewis and Clark, was once a reservation for Native tribes pushed out of the Chicago area as the city was incorporating. Fort Kearny, Nebraska, was a legendary frontier outpost and stop on the storied Pony Express.

To understand the Mormon Pioneer Trail's place in the picture, you must understand the origins of Mormonism, America's largest homegrown religion. The story began in 1827 in the hardscrabble hills of western New York State. It was here

Sleep here...

It's worth spending at least a night in Salt Lake City, the ultimate destination of the Mormon Pioneer Trail, as well as spending time at the trail's beginning in Nauvoo, but look for camping and alternative lodging in the Wasatch Mountains and Wyoming to get the best sense of the journey taken by Brigham Young and his followers.

 Camping in Guernsey State Park, Wyoming
There are no official trail campsites, but this pleasant spot along a reservoir near Fort Laramie, Wyoming, is one of numerous state- and privately-run sites along the route.

Hotel Nauvoo, Illinois
In the historic city center of Nauvoo, Illinois, at the trail's start, this gracious inn's main building was constructed by an early Mormon pioneer. Rooms all have modern conveniences.

Magnolia Hotel, Nebraska
Don't rough it like a pioneer while visiting Winter Quarters in Omaha, Nebraska; stay at this grand 1923 hotel. It's one of the comfiest sleeps in the Great Plains.

 Anniversary Inn, Utah
Close to the trail's terminus in Salt Lake City, this beyond-quirky small chain with two locations has elaborately themed rooms. The Wild West room, with a wagon bed and saloon-style bathroom doors, is appropriate for the occasion.

Toolbox

When to go
Since this trail is mostly about driving from point to point, season is less relevant. Still, avoid winter in mountainous areas, when roads can be treacherous.

Getting there
The trail starts in the small town of Nauvoo, Illinois. The nearest major airport is the Quad City International Airport, 100 miles away in Moline. The trail ends in Salt Lake City, Utah, an air, rail and bus hub. You'll need a car to follow the route.

Practicalities
Length in miles: 1300
Start: Nauvoo, IL
End: Salt Lake City, UT
Dog friendly: Yes
Bike friendly: No
Permit needed: No
States covered: IL, IA, NE, WY, UT

that a 21-year-old treasure hunter named Joseph Smith claimed an angel named Moroni came to him in a dream and told him the location of golden plates bearing the true message of God. This would become the Book of Mormon, the scripture for Smith's new church.

The handsome, charismatic Smith soon attracted followers. He also attracted opposition, and the threat of mob violence drove him and his infant church from state to state across the Midwest. After an arrest in Missouri, Smith escaped and set up a new city in Illinois he called Nauvoo. Here he began to speak of a new revelation: the doctrine of 'plural marriage' (which today's Mormons reject). Amid rising tensions both internal and external, Smith was arrested and jailed. On June 27, 1844, a mob broke into the jail and murdered him.

Smith's successor, Brigham Young, needed refuge for his 15,000 followers. In 1846, 500 of them headed west toward parts unknown; many more would follow. Thus began the Mormon Pioneer Trail.

For modern travelers, the trail begins with the Nauvoo Historic District, today a pilgrimage site for Mormons. Wander downtown's restored shops and houses, including Brigham Young's redbrick home and a gleaming white temple built in 2002. Crossing the Mississippi River into Iowa and passing through several Mormon way stations, you'll come to Mt Pisgah. Once a semipermanent encampment of 2000 settlers, today it has a 9-acre park with exhibits and a reconstructed log cabin.

Entering Nebraska, you'll come to Winter Quarters. The winter of 1846 was vicious, and the woefully underprepared pioneers were forced to make camp. Some 3500 of the faithful wintered here, and hundreds died of malaria, dysentery, scurvy and plain brutal cold. The encampment is now part of the city of Omaha; visit the interpretive center to see pioneer artifacts and a log cabin diorama. In front is a statue commemorating the 'handcart pioneers,' poor European converts without horses who went west on foot, pulling their belongings and children in two-wheeled carts. Many never made it.

In western Nebraska, stop along the broad, muddy North Platte River to see the 'ancient bluff ruins.' These craggy buttes, a trail landmark, reminded English Mormon converts of the ruined castles in their home country. You can also see the ruts left by pioneer wagons.

The Wyoming section of the trail is lined with historic way stations and dramatic geologic features – you can touch the enormous bald boulder of Independence Rock, where pioneers carved their names; hike through the narrow gorge called Devil's Gate; gaze up at the jagged rock formation called the Needles, where Brigham Young became sick with a mysterious fever. Check out the historical reconstruction of Fort Bridger, a onetime fur-trading post built by legendary mountain man Jim Bridger and later bought by the Mormon church.

Now it's time to cross into Utah, the holy land. You'll descend through the canyons amid the Wasatch Range and into the Salt Lake Valley. Today the valley is lined with suburban subdivisions, but the landscape still retains its eerie lunar feel. The final stop on the trail is This Is the Place Heritage Park, with costumed interpreters and replica settler homes. It's named for the words spoken by Brigham Young when he first saw the valley. The journey was over. The pilgrims were home.

Highlights

After a historic beginning in Illinois, the trail kicks up out West as passes the Needles and nears the pine-forested and snow-covered peaks of the Wasatch Mountains approaching Salt Lake City. Interspersed are old pioneer remnants.

GREAT SALT LAKE
Vast, shallow and so salty that swimmers bob around like corks, Utah's Great Salt Lake is America's Dead Sea. Its islands are prime wildlife-spotting territory.

OMAHA
This charming but underrated midsize Nebraska city has one of America's best zoos, a fun railroad museum and a walkable riverfront with a park dedicated to Lewis and Clark, who landed here in 1804.

INDEPENDENCE ROCK
This rounded granite monolith in Wyoming looks like an enormous sleeping turtle. Pioneers bound for Utah, California and Oregon would stop to carve their names here.

GUERNSEY RUTS
So many wagon train pioneers rolled along the banks of Wyoming's North Platte River that their wheel ruts have become part of the topography.

WASATCH RANGE
The pioneers crossed this handsome northern Utah range on their way to the valley. Today you can hike here amid firs, spruces and quaking aspens.

Aspens display their yellow foliage in the Wasatch Mountains.

Resources

O1 Mormon Pioneer National Historic Trail
www.nps.gov/mopi
The National Park Service's official website for the trail, with maps, info and an audio guide.

O2 Church of Jesus Christ of Latter-Day Saints
https://history. churchofjesuschrist.org/ landing/historic-sites
The Mormon church's website has a useful guide to various Latter-Day Saints historic sites on the trail.

O3 *No Man Knows My History: The Life of Joseph Smith*
Fawn Brodie's 1945 biography of the Mormon church founder is essential reading for anyone who wants to understand the religion's origins.

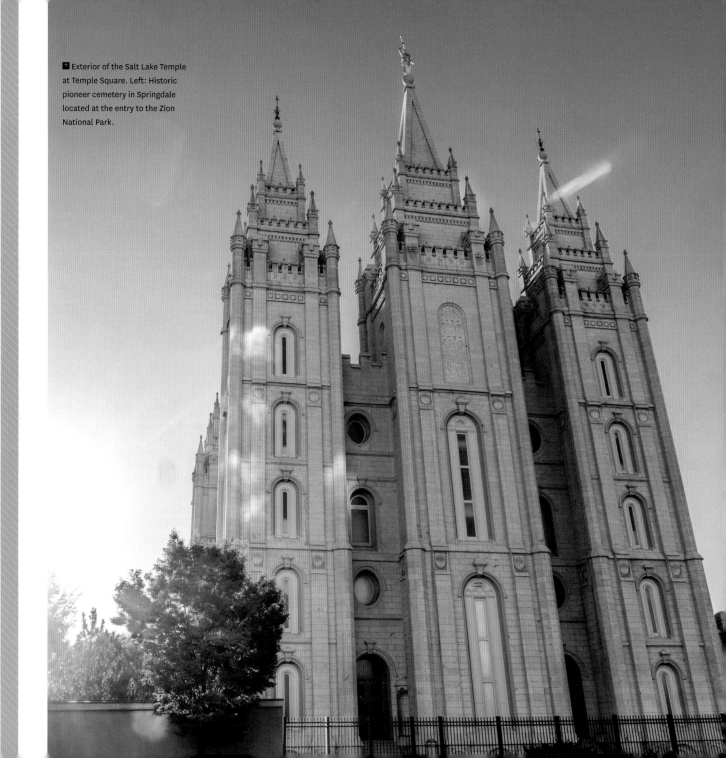

Exterior of the Salt Lake Temple at Temple Square. Left: Historic pioneer cemetery in Springdale located at the entry to the Zion National Park.

Hike this...

Mainly an auto route, there are nonetheless good stopping points to stretch your legs along the length of the Mormon Pioneer Trail.

➡ *Journey's End* statue at the This is the Place Heritage Park, in Salt Lake City.

01
Bridle Trail, Wyoming

You'll want to visit Casper on your Mormon Pioneer trip, an amiable cowboy and oil town on the edge of the North Platte River in Wyoming. Here the excellent National Historic Trails Interpretive Center brings to life the history of the half-million people who passed through here along the Oregon, California, Mormon and Pony Express Trails between 1841 and 1868. It's also the site of the well-loved Bridle Trail, a 4.5-mile loop hike beginning in Rotary Park at the base of Garden Creek Falls. It takes about three hours for the full loop, and requires moderate effort (there's elevation gain), as the hike goes up Casper Mountain. A shorter loop is available on the west side. Split Rock is the highlight. Dogs are allowed on the trail if on leash. For a shorter hike (less than 300 yards), the National Park Service recommends Avenue of Rocks, also known as the Devil's Backbone, on Poison Spider Road west of Casper, an easy jaunt from and to your car.

02
Big Mountain Pass, Utah

One of a number of excellent hikes at the trail's western end, this 4.5-mile path in Utah crosses Big Mountain in the Wasatch Range. It follows in the footsteps of the original 1847 pioneers. Topping out at nearly 7500ft above sea level, it's a lung-burning climb that begins at 6040ft. The pioneers had to use all their oxen to pull the wagons one by one up the mountains with rope. They were lucky, though; the infamous Donner party had passed this way a year earlier, blazing the trail, and found the route so arduous they couldn't make it across the Sierra Nevada before winter. Snowbound, they resorted to cannibalism.

The prospects are cheerier for you: once achieved, the summit offers panoramic views of the Wasatch and Oquirrh Ranges and the Salt Lake Valley. Spring is especially heavenly, when the slopes bloom with columbine and wild hollyhock. It's a popular route for mountain bikers, with steep switchbacks near the pass. Road access closes during the winter, but it's still hikable in late fall.

03
Antelope Island, Utah

This craggy, grass-covered island is a nature photographer's dream, packed with fauna like bison, bighorn sheep, bobcats and coyotes. The bison were introduced in the late 19th century as a tourism and hunting attraction; today the herd is allowed to roam free when not being used as breeding stock. At 42 sq miles, Antelope is the largest of the 10 islands in Utah's Great Salt Lake. City folk come here to hike, bike, ride horses and bird-watch. The island is also an official International Dark Sky Park, which means it's one of the best places on earth for stargazing without the light pollution of civilization. After sundown, the sky feels like an enormous IMAX screen showing constellations all night long. To get to the park (25 miles north of Salt Lake City, 10 miles south of Ogden), head west from I-15 exit 332 and follow the signs; a 7-mile causeway leads to the island. For more info on the island's wildlife, hiking trails and activities, drop by the visitors center.

32

Mountains-
to-Sea Trail

Spanning 1175 miles across North Carolina, this trail offers an authentic experience of the natural beauty and rich history of the whole state.

➡ Blue Ridge Mountains.
Right: The sand dunes of
Jockey's Ridge State Park,
Outer Banks.

The Mountains-to-Sea State Trail (MST) spans the entire length of North Carolina from its rugged mountains to its exceptional coastline, offering the opportunity to hike, bike or paddle this beautiful and captivating state. The current route includes 700 miles of forested trails, greenway or beach and 500 miles of connecting roads that can be biked or walked by the diligent hiker. There is also an optional 100-mile water route on the Neuse River for kayakers or canoeists. Covering the trail's full distance allows hikers to experience close-up the state's vastly different landscapes.

The MST was made official in 2000 and is maintained primarily by the Friends of the Mountains-to-Sea Trail. With help from trail groups, land trusts, federal and state land agencies and private landowners, new miles are being added every year. The goal is to create a continuous off-road trail across the entire state. The MST is still in its infancy, but with the help of volunteers, trail groups and landowners, it has continued to establish itself.

As the most visited national park in the nation, Great Smoky Mountains National Park does not disappoint as the starting point for the 1000-mile trek to the coast. The trail starts at Clingmans Dome (actually in Tennessee) on the border of the state, at the highest peak in the park and the highest point on the iconic Appalachian Trail. Rushing waterfalls, craggy outcroppings and glorious sunsets are highlights along the 300 miles of trail through western North Carolina. The gorgeous terrain also includes many of the most popular outlooks on the famous Blue Ridge Parkway.

The mountains aren't the only wonderful

Sleep here...

A flagship trail necessarily has flagship stopovers, but some of the best stops on the Mountains-to-Sea Trail are the most unassuming, from campgrounds on the beach to those in the mountains. The connections with other hiking and outdoors enthusiasts are priceless, and it's recommended to try and connect with a trail angel via www.mountainstoseatrail.org/the-friends.

Beach Campgrounds
Love going to sleep to the sounds of the ocean and beach? There are several campgrounds on the coast perfect for an overnight – check out the Ocracoke Campground on the Outer Banks, open April–November.

Couch Surfing
Ever heard of trail angels? There are also many people in the state with whom you can stay, courtesy of the Friends of the Mountains-to-Sea Trail website, couch-surfing style.

Inn at Teardrops, Hillsborough
If Colonial-era towns are your thing, consider a stay at the Inn at Teardrops in historic Hillsborough and check out the Eno River Farmers Market, first established in 1754.

Camping on Shortoff Mountain
Grab a permit and spend the night on Shortoff Mountain in Linville Gorge, known as the Grand Canyon of the East, in western North Carolina. It just might be the highlight of your trip.

© Serge Skiba / Shutterstock; © karenfoleyphotography / Getty Images

Toolbox

When to go
This trail is enjoyed year-round; however, March until November will have the best weather for the rugged mountains and coastal marshes. North Carolina summers get muggy – enjoy the eastern waterways in spring or fall.

Getting there
The path traverses the entirety of North Carolina from the Great Smoky Mountains on the border of Tennessee to the Outer Banks of the eastern coast. You are never more than two hours from an access point in the state!

Practicalities
Length in miles: 1175
Start: Clingmans Dome in Great Smoky Mountains National Park
End: Jockey's Ridge State Park on the Outer Banks
Dog friendly: Yes, except for Great Smoky Mountains National Park
Bike friendly: Roughly two-thirds is bike friendly, excluding most of the mountain trails in the west.
Permit needed: Hiking permit needed for Great Smoky Mountains National Park
States covered: North Carolina

Boardwalk to the Pamlico Sound, the largest East Coast saltwater lagoon and estuary.

parts of the state, though. The coast, the wetlands and the Piedmont area have landscapes that are delightful, tranquil and unique. You will see rolling Piedmont farms, picturesque Colonial towns, the distinct knob of Pilot Mountain, many small churches, weathered tobacco barns, old lighthouses and marshy boardwalks: all add to the diversity of the MST. The walk can feel surreal as you pass by time-worn houses near languid marshes, with long Spanish moss hanging from the trees. Near the coast, those making the full trek to the Outer Banks even have the treat of a ferry ride as a break for their tired muscles.

While the Mountains-to-Sea Trail delivers a treat for the eyes, it also offers a physical and mental test for many who venture onto its path. The greenways on the trail are relaxing; but even though the road walking is flat, it provides no variation for the feet, and asphalt can make any normal muggy day feel even more intense. This alone is why many choose to bike the majority of the eastern path. However, riders and hikers should take caution when crossing any of the long bridges in the east, including the 2.8-mile Marc Basnight Bridge (which replaced the Herbert C Bonner Bridge) spanning the Oregon Inlet between Bodie Island and Pea Island on the Outer Banks. Smaller bridges, meanwhile, can have narrow shoulders for non-vehicular traffic.

Adding to the challenge, the variability of southern weather patterns makes for a real adventure. There have been powerful hurricanes, ice storms in March or 100°F days in the fall. If travelling in hurricane season, always check the forecast ahead of time. And always bring your bug spray! It's no wonder that Diane Van Deren, an accomplished ultramarathoner, claimed

the MST as some of the hardest trail running because of its varying landscape and unpredictability. A rainy day in the mid-50s in the mountains can be dangerous if you do not have the proper gear; rocks and roots will get slick, making the hiking very technical. This terrain will surely give you new muscles you never knew you had.

Physical challenges aside, the MST is a great way to indulge if you wish to experience the history, culture and delicious food of the Tar Heel State. With everything from fresh coastal seafood to mouthwatering barbecue to local beer, this is a great trail for foodies to explore. North Carolina is also rich in Colonial and Civil War history, and the trail bisects two battlefields, including Bentonville Battlefield. It passes through many historic districts and towns with local history museums, from the Textile History Museum near Burlington to the Graveyard of the Atlantic Museum at the southernmost point of Cape Hatteras.

You don't really know what you might see around every corner on the back roads of North Carolina, but it is sure to be an experience. The trail is unapologetically authentic in what it offers; you may observe every type of neighborhood, see giant turkey farms that most certainly supply some of the nation's Thanksgiving birds, or hear the many forms of friendly 'y'all' from the locals.

During the hike, one of the most unexpected yet appreciated aspects of the trail is the generosity of the people you meet when you pause a moment to hear their stories and understand a bit about their lives. This is a trail that makes you think in new ways about the life you live.

Highlights

Above all – literally – it's the magnificent mountains that make North Carolina special. Oh, and the dunes, marshes and wildlife refuges along 70-mile Cape Hatteras National Seashore. But don't forget everything in between: people, food and history.

NEUSIOK TRAIL
Cross boardwalks over dense swamp on the 21 miles of the Neusiok Trail, the longest continuous hiking trail on the coastal plain of the state.

JOCKEY'S RIDGE
North Carolina boasts the tallest active sand dune on the East Coast, Jockey's Ridge, a 0.5-mile hike from the main drag in Nags Head.

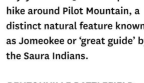

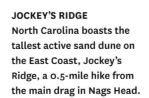

PILOT MOUNTAIN
Enjoy a 1.6- or 3-mile loop hike around Pilot Mountain, a distinct natural feature known as Jomeokee or 'great guide' by the Saura Indians.

WATERROCK KNOB
Near the Blue Ridge Parkway, one of the highest points on the MST offers a gorgeous four-state view just a 0.3-mile side trip off of the main trail.

BENTONVILLE BATTLEFIELD
Stroll a 2.3-mile self-guided trail that brings to life the site of the largest Civil War battle in North Carolina.

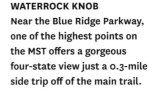

33
Natchez Trace National Scenic Trail

This is one of the oldest roads in North America, following a natural ridgeline used by animals as a grazing route; later, it was a footpath and trading route for Native American tribes.

Biker on the Natchez Trace;
Right: Natchez Trace Parkway
Bridge near Franklin, Tennessee.

The Natchez Trace is not a thru-trail. But what it lacks in continuity, it makes up for in the sheer weight of its history. The Trace runs from Tennessee to the Mississippi River where the Indigenous people known as Mound Builders made their home. From AD 800 to 1500 the mound building culture flourished in what is now Mississippi, Alabama and Tennessee while its people navigated the path now known as the Natchez Trace, following in the footsteps of buffalo, elk and other large game animals. The people were hunters and gatherers and the route was an elemental part of their daily lives. Over time, cultural centers and sacred sites dotted the active byway. Eventually the trail was used by the Chickasaw, Choctaw and Natchez peoples, established as a trading route between different villages. Once Tennessee became a state, the Trace went on to be used as a mail route and by 1809 it was established as a fully navigable wagon route linking the very remote Mississippi to more settled areas of the United States further east. The ancient forest path was now a major roadway of the young USA, though today you can still use it to get a glimpse into the region's life before Europeans arrived here.

If you start your journey at the northern terminus in Tennessee, the best-known signposts on the Trace focus more on its recent history, however, starting with the very first at milepost 438's Birdsong Hollow: the nation's first double arch concrete bridge, spanning 1648ft. Completed in 1994, driving over this feat of modern engineering offers unmatched views of the hilly Tennessee countryside blanketed with trees. Getting above Tennessee's thick canopy of green is a treat

Sleep here...

Pay attention to the National Park Service notice about lodging, in place to keep an unspoiled feel: 'There is no lodging available on the Natchez Trace Parkway itself, but the communities along the Parkway may provide hotels.' Natchez has especially pleasing historic options for overnight stays, and there are some wonderful stops along the way and in Nashville, the other end point.

The Germantown Inn, Nashville
Germantown's oldest house, a shoemaker's cottage dating to 1865, has been flipped into a charming 10-room inn steeped in local design. Exposed brick and natural light are abundant throughout the cozy hideaway.

French Camp Historic District, Mississippi
Reminiscent of life for settlers along the Natchez Trace in the mid-19th century, French Camp has buildings to tour as well as a B&B with several cabins made from 19th-century materials.

Historic Oak Hill Inn, Natchez
At this B&B you can sleep in an original 1835 bed and dine on pre–Civil War porcelain under 1850 Waterford crystal gasoliers. It's all about purist antebellum aristocratic living.

Meriwether Lewis Campground-Natchez Trace
A stone's throw from the parkway in the middle of its path through Tennessee, this much-loved campground is run by the National Park Service and is first come, first served. RVs should look elsewhere; the Natchez Trace RV Campground is nearby.

Toolbox

When to go
There is always a chance of rain in the south, and summers are hot and humid. Best go in the fall after the heat of summer but before the weather turns cold, from September to early November. In general, however, there is no wrong time of year.

Getting there
The Natchez Trace Parkway runs from Nashville, Tennessee for 444 miles south to Natchez, Mississippi. Most visitors arrive by car.

Practicalities
Length in miles: 60 miles of hiking trails, 444 miles of parkway
Start: Nashville, TN
End: Natchez, MS
Dog friendly: Yes
Bike friendly: Yes; drivers should use caution and share the road
Permit needed: No
States covered: Tennessee, Alabama and Mississippi

worth savoring.

Coming from Nashville, Garrison Creek trailhead at milepost 427 is the best place to start hiking; it leads to the Highland Rim Trail, which continues for 25 miles to the Shady Grove trailhead at milepost 408. Traditionally Chickasaw land, just south of the Garrison Creek trailhead you'll cross the boundary that was established between the US and Chickasaw territory when Tennessee became a state in 1796; two decades later, Andrew Jackson would force the sale of the remaining Chickasaw land in the Treaty of Tuscaloosa, a precursor of the removal project to come under his Presidency. Further along the Trace, Te-lah-nay's wall commemorates the Chickasaw's tragic eviction from their native lands and is a worthy stop to pay your respects.

This first 25-mile section of the trail offers multiple picnic sites and an overlook and has portions especially beloved by horsebacks riders, as well as encompassing the venerable Old Trace at milepost 426.3. Visitors will find 60 miles suitable for walking or riding scattered along the Parkway's route; the hikable part of the National Scenic Trail is broken up into roughly five sections stretching from Nashville, Tennessee to Tupelo, Mississippi. Other spots offer lovely views; Baker Bluff to Jackson Falls at milepost 404.7 is a 1.5-mile round-trip jaunt worth making.

For drivers who are history buffs, the next notable stop might be Meriwether Lewis' gravesite at milepost 385.9. After playing his part in the Lewis & Clark expedition, Lewis was traveling on business related to his new post as Governor of Upper Louisiana when he died of gunshot wounds near Grinder's Stand, a possible suicide. A monument marks the spot.

Further on, the Trace leaves Tennessee and the landscape changes accordingly. Experience its southern ambiance in Mississippi's Canton area with a detour at milepost 122 for Cypress Swamp on the Pearl River. The wide-trunked tupelo and cypress trees stick out among the dark water like legs in a pool, reflecting in the glass-like surface of the water. View its eerie beauty from the wooden boardwalk winding through the swamp.

If driving, the parkway makes a beautiful day trip or extended road trip from Nashville, running for 444 miles through three states until reaching its eponymous Mississippi end. The town of Natchez sits on the bluffs of the Mississippi River, and is known for its lavish plantation and antebellum homes. But part of the story that can't be forgotten is that of the people whose unpaid labor generated this wealth. The Forks of the Road site, on the grounds of a former slave market – the largest in the state and one of the largest in the nation – tells part of this story. Visitors can read the information panels about the slave trade in Natchez and beyond. The chains set in concrete are a haunting reminder of this dark part of American history. It's all part of the story of the Trace.

Of the many highlights along the way, the Double Arch Bridge near Franklin, the Fall Hollow and Jackson waterfalls and the Tennessee River stand out, and can easily be visited in a day. There's a helpful visitors center outside Tupelo. The parkway is extremely popular with cyclists, who come from surrounding states to ride the miles of truck-free highway. Remember to share the road – and to get out, stretch your legs, and experience the scenic trail as well.

Highlights

This is a lovely, scenic drive that traverses a wide panoply of Southern landscapes: thick, dark forests, soggy wetlands, gentle hill country and long swaths of farmland. The original Trace has an almost canyon-like feel, echoing with history.

PHARR MOUNDS

This is a roughly 2000-year-old, 90-acre complex of eight Indigenous burial sites. Four were excavated in 1966; other mound sites can be found on the Trace as well.

CYPRESS SWAMP

At milepost 122 a wooden boardwalk winds through cypress and tupelo trees that jut from the water's glassy surface. Watch for alligators sunning themselves along the banks.

SUNKEN TRACE

At milepost 41.5 is a small reminder of the long legacy of the Trace. Here the earth has been worn away from thousands of years of use, making a small canyon through the earth.

ELVIS' BIRTHPLACE

Between the little cottage where Elvis was born, the Tupelo hardware store where he bought his first guitar and a small, thriving restaurant scene, Tupelo is a great stop.

TE-LAH-NAY'S WALL

The Yuchi tribe was forced on the Trail of Tears to Oklahoma. One woman, Te-lah-nay, walked right back. Her great-great-grandson built a wall in her honor at milepost 338.

Sunset at the Natchez Trace Parkway near Nashville, Tennessee.

Resources

01 Natchez Trace National Scenic Trail site
www.nps.gov/natt
The NPS website includes helpful trail maps and advisories on current conditions.

02 *A Way Through the Wilderness: The Natchez Trace and the Civilization of the Southern Frontier*
This history by William Davis looks at the growth of the Mississippi Territory from 1798 to the 1830s through the lens of the Trace.

03 *Last Train to Memphis: The Rise of Elvis Presley*
Fans of Elvis who are tracing his steps from Tupelo on can dive deep into his early years in this biography by Peter Guralnick.

Silver Street at the Mississippi River, Natchez, Mississippi. Left: Birthplace of Elvis Presley.

Hike this...

As the Natchez Trace Parkway is one of the country's most famous scenic drives, it gets more attention for its roadway than for the parallel scenic trail, but there are over 60 miles to hike here over five separate trails.

➡ A man stands in front of Jackson Falls on the Natchez Trace Parkway.

01
Highland Rim Trail, Tennessee

The northernmost section for hikers on the Natchez Trace runs from milepost 408 to 427. Tennessee visitors will want to set their sights on this 25-mile stretch that includes an old section, the aptly named Old Trace. It can be approached in a variety of ways depending on the amount of time you have to spare, and whether you intend to hike or ride the trail.

Some sections of the Highland Rim Trail are open to horseback riders as well as hikers; the trailhead at Highway 50 is open to both, with parking for trailers, hitching posts, and water for horses available. Milepost 416's Fly trailhead has fewer amenities but is shared by equestrians and bipedal visitors as well.

Hikers wanting views rather than history can head to the Tennessee Valley Divide trailhead at milepost 423.9, with a 3-mile round-trip hike to Burns Branch offering vibrant scenery in spring and fall. However, not visiting the Old Trace would really be a shame.

02
Potkopinu Trail, Mississippi

This sunken 3-mile stretch near the southern terminus of the Natchez Trace in Mississippi is the longest remaining section of the Trace as it once was, the path worn down by successive generations of animals and humans passing through these woods over the course of many centuries. It's the origin story of the Natchez Trace.

If you want a taste of the trail as it used to be long before recorded history, this is the spot. It can be accessed at either milepost 17 (south of Coles Creek picnic area) or milepost 20, the Road 553 trailhead, the larger trailhead with paring on the shoulder of the road.

Potkopinu (Pot-cop-i-new) Trail features some embankments up to 20ft high, and takes its name from the Natchez Indian word for 'little valley'. For an easy, year-round hike through the forest, there's a deep reverence to the trail here. It's accessible on foot only; there's no equestrian access here. Look out for stream crossings, whose depth varies based on recent rainfall or lack thereof.

03
Blackland Prairie Trail, Mississippi

Just opposite the Tupelo Visitors Center for the parkway at milepost 266 is the northern trailhead of this 6-mile out-and-back trail (12 miles round trip) for hikers only that runs parallel to the parkway, and requires walking via the road at creek crossings. It's a nice add-on to a stop at the visitors center, and can be as short or long as you choose; just turn back when you've covered half your preferred distance on this one-way trail. You can walk to the Old Town Overlook at milepost 263.9 or the Chickasaw Village Site at milepost 261.8, with interpretive signs available.

Almost directly in the center of the parkway, with helpful rangers at hand to offer advice on what approach suits your needs best, any stretch of the Blackland Prairie Trail is a great place to experience a sampling of the National Scenic Trail that accompanies the more frequently driven two-lane parkway. There's great benefit in combining both a driving tour with a scenic trail hike.

34

Natural Bridge Trail and Red River Gorge

Double Arch rock formation at Red River Gorge in Kentucky at sunset. Right: Enjoying the view of Red River Gorge in Daniel Boone National Forest.

The Red River Gorge in Kentucky's Daniel Boone National Forest is a geologic masterpiece with trails that pass enthralling rock formations from millions of years ago.

The soft earthy trail cushions your footsteps as you walk down into a forested ravine. Sherbet-colored mushrooms perch on nearby fallen logs while gossamer spiderwebs hanging from a nearby branch sway in the breeze. You walk farther and a large sandstone outcropping appears, its sides scored and scalloped by millions of years of running water and wind. Additional exploration reveals a stone archway stretching across the path, appearing delicate despite its strength and size. This is Red River Gorge.

Kentucky is home to fascinating geology, with limestone karst hillsides setting the foundation for the rolling hills of the western and central parts of state. They abut the rippled ridges of the Appalachian Mountains, the continent's oldest mountain system, thought to be over 400 million years old. Here, at the meeting point of the hills and mountains, is Red River Gorge, a zigzag canyon framing its namesake river. This place may seem understated at first glance, but it harbors ecological wonders as well as three intertwined trails: the Red River Gorge Trail, Natural Bridge Trail and a section of the 270-mile Sheltowee Trace.

The Red River Gorge Trail sprawls across its namesake canyon like a neural network, a backcountry route that twists and turns through a variety of mammoth stone formations shaped over many millennia. The geologic area is estimated to contain over 150 natural stone arches, outnumbered in the US only by Utah's Arches National Park.

The gorge has a storied human history as well as an environmental one; it's thought that people have occupied the region for nearly 12,000 years, and it served as home

Sleep here...

While camping is allowed in Red River Gorge, indoor accommodations are relatively few. Other options are a bit farther from the trails but are worth booking to get a well-rounded taste of this part of Kentucky.

Hemlock Lodge
Run by Kentucky State Parks, the lodge is simply designed, but it's pet friendly and close to the Red River Gorge and Natural Bridge trailheads. It also offers cabin accommodations.

Snug Hollow Farm
This cozy B&B east of Berea sits on 300 Appalachian acres and consists of two guest cabins and a main house. Guests have access to nearby walking trails, and meals are prepared from harvests from the on-property garden.

Red River Gorge Cabins
A small, family-owned operation, this outfit has four cabins of varying sizes and styles, all with atmospheric wood accents and budget-friendly rates.

21c Museum Hotel Lexington
For those looking to balance outdoor adventure and culture, Lexington's contemporary art museum hotel packs a big punch. Rooms and public spaces are decorated with regularly changing artworks, and 4ft-tall plastic penguins dot the property, changing positions each night.

Toolbox

When to go
The trails are accessible most of the year, but the area is at its best in transitional months. Spring introduces life in the form of wildflowers, multicolored mushrooms, babbling brooks and misty waterfalls, while fall carpets the landscape in leaves of various hues and turns scenic lookouts into prime leaf-peeping spots.

Getting there
The Red River Gorge and Natural Bridge are in Daniel Boone National Forest, where central Kentucky meets Appalachia. The nearest airport is in Lexington, only an hour's drive from the trailheads.

Practicalities
Length in miles: 34 (gorge), 0.5 (Natural Bridge)
Start: Hemlock Lodge, Slade, KY
End: Same
Dog friendly: No dogs allowed on Natural Bridge Trail; permitted (leashed) in Red River Gorge
Bike friendly: No
Permit needed: Only for camping
States covered: Kentucky

to indigenous people for centuries before the arrival of European colonists. Many artifacts have been found in the gorge's rock shelters, as they offered protection from the elements for the area's early residents.

Fast forward to the 1960s when human interference almost resulted in the gorge being entirely underwater. In 1967 the Army Corps of Engineers planned to build a flood control dam that would have submerged the Red River Gorge and its unique flora and fauna. The Sierra Club and Supreme Court Justice William O Douglas participated in a protest hike that brought national attention to the case and eventually stopped the dam's development. The gorge has been untouched by industry ever since.

Hikes are plentiful here. The area is within the massive Daniel Boone National Forest, and its wild crags, rugged ravines and gravity-defying sandstone cliffs make the term 'foothills' seem weak indeed. Head up the Auxier Ridge Trail for some of the best views of the area's rocky bluffs and rumpled landscape, or wind your way down to the statuesque Gray's Arch to see one of the many impressive sandstone arches in this part of the forest. Rock shelters, caves and waterfalls also abound, creating microclimates in which you'll find rare flowers, flattened salamanders and spongy green moss that glistens with water droplets from nearby streams and waterfalls. Primitive or backcountry camping (with no amenities; carry in what you need) is allowed in various places throughout the gorge, but be mindful of your tent location – abrupt cliffsides are numerous and pose a threat to sleepwalking campers.

Today hikers and campers aren't the only ones flocking to this mountainous oasis; Red River Gorge is considered one of the premier rock-climbing spots in the country, thanks to its impressive number of sheer rock faces, relatively temperate weather and well-developed climbing infrastructure. Affectionately known as the Red, the gorge is a hub for sport climbing, and bouldering and trad-climbing options are popular as well.

The shining star of the area's geologic marvels is the Natural Bridge, and it's also the gorge's most accessible. Located in Natural Bridge State Resort Park just to the south of the Red River Gorge Geological Area, the bridge is accessible to visitors via a relatively short hike (less than a mile, though much of that is directly uphill) or a motorized skylift, an excellent option for those with mobility challenges. Trails lead right up to and over the Natural Bridge, giving you the sensation of being very small in a very big place. For the best views of the entire formation, head to the nearby lookout off of the Laurel Ridge Trail in late afternoon – the setting sun turns the sandstone gold. Hemlock Lodge at the trailhead is equipped with maps of the local network of trails.

One of the best things about Red River Gorge and Natural Bridge is that they are roughly an hour from two cities that are worth visiting in their own right and also serve as convenient jumping-off points for your outdoor adventure. Located directly to the west, Lexington is a college town with Kentucky flair, home to horse farms, breweries and bourbon distilleries. Southwest of the gorge lies Berea, a small town known for its thriving artisan community and environmentally sustainable practices.

Highlights

In the Appalachian foothills of eastern Kentucky, hiking, rock climbing, camping, boating and fishing are the big to-dos; Natural Bridge State Resort Park alone offers 20 miles of mostly short hiking trails. Simply enjoying the fresh air is a must too.

WHITE-HAIRED GOLDENROD
This plant with bright yellow flowers, unique to the rock shelters of the gorge, grows nowhere else in the world. The rare plant was once listed as endangered but is recovering.

NATURAL BRIDGE
This sandstone arch is one of the most striking rock formations in the area. It's an impressive 78ft long and 65ft high, and is believed to be at least a million years old.

CLIFTY WILDERNESS
Within the Red River Gorge Geological Area, the Clifty Wilderness prohibits motorized vehicles and mountain bikes on its trails, guaranteeing time for silent contemplation.

AUXIER RIDGE
Follow this 2-mile trail to one of the best lookouts in the gorge from Auxier Ridge, with views of Courthouse Rock, Double Arch and Haystack Rock.

MIGUEL'S PIZZA
While not part of the gorge trail system, this homey pizza joint in Slade is a staple for local hikers and climbers. Order a pie and an Ale-8-One soda after a long day outdoors.

35

New England National Scenic Trail

You'll walk by rural towns, farmlands, forests, mountains and valleys on this 215-mile path stretching from the Long Island Sound in Connecticut to the Massachusetts–New Hampshire border.

➡ Faulkner's Island Lighthouse in the Stewart B McKinney National Wildlife Refuge, Connecticut. Right: Pattaconk Reservoir, Cockaponset State Forest, Connecticut.

The Heublein Tower in Simsbury, Connecticut, sits at the top of Talcott Mountain, a 1000ft promontory. Hike to its base and then climb the stairs to the observation deck for 360-degree views of the lush Farmington River valley and the rolling Connecticut landscape. If it's fall – the best time to go – the woods will be ablaze with fiery colors, and migrating hawks will soar overhead. On clear days it's said that you can see 1200 sq miles, with views of Mt Monadnock in New Hampshire, the Berkshires in Massachusetts, and Long Island Sound to the south. It's a landscape that inspired some of America's first painters and writers. Today you can also see the modern Hartford, Connecticut, and Springfield, Massachusetts, city skylines.

This all-in-one, urban-mountain-valley-farmland-water view epitomizes the New England Trail, a 215-mile path that includes an amazing diversity of landscapes as it travels 215 miles through densely populated southern New England.

The New England National Scenic Trail, also known as NET, MMM or 3M, is the combination of three trail systems: the Mattabesett, Metacomet and Monadnock Trails. The trail travels along back roads, through fields, forests and farmlands, and across mountain peaks and ridges. It also crosses streets and meanders through 39 communities, sometimes through private properties, with the cooperation and permission of owners. Few people hike its entirety at one time. It's best done as a series of shorter overnight trips or day hikes from places where trailheads are easy to access. In fact, nearly two million people live within 10 miles of the trail.

The southern section of the NET begins

Sleep here...

The trail passes through several charming New England towns, so there are plenty of nearby hotels and motels. Make a literary pit stop out of a visit to Amherst from a Mt Holyoke base (or do college visits in this densely academic cluster). If you prefer camping on the trail, consider one of the below options.

 ### Rockland Preserve Campsite, Connecticut

There are tent platforms surrounded by woods, as well as a campfire ring, at this campsite in section 9 in Connecticut.

 ### Mt Holyoke Outing Club Cabin, Massachusetts

The cabin in section 7 in Massachusetts has six cots and one queen air mattress, electricity and kitchen supplies. It's open from September to April.

 ### Richardson-Zlogar Cabin, Massachusetts

Located in section 17 in Massachusetts, the backcountry log cabin has cushioned benches, three twin beds, tent platforms and picnic tables – plus great mountain views. Reservations are required.

 ### Wendell State Forest Shelter, Massachusetts

A lean-to, this shelter in Section 15 in Massachusetts has room for six to eight hikers. There's a firepit, water access and an outhouse.

Toolbox

 ### When to go
Parts of the trail get very busy with day-trippers during the summer months. Shoulder seasons are best. Spring brings wildflowers and migrating birds, while fall boasts spectacular foliage and crisp, clear days.

Getting there
The southern terminus is in Guilford Harbor in historic Guilford, Connecticut, on picturesque Long Island Sound, about an hour from Bradley International Airport. There are many additional access points along the trail. The northern terminus is only close to regional airports, but is under three hours from Boston Logan International Airport.

Practicalities
Length in miles: 215
Start: Guilford Harbor, CT
End: Royalston Falls, MA
Dog friendly: Yes, some sections
Bike friendly: Yes, some sections
Permit needed: No
States covered: Connecticut, Massachusetts

in the historic town of Guilford, Connecticut. Pick up the path from waterfront Chittenden Park and meander past Colonial homes and the scenic town green. Heading north out of town, the path follows the tidal East River into the East River Preserve, under a canopy of soaring white oaks. From here, the trail links a number of preserves and forests, including the Cockaponset State Forest, Connecticut's second largest with more than 17,000 acres, and Tri-Mountain State Park, accessible only by foot. The trail now heads to the southern mountain peaks. Mt Higby is first, a steep scramble up a ridgeline and through Preston Notch that has pretty views of the distant mountains. Next comes Ragged Mountain Memorial Preserve.

Just outside of New Britain, Connecticut, the trail climbs to Rattlesnake Mountain and Pinnacle Rock, where you'll walk through an old orchard to reach Will Warren's Den, a giant boulder field. Take time to explore the boulder caves and then continue to the summit of Pinnacle Rock, with a bird's-eye view in all directions.

One of the NET's most popular sections in Connecticut lies farther north, traveling through Talcott Mountain State Park, home to the Heublein Tower. The former summer home of a wealthy Connecticut businessman has an observation deck overlooking the lush Farmington River valley.

Trekking north from Heublein Tower, you'll reach Massachusetts. Crossing the state border brings you to a diverse landscape – fields, farms and forests crisscrossed with rivers and dotted with ponds and back roads – before you enter the Mt Tom Reservation, one of the finest sections of the trail. Hike the strenuous path up the volcanic ridgeline for views of the

Berkshires and the Connecticut River valley.

In the Mt Holyoke Range in Massachusetts, the trail passes the spot where 19th-century artist Thomas Cole created *The Oxbow*, considered a masterpiece of American landscape painting. The area is also home to the Seven Sisters, a necklace of ridgeline summits with beautiful mountain-to-valley vistas.

Further north, the trail climbs 1106ft Mt Norwottock, the highest peak in the Holyoke Range, and leads to Horse Caves, a rocky jumble said to have been a hideout during Shays' Rebellion (1786–87). Then the trail meanders down roads and through fields and woods, crossing several brooks by the Quabbin Reservoir and zigzagging through forests including Wendell, Northfield and Mt Grace State Forests.

The NET officially ends at Royalston Falls, though you can continue on the Monadnock Trail to the open summit of Mt Monadnock in New Hampshire, a National Natural Landmark. The 3165ft peak and the sweeping views from its summit were an inspiration to Henry David Thoreau, Ralph Waldo Emerson and more. Monadnock derives from an Abenaki tribal word meaning 'special' or 'unique.' The word is now used geologically to describe a residual hill that rises alone on a plain.

Whether you continue to Mt Monadnock or not, you'll want to linger awhile at Royalston Falls, which hugs the New Hampshire–Massachusetts border. Follow the trail through a lush, misty river valley, past rippling brooks and cascades, to a rocky gorge framed by dense forest, mosses and ferns. Here Royalston Falls, carved by Falls Brook, plunges 45ft into a frothy basin. It's a perfect, cooling respite and a fine ending or beginning to the NET.

Highlights

New England's plethora of peaks offers ample enticement to don a knapsack and hit the trails. And New England is intrinsically tied to the sea – historically, commercially and emotionally. To see this connection firsthand, start at the coastline.

MT TOM RESERVATION
Ridgeline views of the Berkshires and the Connecticut River Valley make this section in Massachusetts one of the trail's finest.

TALCOTT MOUNTAIN
Climb the 165ft Heublein Tower on top of this mountain in Connecticut for expansive views of the Farmington River valley and beyond. It's especially pretty in fall.

ROYALSTON FALLS
At the Massachusetts–New Hampshire border, you can hike through a luxuriant river valley to Royalston Falls, which plunges 45ft into a frothy basin.

GUILFORD
Meander through the coastal town of Guilford, Connecticut, exploring its museums and historic homes and taking in views of Long Island Sound.

MT MONADNOCK
Just past the NET, the summit of Mt Monadnock is a breezy rock pile ready-made for picnicking, view-appreciating and, well, selfie-taking.

→ Enjoying the sunset from the top of a New England peak.

Resources

O1 New England Trail
www.newenglandtrail.org
Visit the official website for up-to-date information, including trail descriptions and maps, trail conditions and events.

O2 Appalachian Mountain Club (AMC)
www.outdoors.org
The Berkshires chapter of the AMC in Massachusetts promotes and maintains large portions of the NET.

O3 Connecticut Forest & Park Association (CFPA)
www.ctwoodlands.org
The nonprofit organization works to protect forests, parks, walking trails and open spaces in Connecticut, and helps sustain the NET.

O4 *New England Trail Map & Guide*
This collaboration between the AMC and CFPA is a good reference.

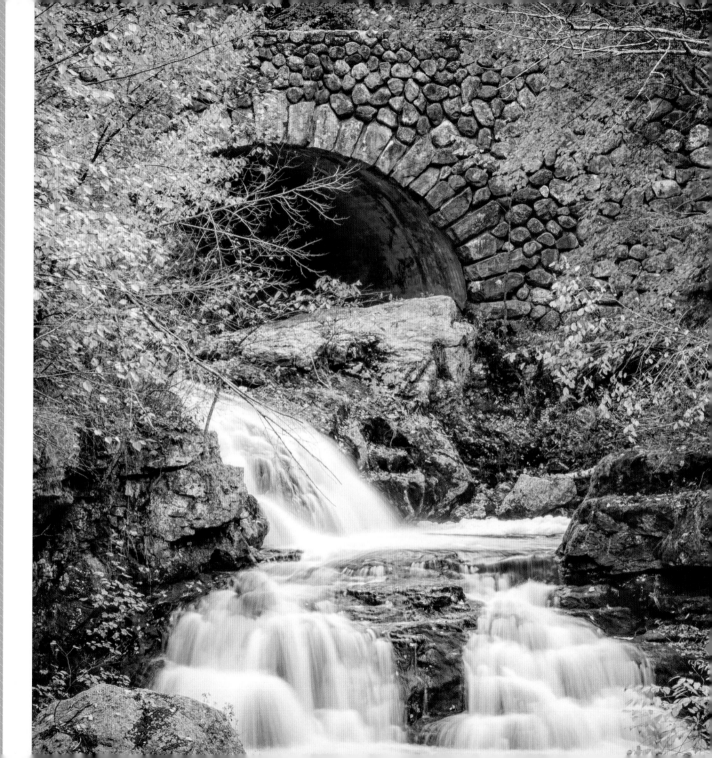

Hike this...

Try to time your hikes to the legendary brilliance of fall in New England. Scarlet and sugar maples, ash, birch, beech, dogwood, tulip tree, oak and sassafras all contribute to the carnival of autumn color.

→ Bluff Head ridge along Mattabesett Trail. Opposite page, from left: Mattabesett Trail NET sign; Royalston Falls in Massachusetts.

01
Ragged Mountain, Connecticut

North of Mt Higby and south of Rattlesnake Mountain on the NET, the Ragged Mountain Memorial Preserve offers a fairly strenuous, huff-and-puff climb to the summit of Ragged Mountain (761ft). The hike gains only 560ft in elevation but rewards with open views of the surrounding bluffs, the Quinnipiac River valley and the Wassel Reservoir. Ragged Mountain was formed of igneous traprock, or basalt, at the end of the Triassic Period and the ascent includes some scrambles. See the cliffs and you won't wonder why the Preserve is the most popular rock climbing region of the state. Taking a 5.5-mile loop trail brings you onto a stretch of the Metacomet Trail before returning back down. Start from the trailhead on West Ln in Berlin. Three miles west of New Britain, Ragged Mountain Memorial Preserve is located near the towns of Southington and Berlin, and is part of the extended Metacomet Ridge. In winter, it can be tackled by snowshoe.

02
Seven Sisters, Massachusetts

Walk the set of summits sprawling across the ridgeline of the Mt Holyoke Range in Massachusetts on this 6-mile or so section of the MMM/NET that crosses Skinner State Park and Mount Holyoke Range State Park. Technically, there are ten summits (despite the name), and you'll climb 4000ft overall. Along the way, you'll have mountain-to-valley views.

The hike is one-way, meaning you will need to park a car at each trailhead or catch a rideshare back to your car at your starting point. At the trail's eastern trailhead, the Notch Visitor's Center on Rt 47 by Mt Holyoke College has ample parking. Then it's up 650ft to Bare Mountain (1014ft), the first summit.

By the western edge of the trail is Holyoke House. There's also a Summit House at Mt Holyoke (940ft), with views of the Connecticut River below. And if you loved the experience, maybe you'll want to run in the Seven Sisters Trail Race, 12 miles (out and back again) of trail running along the Holyoke Range ridge.

03
Farley Ledges Loop, Massachusetts

In section 16 of the NET, you can take a 2.4-mile loop trail along the ridge of Rattlesnake Mountain (1067ft) near Erving. Farley Ledges can be found here, a wide, 220ft-high precipice of sheer rock especially popular for climbing and bouldering. Briggs Brook Falls is also just off the MMM Trail here.

Dogs should remain leashed; some portions of the trail go by public property, and it's important to behave respectfully while using the trail recreationally. Park off Rt 2 at the Farley Ledges trailhead. Parking can fill up; try to arrive by 10am. Alternatively, take the Erving Ledges–Hermit Mountain path instead, for 4.8 miles with a 1020ft elevation gain. It's a good snowshoeing route as well. This popular (and practical) New England pastime that fits well with the region's scenic trail.

Another trail option in Franklin County near Erving is the Mohawk Trail, which runs east–west along Rt 2 using an old Native American trading route and has some hiking segments.

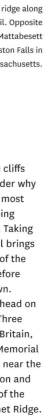

3.6

Nez Perce National Historic Trail

This trail recalls the tragic struggles of the Nez Perce even as it passes through some of the West's most beautiful landscapes, mostly in Montana.

Alpenglow on mountains over Sawtooth Lake at sunrise, Idaho. Right: Northeastern Oregon's Wallowa Valley.

The Nez Perce Trail is somewhat of an oddity among the National Historic Trails. First, it's managed by the Forest Service and not the National Park Service, but that's the least notable difference. What makes it more unusual is that it commemorates what is undeniably a low moment in American history. Most trails emphasize the nation's moments of triumph, whether it's the 240 settlers led by Juan Bautista de Anza from 1775 to 1776 across the Southwest and through California or the civil rights activists who marched across Alabama in 1965. Yet there was often a silent loser on those marches of expansion: the continent's Native peoples.

The Nez Perce Trail, on the other hand, shines a light on the cruelties and injustices of the Indian Wars of the late 19th century. It follows the route of the Nez Perce Indians as they attempted to outrun the US Army in 1877. Unlike the pioneers who moved to settle a remote corner of the West, the Nez Perce were trying to flee the country. For them, the land of promise was not America but Canada, where they hoped Chief Sitting Bull of the Lakota would be able to help them – yet they would never make it there. After 127 days, they were stopped 40 miles from the border in the Battle of Bear Paw.

The dispute with US authorities began with the government breaking its treaty with the Nez Perce – an act described at that time as a 'gigantic blunder and a crime' by the *New York Times*. The journey of the Nez Perce ended with the heartbreaking surrender speech by Hinmatóowyalahtq'it, also known as Chief Joseph, which captured his feeling of total defeat: 'I am tired; my heart is sick and

Sleep here...

Rates for accommodations are noticeably higher in the Yellowstone region than in the surrounding areas of Wyoming, Idaho and Montana, particularly in the high-season months of July and August. Yellowstone itself remains the biggest headache, with accommodations booked up months in advance. The key is to reserve well ahead, though around half the campsites in Yellowstone are on a first-come, first-served basis.

 Camping in Sawtooth National Forest
This national forest in Idaho is part of the 756,000-acre Sawtooth National Recreation Area, which is almost the size of Rhode Island. A plus of camping here is easy access to nearby hot springs.

 Old Faithful Inn
Built in 1903 and 1904, this National Historic Landmark in Wyoming's Yellowstone National Park has signature rustic resort architecture and is still a beloved base for exploring the park.

 Lodging and Camping in Nez Perce–Clearwater National Forests
Rustic cabins are for rent in these Montana national forests, or you can choose from a variety of camping options: RV hookups, campgrounds and dispersed camping (anywhere within 300ft of the median line of certain roads).

 Grand Union Hotel
Montana's oldest operating hotel opened in Fort Benton in 1882, just five years after the epic journey of the Nez Perce. It reopened in 1999 after an extensive restoration.

Toolbox

 When to go
Summer is the best season – it's that simple. There will be bigger crowds at parks in peak season, and you will pay more for rooms, but there's a reason it's so popular: the warm, sunny and long days are hard to beat.

Getting there
Both ends of this trail are off the beaten path. The closest major airport to Wallowa, Oregon, is in Walla Walla, Washington. The best option from Chinook, Montana, at the other end of the trail, is the Great Falls International Airport, Montana.

 Practicalities
Length in miles: 1170
Start: Wallowa Valley, OR
End: Chinook, MT
Dog friendly: Yes, in portions
Bike friendly: Yes, in portions
Permit needed: Some campgrounds
States covered: Oregon, Idaho, Wyoming, Montana

→ Part of the Nez Perce National Historic Trail in Wyoming

sad. From where the sun now stands, I will fight no more forever.'

It is perhaps ironic that the scene of this tragic moment in American history passes through some of the most beautiful parts of the country. While it is not possible to follow the exact trail of the Nez Perce – much of it is on private land – many of the portions that are accessible pass through dense woods and rich pastureland, with snowcapped peaks on the horizon. The route includes one of the jewels of the National Park System, Yellowstone, which was five years old at the time of the Nez Perce War. Today the wild and scenic Clarks Fork of the Yellowstone River runs along much of the Chief Joseph Scenic Hwy (Hwy 296), linking Cody (via Hwy 120 N) with the Beartooth Hwy and Yellowstone National Park's Northeast Entrance. Chief Joseph eluded the US army and escaped through Clarks Fork here in 1877. If you decide to stop and hike, the bluntly named Dead Indian Pass (8048ft) will lead you to Clarks Fork Canyon, home of a breathtaking waterfall, and 1200ft granite gorge.

The trail, and the saga of the war, begin in Oregon's Wallowa Valley. Even today it is easy to see why this fertile land in the shadow of the Wallowa Mountains would have been coveted by the white settlers who petitioned the US Army to move the local Nez Perce Indians to their reservation in Idaho, in violation of the Walla Walla Treaty of 1855. The valley's towns, like Wallowa and Joseph (originally Silver Lake, but later renamed for Chief Joseph), retain an Old West atmosphere, their streets lined with historical buildings with typical western false fronts.

The first battle of the Nez Perce War took place just across the border in Idaho, at White Bird Canyon. It resulted in a defeat for the US Army despite the fact that they outnumbered the Nez Perce and had superior weapons. Today the site is one of 38 that make up the Nez Perce National Historical Park. A short trail at the battlefield brings to life the events of June 17, 1877.

The largest confrontation of the war took place on August 9 and 10 at Big Hole, after the Nez Perce had crossed over into Montana. A predawn raid resulted in somewhere between 60 and 90 dead men, women and children on the Nez Perce side, and it shattered any hope that the residents of the Montana Territory would allow the Nez Perce to make their way peacefully to the Canadian border. Today the battlefield site covers more than 1000 acres (though a third of it is privately owned) and sits due east of the Nez Perce Reservation – Idaho's largest, though it is about one-twentieth of the size of the reservation originally promised to the nation.

The final confrontation took place at Bear Paw, just over 40 miles from the border with Canada, near Chinook, Montana. The Nez Perce had traveled almost 1200 miles and faced the US Army in multiple confrontations. Their last hope was that Sitting Bull, chief of the Lakota, would send reinforcements. He didn't, and when the Nez Perce were told they would be allowed to return to the Wallowa Valley if they gave up their arms, they surrendered.

It would be yet another broken promise on the part of the US, as the Nez Perce who didn't escape to Canada were taken to Fort Leavenworth, Kansas. Today you can visit the Bear Paw Battlefield at the trail's end to pay honor to the valiant history of the Nez Perce nation.

Highlights

Goodbye suburban strip malls, hello unblemished wilderness...and tragic tales from the 1877 close of the Nez Perce War. The quixotic, beyond-brave stand of Chief Joseph may have failed in its ultimate goal, but it's paid tribute along this route.

VIRGINIA CITY
Visiting Virginia City in Montana requires a detour from the trail, but the reward is a ghost town reborn as a living museum of the West.

HISTORICAL MUSEUM AT FORT MISSOULA
The original fort in Missoula, Montana, was established in 1877 during the Indian Wars; the museum also covers its role as an internment camp during WWII.

YELLOWSTONE NATIONAL PARK
The park, the first in the National Park System, is not only a highlight of the trail (the Nez Perce passed through it on their flight) but also of the West generally.

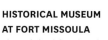

BANNACK STATE PARK
While it is not on the Nez Perce Trail itself, this Montana park sits on the parallel route followed by US Army forces in pursuit of the Nez Perce. Today Bannack is a ghost town.

WHITE-WATER RAFTING
Take a break from driving with a half day or full day of rafting on the Gallatin, Madison or Yellowstone Rivers. There are many outfitters in Bozeman.

Pictured Rocks National Lakeshore. Right: Canoer on Cross Bay Lake in the Boundary Waters.

3.7

North Country National Scenic Trail

The US–Canada border along the Great Lakes is the backdrop for the longest National Scenic Trail as it winds through the heartland's diverse landscapes.

The glacially carved landscape along the Great Lakes – Ontario, Erie, Huron, Michigan and Superior – inspired the North Country National Scenic Trail (NCT). Conceived by the USDA Forest Service in the 1960s and designated in 1980, this trail meanders through northeastern mountains and forests, past midwestern farms, northern lakes and streams, and across the grasslands of the Great Plains. A dozen national forests and numerous state parks offer wilderness and near-wilderness experiences.

The NCT is an evolving combination of mostly off-road trails and on-road miles. In 2019 Vermont became its eighth state, with an addition of between 40 and 60 miles. Although it's not yet marked on the ground, the new portion will link Maine Junction on the Appalachian National Scenic Trail with Vermont's Long Trail and continue north through the Green Mountains to Lake Champlain.

The other seven state segments are New York (706.2 miles), Pennsylvania (278.5 miles), Ohio (1063.3 miles), Michigan (1160.1 miles), Wisconsin (209.7 miles), Minnesota (853.5 miles) and North Dakota (438 miles).

From Crown Point State Historic Site in New York, the trail traverses northeastern New York's Adirondack Park. One of America's oldest preserves, the park comprises public forests and privately owned land, with 12 distinct regions offering their own recreational opportunities. Following towpaths and abandoned railways, the trail joins the Finger Lakes Trail and follows it through Allegany State Park.

Northwestern Pennsylvania's first hundred miles traverse the rolling hills of Allegheny National Forest, passing

Sleep here...

Though the terrain isn't necessarily the most grueling (although sometimes challenging) the stamina needed makes this an advanced hiker's trail. Plan carefully and do extensive research on the backcountry sections. Killington, the eastern terminus in Vermont, is chockablock with ski resorts and presents a luxurious start.

 Adirondack Great Camps, New York

Between the 1880s and 1920s, architects designed three dozen grandiose private compounds called 'great camps' in New York's Adirondack Park. Today six of these historical camps welcome guests.

 St Croix National Scenic Riverway Camping, Wisconsin

Multiday rafting in northwestern Wisconsin is feasible by staying at primitive campsites along the river's shoreline. Some sites are accessible only by the river, and many are relatively isolated.

 Pictured Rocks Camping, Michigan

Three campgrounds near or along Lake Superior's Michigan shoreline are accessible by vehicle. Another dozen backcountry campgrounds are every 2–5 miles along the Lakeshore Trail.

 Boundary Waters Canoe Area Wilderness Campsites, Minnesota

To preserve the remote, pristine landscape of Minnesota's Boundary Waters, camping is only permitted at designated lakeside campsites, with each lake having between one and five individual sites.

Toolbox

 When to go
The trail sees hikers between April and November, with July and August being the peak months despite hot and often humid days. Thru-hikers usually complete the trail over two years, hiking five months each year.

Getting there
New York, Pittsburgh, Columbus, Detroit, Minneapolis, Duluth (Minnesota) and Fargo (North Dakota) have airports with convenient interstate access to drive to various trail segments. US 131 provides access through Michigan, as does Hwy 28 through the Upper Peninsula.

 Practicalities
Length in miles: 4709 (3129 trail miles and 1580 road miles, excluding VT)
Start: Maine Junction near Killington, VT
End: Lake Sakakawea, ND
Dog friendly: Yes; some segments
Bike friendly: Yes; some segments
Permit needed: Yes; some segments
States covered: VT, NY, PA, OH, MI, WI, MN, ND

➡ The Carp River as it meanders through the Porcupine Mountains Wilderness State Park in the Upper Peninsula of Michigan.

old-growth hemlocks in Tionesta National Scenic Area and heading into Cook Forest State Park. Heading through state parks into the Slippery Rock Gorge north of Pittsburgh, the route turns to Ohio.

Here, it's not a wilderness trail. It follows abandoned canals and railways and existing trails through state parks and Wayne National Forest, joining the Buckeye Trail for more than 800 miles through southern Ohio's hills before turning north onto the Wabash Cannonball Trail.

In Michigan's Lower Peninsula, hikers ramble through farmland to Manistee National Forest on Lake Michigan's eastern shore. Continuing north through state forests, the trail crosses the Mackinaw Bridge to reach the Upper Peninsula. Changing from rural landscape to wilderness path, you'll run through the Hiawatha National Forest to Lake Superior's shore and traverses Pictured Rocks National Lakeshore, one of the NCT's most picturesque segments. Hikers cross rivers and gorges through Porcupine Mountains Wilderness State Park, home to the largest old-growth hardwood and hemlock forest in the Great Lakes region.

Dipping into Wisconsin's remote Northwoods and meandering through the quartzite hills of the Penokee Mountains, the NCT follows a westerly course. The route passes through Copper Falls State Park, with its many beautiful waterfalls that tumble over ancient lava, before entering the lake-dotted Chequamegon-Nicolet National Forest and Brule River State Forest. The track follows the St Croix National Scenic Riverway, popular with paddlers, before turning north through wetlands and over wooded ridges toward Duluth.

Entering Minnesota south of Duluth, the trail heads to Jay Cooke State Park near Lake Superior's western tip. Following the lakeshore northeast to the US–Canada border along the scenic Superior Hiking Trail, the trail ventures deep into the Boundary Waters Canoe Area Wilderness and Superior National Forest, where it navigates myriad lakes and rivers any angler or adventurer would love. In this wild country, the Border Route Trail and the Kekekabic Trail between Grand Marais and Ely are rugged, remote and primitive, and should be attempted only by experienced backpackers. Heading southwest, the NCT makes its way to Chippewa National Forest. Chippewa is half water, and America's most aquatic national forest. The trail continues west through state forests where a detour to the Mississippi River's source (Lake Itasca) is possible. Turning southwest, pass through Tamarac National Wildlife Refuge – an important migratory bird breeding ground whose landscape encapsulates the transition from northern forest to tallgrass prairie – and enter the Red River Valley.

In southeastern North Dakota is the Fort Abercrombie State Historic Site, a relic of traders heading to Canada and prospectors heading to Montana's gold mines. Meander the Sheyenne National Grassland with its bur oak savanna, riverine hardwood forests and tallgrass prairie hosting greater prairie chickens and sandhill cranes. Then follow the Sheyenne River valley through Fort Ransom State Park and along man-made Lake Ashtabula. North Dakota's grasslands, where millions of bison once roamed, are one of the great waterfowl nesting areas in the US. Crossing the Lonetree Wildlife Management Area, the NCT meets the Audubon National Wildlife Refuge and Lake Sakakawea, its western terminus.

Highlights

From the hills to the lakes to the plains, the North Country Trail meanders from Vermont to western North Dakota. Hikers must tirelessly traverse trail the winding shoreline of Lake Superior on their way to the grasslands of the west.

SHEYENNE NATIONAL GRASSLAND
Wend through the wide-open spaces of North Dakota's tall-grass prairie, which is home to abundant flora and fauna and migratory songbirds.

ADIRONDACK PARK
Upstate New York's forested Adirondacks, encompassing 6 million acres and forming the largest protected area in the contiguous US, is an ideal outdoor playground.

FINGER LAKES
The glacial topography of New York's Finger Lakes region offers 11 lakes, many colorful gorges and waterfalls, forests and rolling countryside with sweeping vistas.

PICTURED ROCKS NATIONAL LAKESHORE
Lake Superior's 42-mile-long wild shoreline along Michigan's Upper Peninsula boasts towering, forest-topped sandstone cliffs above pristine beaches.

BOUNDARY WATERS CANOE AREA WILDERNESS
In this remote corner of north-eastern Minnesota where no motors are allowed, more than 1000 lakes are connected only by trails and portages.

3.8
Old Rag Mountain

A view of Old Rag Mountain at Thorofare Overlook in Shenandoah National Park, Virginia. Right: Ridge Trail, Old Rag Mountain.

It's worth getting out of your car on Skyline Drive for a closer look at Old Rag Mountain, whose imposing summit towers over this region of the drive.

The earliest parks in America's National Park System had a decidedly Western focus. Yellowstone in Wyoming, the Grand Canyon in Arizona and Crater Lake in Oregon were among these – technically, all were established so early that they preexisted the National Park System itself. In 1925 President Calvin Coolidge began the process of creating Shenandoah National Park, located 75 miles from Washington, DC, as well as Great Smoky Mountains National Park in Tennessee and North Carolina. These were the first southern parks in the system.

Acquiring the parcels of land that would make up Shenandoah National Park would take 11 years, and the result was a long, narrow park with the Shenandoah River and Shenandoah Valley on one side and the rolling blue hills of the Virginia Piedmont on the other. The park's most famous feature is Skyline Drive, a 105-mile scenic highway that runs the length of the park, but there are also 500 miles of hiking trails. The most popular is the circuit trail to the summit of Old Rag (around 3300ft), at the northeastern end of Shenandoah. The hike to the rocky summit is one of the best in the state. A rocky scramble and an elevation gain of 2415ft make this a strenuous hike. This isn't for novices or the unfit, and families with young children should probably give it a miss. Even though the entire loop is only 9.2 miles, you should arrive early and be prepared to hike a full seven to eight hours. Try to hike on weekdays, as the trail can be unpleasantly crowded on weekends. The payoff justifies the effort: sweeping views of the Shenandoah.

For geologists, the hike offers lessons in the forces that formed the peaks of the

Sleep here...

The park has two lodges, five campgrounds, a number of rental cabins and free backcountry camping. Camping is possible at five NPS campgrounds; four cater to individuals, one is for larger groups only. Most are open from mid-May to October. Camping elsewhere requires a backcountry permit, available for free from any visitors center.

Camping in Shenandoah National Park
The park has five campgrounds with fire grates, showers and other amenities. These are open seasonally, with different schedules; some open in March, and all close in late fall.

Backcountry Camping in Shenandoah National Park
If you're a more experienced camper and want some solitude in the backcountry, you'll need to get a permit from the park's visitors centers or an entrance station.

Fairfield Inn & Suites by Marriott
This reliable option to the west of the park in Harrisonburg is great for families, thanks to its pool and spacious rooms. It's also convenient to local sights like the Explore More Discovery Museum.

Hotel Laurance
In a building from 1830, the 12-room hotel in Luray has been thoroughly renovated and given a contemporary makeover, but it retains many charming details like hardwood floors and some antique mantels.

© Jon Bilous / Alamy Stock Photo; © Natural History Library / Alamy Stock Photo

mid-Atlantic. The name itself is a reference to the mountain's geologic history: Old Rag is the granite that underlies the peak. Formed around a billion years ago, the granite has a resistance to erosion that explains why the mountain is taller than its neighbors. A geologically themed walk begins as soon as you start to ascend the trail – enormous boulders, created by a process of lichen and water splitting the granite, dot the lower slopes. The boulders make their way downhill through frost heave: they are pushed slightly uphill when the water beneath them freezes each winter, and then they slide almost imperceptibly in spring when the ice melts.

As you ascend Old Rag, you may notice another, darker rock. This rock, charnockite, is formed from the same magma that created the granite, but the process of fractionation results in different minerals being forced from it as it cools. Two rocks that sit side by side and have their origins in the same geologic events can have different compositions. When you reach the peak of Old Rag, look closely at the stone for white feldspar, black mica, red garnet and blue or gray quartz. An insider's tip: if you are primarily interested in the geologic history of Old Rag, a hike in winter, when trees are bare, offers the best views of the area's topography.

A hike focused on the flora and fauna begins with the trees on the lower slopes: hemlock, hickory, maple, oak and white pine. They create a shaded woodland setting, though none of this is old-growth forest. Most of the area was farmland in the early 20th century, and the trees you see today were almost all planted after Shenandoah became a park in 1935.

After the trees took root, wildlife followed: white-tailed deer, squirrels, chipmunks, wild turkey, gray and red foxes, bobcats and black bears. The foxes and bobcats tend to be elusive, and a spotting is rare. If you come across black bears, they will most likely amble away. If one stands its ground, slowly walk backward while facing the bear.

As you continue your ascent, mountain laurels line the trails. These large shrubs with dark green leaves put on a spectacular display in spring and summer, when their showy pink blossoms scent the air. At the highest parts of the trail, evergreens are common and the deciduous trees of lower elevations rare. Crossing the rock scramble before reaching the summit is the challenging part of the hike, after which you can admire a simply extraordinary view over the national park.

Birders will want to bring their checklists and keep their eyes open for wild turkeys, grouse, woodpeckers, warblers and other species. Roughly 30 species live in the park year-round, while another 160 species use the park as a stop on a migratory route or as a breeding ground. The park also has two animals that appear on few visitors' checklists: poisonous timber rattlesnakes and copperheads. Don't let these snakes scare you away. If you hike in shoes or boots rather than sandals, you have eliminated most of the risk of a bite, which is a rare event: one usually occurs only if someone taunts or pokes at a snake. The risk is well worth the reward of Old Rag's views over this gorgeous expanse of forest. What's more, as a day hike, this leaves you plenty of time to explore Shenandoah. With more than 500 miles of trails, including 101 miles of the Appalachian Trail, there is much to do and see.

Highlights

One of the most spectacular national parks in the country, Shenandoah is like a new smile from nature: in spring and summer the wildflowers explode, in fall the leaves burn bright red and orange, and in winter a cold, starkly beautiful hibernation period sets in.

NATURAL STAIRCASE
At roughly one-third of the way along the circuit, this natural staircase consists of steps, known as columnar joints, that formed as magma cooled and contracted.

OLD RAG SUMMIT
Midway along the trail, the summit of Old Rag is roughly 3300ft above sea level and offers sweeping views of the Blue Ridge Mountains.

VILLAGE OF OLD RAG
The Shenandoah Valley's human history goes back a long time. All that remains of this village, established around 1750, are the foundations of several buildings.

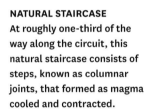

BYRD'S NEST SHELTER
This trailside hut offers shade from the summer sun or shelter from the rain. The flagstone structure was constructed in 1934 by the Civilian Conservation Corps.

SHENANDOAH NATIONAL PARK VISITORS CENTERS
The park's visitors centers at mile 4.6 and mile 51 on Skyline Drive have exhibits about the area and bookstores selling guides and maps.

39

Old Spanish National Historic Trail

An old trading trail that dates from 1829 connects Santa Fe and Los Angeles, and along the way passes through the Southwest's stunning desert landscapes.

Road leading towards Snow Canyon, St George, Utah. Right: Aerial view of a massive highway interchange in Los Angeles.

Although Spanish settlements and missions in California date back to the 18th century (San Diego was founded in 1769), and New Mexico is even older (Santa Fe was established in 1610), an overland route connecting these two different parts of Spain, and later Mexico, wasn't established until 1829–30. Military expeditions, missionaries and explorers had followed portions of the larger, 700-mile-long Old Spanish Trail, but it was Antonio Armijo, a Mexican trader, who first successfully led a commercial caravan from New Mexico (starting at Abiquiú, near Santa Fe) to California (ending at the San Gabriel Mission, 10 miles from Los Angeles).

The extreme conditions of this part of America explain why it took so long to establish the route. The Old Spanish Trail crosses soaring peaks, remote canyons and the Mojave Desert, the driest desert in North America. It took Armijo – and his 60 men and 100 mules – almost three months to make the journey. It included days without water and other days when, as food supplies dwindled, the men resorted to killing some of their horses and mules to survive. After a month in California, Armijo turned around and retraced his route, though in about half the time as his journey west.

After that first successful crossing, thousands of other trading journeys followed. Most were bringing blankets and other textiles west to California and returning east with horses and mules. Because the trail passed through harsh and remote territory, however, it also became a favorite of traders dealing in contraband goods, including Native American slaves.

The Old Spanish Trail came to consist of three different main routes. Along with

Sleep here...

Your path on the North Branch, Northern Route, Armijo Route or Mojave Road will dictate your options to an extent. On the Northern Route, all of the 150,000 hotel rooms of Las Vegas are at your disposal. The routes merge at Barstow en route to Los Angeles; both cities offer many options for visitor lodging. Closer to the trail's start, the Southwest is a camper's dream destination. You should always reserve months ahead for national parks and if you're in an RV.

 ### Hole-in-the-Wall Campground, California
Count the many stars in the sky at this campground located at 4400ft (making it cooler than the desert floor) in California's Mojave National Preserve. Surrounded by volcanic rock formations, your campsite guarantees a night to remember.

 ### Rancho Nambe, New Mexico
Santa Fe has many Spanish Colonial Revival hotels, but Rancho Nambe, on the road toward Abiquiú, New Mexico, is the real deal: a 300-year-old hacienda with views of the Sangre de Cristo Mountains.

The Lodge at Bryce Canyon, Utah
This 1920s lodge is the only hotel inside Utah's Bryce Canyon National Park. It books out far in advance; reserve your room before you buy your plane tickets.

 ### Red Mountain Resort, Utah
Along much of the trail, you'll have to make do with budget chains or camping, but this is a pampering resort with fitness classes and a spa in a spectacular desert setting near St George, Utah.

Toolbox

 When to go
Traders would travel west to California in November, when water was most abundant and temperatures were the coolest. Even if you aren't relying on creeks to refill your bottles, winter and spring are the most pleasant seasons to explore the route.

 Getting there
Both ends of the trail, Los Angeles and Santa Fe, New Mexico, are served by airports, though the latter is far smaller. Albuquerque, which has a larger airport than Santa Fe, is just over an hour's drive away. Per the NPS, trail segments are accessible via Route 25 in New Mexico, I- 70 in Colorado, Utah, and Nevada and Route 5 in California.

 Practicalities
Length in miles: 2700
Start: Santa Fe, NM
End: Los Angeles, CA
Dog friendly: Yes, in portions
Bike friendly: Yes, in portions
Permit needed: Some campgrounds
States covered: AZ, CA, CO, NM, NV, UT

1000-year-old Taos Pueblo.

Armijo's trail, there's a Northern Route first mapped in 1831 that heads north into central Utah, where water was more abundant; it avoided areas controlled by the Navajo. The route rejoins Armijo's near present-day Las Vegas. Confusingly, there's also a Northern or North Branch that heads north from Santa Fe to Taos, makes its way along trails that had long been used by trappers, and then rejoins the Northern Route near Green River, Utah. It had the advantage of being far from some mountain passes that were, well, impassable after winter storms. There was also an alternate route through the Mojave Desert that followed trails long used by Native Americans and Spanish missionaries.

In the two decades that the Old Spanish Trail was in active use, there were other variations, many of which are lost to history. While the trail helped make Santa Fe a commercial center of the Southwest, its time as an important trade route was short. In 1848, at the conclusion of the Mexican-American War, Mexico ceded all of its territory north of the Rio Grande to the US. Newer stagecoach and then rail routes replaced the Old Spanish Trail.

The Old Spanish Trail's abandonment – as well as geographical conditions that assured the territory it passed through would never be developed – means that visitors today can see landscapes largely as they would have appeared to those early traders. Fortunately for modern-day travelers, sites that were perilous obstacles to the traders of the 1830s can now be appreciated as natural wonders. Different routes pass through, or at least near, some of the Southwest's most stunning national parks and recreation areas: Mesa Verde, Glen Canyon, Bryce Canyon and Zion among them.

A journey along the trail also presents an overview of the diverse cultures and peoples of the Southwest. Traveling from east to west, the trail starts in Santa Fe, the oldest state capital and third-oldest city in the US. With the Palace of the Governors on its main plaza, and with the city's many historic adobe buildings, much of Santa Fe looks like it would have during the days of the Old Spanish Trail. The nearby pueblos of the Pueblo Indians give glimpses of a civilization that predated the arrival of the Spanish and Mexicans. As the trail passes through Utah, historic sites provide introductions to the Mormon settlers who played such a significant role in settling the West. The southernmost route, Armijo's original trail, passes through Navajo country, and fell into disuse when tensions arose with the Navajo that made it impractical.

As the trail heads into Nevada, two very different places embody the desert Southwest today. There's enormous, man-made Lake Mead, sitting behind Hoover Dam, a playground for boaters but also crucial in transforming Southern California into the country's irrigated orchard. And then there is glittering, neon-lit Las Vegas. While the traders making a profit by exchanging blankets and serapes for horses and mules could never have conceived this city emerging from the desert, we think they'd admire it and its free-wheeling reputation. If Vegas might leave them speechless, imagine their response to El Pueblo de Nuestra Señora la Reina de los Ángeles, which has grown from a town of 1680 people in 1841 to the second-largest city in the US today. At pitstop Barstow between the two, the nostalgia of Route 66 dominates.

Highlights

The mule trains that originated this route through Mexican territory in the 1820s passed some incredible scenery (think snowcapped peaks and sage-speckled plateaus), as well as winding past historic sites from Pueblo Indians and, later, Mormon settlers.

AZTEC RUINS NATIONAL MONUMENT
Sitting on the original Old Spanish Trail, this 900-year-old, 400-room great house in Aztec, New Mexico, was inhabited by the ancestors of today's Pueblo Indians.

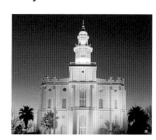

ST GEORGE'S MORMON SITES
This Utah town was settled by Mormons who arrived after 1860. The most significant historic sites are the temple, the tabernacle and Brigham Young's winter home.

TAOS PUEBLO
A Unesco World Heritage Site, Taos Pueblo (on the Northern Branch) in New Mexico is the US's oldest continuously inhabited community. The adobe structures were built between 1000 and 1450.

LAKE MEAD NATIONAL RECREATION AREA
Created in 1935 with the construction of Hoover Dam, the enormous man-made lake in Nevada and its surrounding area offer biking, hiking and boating.

ARCHES NATIONAL PARK
Near where the Northern Route and the Northern Branch meet, this Utah park has some 2000 natural red-stone arches that glow in the desert light.

40

The Oregon Coast Trail

➡ A woman hiking a path near the Oregon coast. Right: Orange crocosmia and purple asters on the shoreline in Yachats, Oregon.

Connecting the lush rainforests, eerie headlands and picturesque beaches that make up the People's Coast, this trail spans all 382 miles of Oregon's western edge from Washington to California.

With otherworldly beaches, ragged headlands and ancient stands of Sitka spruce coated in ferns, it's no wonder the Oregon Coast has been the location chosen by so many Hollywood filmmakers for flicks from *The Goonies* to *Kindergarten Cop* to *Twilight*. Part of the magic of these atmospheric shores isn't just the landscape itself, but the way it's uninterrupted by commercial development for all of the almost 400 miles of the state's Pacific frontage.

That unique public access to the state parks and beaches lining the coast dates back to the beginning of Oregon territory and statehood, when some surprisingly forward-thinking legislators decided to protect what is now the People's Coast before it could be bought up, parceled off and built over by private owners. Originally, the justification of keeping the land public was to set aside coastal lands for Oregon's portion of the iconic Hwy 101. Later, in 1967, the Oregon Beach Bill further protected the coast from private development, saving it for recreational use.

It was a geology professor named Samuel N Dicken who convinced the Oregon Parks and Recreation Department to truly celebrate that unfettered coastline with a hiking trail running from Washington to California. After spending decades exploring the numerous trails snaking through the rainforests between Oregon's Coast Range and the big Pacific, Dicken dreamed of creating an official, connected route that could be enjoyed by section and thru-hikers alike.

Today the Oregon Coast Trail, authorized in 1971, is just 50 miles short of completion. It's absolutely possible to thru-hike from

Sleep here...

Anything from camping (remember it's chilly at night year-round) to gorgeous beachfront condos is available here, but you'll want to reserve in advance whenever possible – and for sure in summer. Check out the below, and in Yachats, the 1894 Queen Anne–style Heceta Head Lighthouse B&B can't help but attract passersby. Located near the lighthouse trail, it's 13 miles south of town on US 101.

 Camping at Fort Stevens State Park

Families especially will love camping at this park in northern Oregon. There's not only military history to dive into but also an old shipwreck looming on the beach that is perfect for all sorts of imaginary adventures.

 Camping at Cape Perpetua Scenic Area

The low-key campground here has attentive camp hosts, clean restrooms and access to excellent hiking trails. The park is also close to some of the Oregon Coast's most iconic attractions, as well as the delightful town of Yachats.

 Yurts at Nehalem Bay State Park

Most Oregon state parks have yurts and cabins in addition to tent and RV sites, if roughing it isn't your thing. The yurts at Nehalem Bay State Park are especially convenient to Manzanita Beach for prime sunset snapshots.

 WildSpring Guest Habitat

An ultra-chill eco-resort hidden in a stand of pines near the ocean, WildSpring blends luxury and privacy, along with the chance to soak up the beauty of Port Orford in southern Oregon. Walk the forest mandala in the mornings.

Toolbox

 When to go

Late May through early September are reliably sunny and dry along the Oregon Coast, and your water crossings will be easier and safer too. Always bring a tarp and raincoat, though – even with no rain, fog inevitably rolls in.

Getting there

The Pacific Coast Hwy runs parallel to the Oregon Coast Trail (OCT); the nearest airports are Portland International at the trail's northern end, and Rogue Valley International in Medford near the southern terminus. Amtrak's Coast Starlight route also serves several cities a short drive from the OCT.

 Practicalities

Length in miles: 382
Start: South Jetty at Columbia River, Fort Stevens State Park, OR
End: California border south of Brookings, OR
Dog friendly: Yes, though on leash in Oregon state parks; dogs prohibited near nesting shorebird sites March 15–September 15
Bike friendly: No
Permit needed: No
States covered: Oregon

one state line to the other, and more hikers are tackling the OCT end to end every year. However, those unfinished 50 miles do mean you'll spend some time taking ferries and walking on the shoulder of the Pacific Coast Highway.

Since 2017, the state has been working on finishing those 50 miles so the entire Oregon Coast Trail will be more of a complete wilderness experience. In the meantime the OCT is growing more popular than ever, as more Oregonians and visitors alike recognize this trail for what it is: a great way to experience the whole Oregon Coast. From the crowds of sea lions near the OCT's northern terminus near Astoria to the scenic lighthouses of Yachats and Heceta Head to the multicolored tidal pools of Gold Beach, there's a lot to see.

While some wilderness purists might prefer to stay shaded by ferns and moss, part of the beauty of the Oregon Coast Trail is the way it weaves in and out of the state's quirky, scrappy, small coastal towns. Where canneries and warehouses once stood, craft breweries, distilleries and farm-to-table restaurants are moving in. Yachats Brewing and Farmstore in Yachats is a particularly great respite, whether you're in the area for a day hike or a well-deserved break from your thru-hike.

The vast majority of the OCT, however, is pure wilderness and gives you a taste of just how diverse Oregon's ecosystems can be. Along your 400-mile journey, you'll travel from the lush rainforests near the Washington border past the much-photographed sea stacks of Cannon Beach. You can swim in the pool at the base of Nehalem Falls or watch the fisherfolk haul in their catches from Barview Jetty.

The famous Octopus Tree at Cape Meares is a welcome sight on the other side of Tillamook Bay. And at evocatively named places such as Devils Churn, Devils Punchbowl, and Thor's Well, you can take in the cinematic ways that geology has shaped the Oregon Coast, and be reminded that the Pacific is still making and remaking this place. As you continue on, snap a photo at Coos Bay, the halfway point between Seattle and San Francisco.

As you travel south, the heavy greenery of northern Oregon gives way to massive sand dunes, some towering as high as 500ft above sea level. That epic scale inspired Frank Herbert to write *Dune*, his sci-fi masterpiece. This area is also a destination for OHV (off-highway vehicle) enthusiasts and an important nesting ground for endangered snowy plovers. No other place on the West Coast is like this, but the area is in its 'last gasp,' as trees and European beach grass are winning the battle against the shifting sands.

History buffs and beachcombers alike will enjoy taking in century-old infrastructure like remnants of a lifeboat launch at Nellie's Cove in Port Orford, now a playground for sea otters and starfish. Take a break to go kayaking before finishing up the last third of your journey.

By the time you reach the California border, the landscape you see starts to more closely resemble the redwood forests of NorCal than the rainforests of the Olympic Peninsula. You'll also probably have a fair amount of sand in your boots from trekking up and down all those beaches and dunes. But you'll also have taken in millions of years of geologic and pioneer history, seeing firsthand the way the Pacific continues to shape every inch of the People's Coast.

Highlights

Can't do the whole trail? Oregon's stunning 360 miles of coastline is the great drive-and-hike destination of the West Coast. It's like bar-hopping, but stopping off for mile-long hikes to reach otherwise out-of-view coves, beaches and bluffs.

OSWALD WEST STATE PARK
In Oswald West State Park, wind past beaches and waterfalls, linking Arch Cape with Manzanita. Smugglers Cove emerges from dense, temperate rainforest here.

SAMUEL H BOARDMAN STATE SCENIC CORRIDOR
Twelve miles of beaches and bluffs hug the ocean between Brookings and Gold Beach on Hwy 101.

THE DEVILS PUNCHBOWL
Five miles south of Depoe Bay, admire the Devils Punchbowl (also known as Satan's Cauldron), an impressive collapsed sea cave that churns with waves and offers good tidepools nearby.

NATURAL BRIDGES COVE
The Oregon Coast Trail passes many stunning sea stacks, arches and rock formations, but Natural Bridges in Samuel H Boardman State Scenic Corridor is one of the best.

SIUSLAW NATIONAL FOREST
This national forest is especially nice, with trails through the dunes and the highest peak in the Coast Range, 4097ft Marys Peak with trails aplenty (though it's off the Oregon Coast Trail).

Resources

01 Oregon Parks and Recreation Department
www.oregon.gov/oprd
The state parks and recreation department website has Oregon Coast Trail maps online.

02 *Oregon Coastal Access Guide, Second Edition: A Mile by Mile Guide to Scenic and Recreational Attractions*
This 2008 guide by Kenn Oberrecht offers a mile-by-mile look at how to use Oregon's publicly owned beaches.

03 *The Oregon Coast Photo Road Trip: How To Eat, Stay, Play, and Shoot Like a Pro*
Rick and Susan Sammon give aspiring shutterbugs their tips on how to get the best of the Oregon Coast, both as a visitor and as a photographer.

⬆ Heceta Head Lighthouse on the central Oregon Coast, between Yachats and Florence. Left: Cape Arago State Park, Coos County.

Hike this...

You know those cliff-cut roads, rocky shores, surf waves and gold-sand beaches of California don't just stop cold when the state line passes by, right? In fact, the terrain only gets more interesting along Oregon's coast. Come see it for yourself.

➜ Walking on Cannon Beach near Haystack Rock.

01
Samuel H Boardman State Scenic Corridor

Ever 'hike-hopped'? The Samuel H Boardman State Scenic Corridor is a 13-mile span of jagged capes and coves, natural bridges and sandy beaches, easily enjoyed by short, easy hikes – none more than a mile. You find the first of a dozen stops about 13 miles south of Gold Beach, where you can pick and choose where to go...or stop off at every point. China Beach and Whaleshead Beach are fun for sand, while sea sprays through a collapsed sea cave at Natural Bridges Cove, accessible with a short half-mile hike. Arch Rock, another short walk to an overlook, was a landmark of the region's Tolowa Tribe, and is part of a legend about the mythical Coyote.

Then there's the aptly named Secret Beach Trail. A local favorite, this moderate hike takes you down to a beach you're likely to have to yourself (living up to its name). It's best accessed at Thunder Rock Cove at mile 345.8 of the Oregon Coast Trail, and is a 1.5-mile round trip journey from the gravel parking lot.

02
Oregon Dunes

The dunes tower up to 500ft and undulate inland as far as 3 miles to meet coastal forests, harboring curious ecosystems that sustain an abundance of wildlife, especially birds. The very northern and southern sections of the dunes are dominated by dune buggies and dirt bikes (off-highway vehicles, or OHVs); avoid hiking in these areas. It's possible to rent vehicles south of Florence and around Winchester Bay. The central section of the dunes is closed to OHVs and preserved for wildlife and more peaceful human activities such as hiking and canoeing.

One trail, a dozen miles south of Reedsport, samples the Umpqua Dunes, where a mile-long loop takes in the rippled sandy habitat of 'tree islands' and dunes that inspired the film *Dune* (the real dunes are more entertaining). If you have the energy, soldier on along the 6-mile round-trip John Dellenback Trail through dunes and forested marsh to the beach. It's a classic, but it can be disorienting, so pack a compass.

03
Cape Lookout State Park

A mere hour and a half west of Portland through the gorgeous Wilson River pass, Cape Lookout State Park is a world away. It's not the westernmost point of the Lower 48, it only feels like it. Running along a forested ridge that juts a full mile into the Pacific, the 4.7-mile out-and-back hike on Cape Lookout Trail over basalt headlands feels positively edge-of-the-worldly. Towards the end, it can be a bit of a rooty scramble, with a big payoff for whale-watching fans. Point explorer-like from the point if you must, but expect some eye-rolls. There's also a beauty of a campground in the state park, which is right along the beach but never feels crowded, thanks to well-positioned sites and plenty of trees (book early).

Just north of here, you'll find 7 miles of sandy beaches (with good clamming spots) on Netarts Bay as the Oregon Coast Trail descends through old spruce forest. The cape is about 10 miles south of Tillamook on the Cape Meares Loop.

The Oregon Coast Trail

4.1

Oregon National Historic Trail

The Oregon Trail, the earliest wagon route to reach the West Coast, lives on in the American legend...with no small thanks to the eponymous computer game. This historic trail follows its path.

➡ The historic Oregon Trail at Scotts Bluff, Nebraska. Right: Covered wagon from the Oregon Trail on display at Mt Hood.

If you are rusty on your history of the American West, you may have forgotten that Oregon was the first territory to be extensively settled by migrants from the eastern US. Until 1848, everything south of the 42nd parallel was (at least nominally) part of Mexico; what is now the state of Washington was claimed by the UK until 1846, and the Great Plains were viewed as unfit for settlement. That left Oregon, which had untouched pine forests, a coastline with natural harbors, and an interior that was not as parched as that of the area to its east.

All this would lead to the Oregon Trail becoming the earliest wagon route from the Midwest to the West Coast, with portions of it later incorporated into the California, Mormon and other trails. Unlike the hundreds of thousands of prospectors and other settlers who poured into California, the numbers on the Oregon Trail were modest. Even the so-called Great Migration of 1843 consisted of only around 875 pioneers, though that's an impressive number compared to the 38 people who made the journey to California that year.

Still, in a sparsely populated part of the continent, when these new settlers were added to those who were already there, they formed the Provisional Government of Oregon. This would prove instrumental in leading Britain to renounce its claims to Oregon and agree to the 49th parallel as the border between British North America and the US. The pace of migration did pick up; even before transcontinental railroads spanned the country, some 500,000 people would traverse the eastern portion of the Oregon Trail, but most took a turn to the south and headed to California as their final destination, in part because of the

Sleep here...

The travelers on this lengthy trek brought their lodging with them in the form of their covered wagons, but drivers following the auto route will have to chart their own course between overnight stays. Try to camp out along the way to get a small taste of roughing it 1800s style, and take advantage of some of the historic lodgings along the way as well.

 Camping in Buffalo Bill Ranch State Recreation Area, Nebraska
In western Nebraska, the Oregon Trail runs alongside the North Platte River. The campsites here have river views, and Buffalo Bill's house is in the state park next door.

 White Eagle Saloon and Hotel, Oregon
Though it's in Portland, north of the trail, and this saloon didn't open until 1905, the 11-room inn offers a festive Old West ambience – a fitting conclusion to an Oregon Trail journey.

 Camping in Three Island Crossing State Park, Idaho
Infamous as a challenging crossing of the Snake River, this Idaho site is now a state park with 82 campsites and an interpretive center dedicated to the history of the Oregon Trail.

Mountain View Hotel, Wyoming
This six-room historic inn built in 1907 is in Centennial, Wyoming. It's not far from the Overland Trail, a branch of the Oregon Trail that was at its busiest in the 1860s.

Toolbox

 **When to go**
The original pioneer settlers of Oregon would make the journey starting in April. Spring to early autumn are still the most pleasant times to visit, and you'll avoid the risk of winter road closures.

 **Getting there**
Independence, Missouri, is next to Kansas City, which is served by many flights each day. At the other end of the trail, Oregon City sits just south of Portland and its busy airport.

Practicalities
Length in miles: 2170
Start: Independence, MO
End: Oregon City, OR
Dog friendly: Yes; portions
Bike friendly: Yes; portions
Permit needed: Some campgrounds
States covered: MO, KS, NE, WY, ID, WA, OR

1848 Gold Rush.

Settlers would typically gather in April around Independence, Missouri, and other points along the Missouri River to begin their trek. At this point in the year, the grass on the beginning of the trail would have grown tall enough for horses and cattle to graze on it. An April departure also meant that settlers would arrive in Oregon by early autumn, before snow blocked mountain passes.

The journey across the plains of Kansas and Nebraska was marked by miles of prairie grass in every direction, often reaching the height of an adult. The greatest challenge in this flat land was getting wagons over the many rivers and creeks. Chimney Rock was, and is, one of the most dramatic landmarks along the route, and it stands not far from today's Nebraska–Wyoming border. Most of the trail across Wyoming follows the line of the Platte River, until it reaches what would become known as the Parting of the Ways. Here two routes diverged, with one heading south toward the Great Salt Lake and the other north into Idaho. After those on the northern route made their way over 'the Big Hill,' a challenge for wagon drivers accustomed to the flat plains, the Clover Creek Camp was a welcome sight. The camp sat near Montpelier, Idaho (not settled until 1864), where curious travelers today can learn more about this portion of the trail at the National Oregon/California Trail Center.

Fort Boise, near today's Idaho–Oregon border, provided a rest stop before the final legs of the journey. Nothing remains of the fort today, though the site is on the National Register of Historic Places; it is a bucolic spot on the banks of the Snake River. There's a reconstruction of the fort in nearby Parma.

If any traveler today is inclined to romanticize this era, the many cemeteries along the route will dispel those notions. Near Walla Walla, Washington, the Whitman Mission National Historic Site is another reminder of the cruelties of frontier life. An obelisk stands as a monument, and stones outline the foundations of a mission founded to Christianize the Cayuse people. In 1847 Marcus and Narcissa Whitman (and 11 others) were killed by members of the tribe, who blamed Marcus for the many deaths from measles that had devastated the Cayuse. The incident would lead to an eight-year war of armed confrontations between the Cayuse and settlers.

Continue on and stop at the National Historic Oregon Trail Interpretive Center, the nation's foremost memorial to the pioneers who crossed the West along the Oregon Trail. Lying atop a hill 7 miles east of Baker City, it contains interactive displays, artifacts and films that stress the day-to-day realities faced by the pioneers. Outside, you can stroll along the 4.2-mile interpretive path system and spot the actual Oregon Trail. The remainder of the Oregon Trail within Oregon runs mostly along the south bank of the Columbia River, with The Dalles presenting a final obstacle for pioneers and a photo opportunity for travelers today. After navigating this series of falls, settlers would arrive in Oregon City. While it would later be overshadowed by Portland (13 miles to its north), the city still celebrates its 19th-century heyday. The Municipal Elevator, built in 1915, carries visitors to the top of a bluff for views of the city and the Willamette Valley.

Highlights

Touring today's National Historic Trail by car is a much easier and less treacherous trek than the historic wagon route stretching nearly 2000 miles from Independence, Missouri, and you can still take in the major sites visited by Western settlers.

ALCOVE SPRING
This spring and pool in Kansas were a popular stopping point for pioneers, many of whom carved their names into the rocks, where they can still be seen today.

HOMESTEAD NATIONAL MONUMENT
The 1862 Homestead Act provided 160 acres of land to anyone who would farm it for five years. See a homestead at this Nebraska park.

FORT KEARNY STATE HISTORICAL PARK
While it has 'fort' in its name, this Nebraska outpost was mainly a supply depot for emigrants. The buildings are reconstructions, though historically accurate ones.

MINIDOKA NATIONAL HISTORIC SITE
Just to the north of the Oregon Trail, Minidoka in Idaho was one of 10 camps where Japanese Americans were interned during WWII.

OREGON TRAIL INTERPRETIVE CENTER
Near this 23,000-sq-ft center in Baker City, Oregon, emigrants would have their first glimpse of the Blue Mountains, a sign they were near their goal.

→ Chimney Rock National Historic
Site, western Nebraska.

Resources

O1 Oregon National Historic Trail
www.nps.gov/oreg
The National Park Service's website for the trail includes an interactive trip planner map and a free app for both Apple and Android devices.

O2 Oregon–California Trails Association
www.octa-trails.org
This organization focuses principally on the Oregon and California Trails, with a wealth of resources about both of them, but the website also covers (in less detail) the Cherokee and Southern Emigrant Trails.

O3 *The Oregon Trail: A New American Journey*
Rinker Buck's 2015 title retraces the path of the trail in a covered wagon; his book about the journey is filled with awe and respect for the pioneers who made the arduous trip.

View of the Historic Columbia River Highway from Rowena Crest overlook, Columbia River Gorge, Oregon. Left: A sandhill crane on the North Platte River.

Hike this...

Modern visitors can stop off at these key Oregon National Historic Trail sites for a little exercise without undue fear of exhaustion, drowning, dysentery or snakebite, unlike those who passed this way in the mid-1800s.

➡ North Platte River, Casper, Wyoming.

01
Scotts Bluff National Monument, Nebraska

It's no coincidence that Scotts Bluff National Monument is a recurring feature of the country's National Historic Trails. This bluff, which rises 800ft above the North Platte River in Nebraska, was a landmark for emigrants on the California and Oregon Trails, and it was also a guidepost on the Mormon and Pony Express routes. Before any of those trails, though, the bluff was significant to Native Americans. Even today, modern-day travelers are struck by the sight, especially given Nebraska's generally flat topography.

The national monument includes 3000 acres and has a number of walking trails that start at an interpretive center that provides some Oregon Trail history. If you aren't feeling up for a hike, a road built in the 1930s by the Civilian Conservation Corps (CCC) goes to the top of the bluff, where you can take in views of Chimney Rock and other nearby formations. The Summit Road is also travelled seasonally by the free Summit Shuttle.

02
Guernsey State Park, Wyoming

The main draw for Oregon Trail buffs at this Wyoming park are the Guernsey ruts, the still-visible wheel tracks of early pioneers' wagons, off Hwy 26. Almost everyone else comes for the reservoir that didn't exist at the time of the trail: the dam that made it possible was built in 1927. The park earned its status as a National Historic Landmark thanks to the buildings and other facilities that were the work of the CCC from 1934 to 1939. There are 14 miles of hiking trails, as well as several beaches if that sounds more appealing.

The trail system starts at the Brimmer Point turnoff, and consists of several scenic loops of moderate difficulty. The park has 245 campsites divided among different campgrounds, most of them overlooking the lake, and there are even four yurts. Check the website for campground reservation information and reserve in advance.

Two miles southeast of Guernsey is trail landmark Register Cliff: settlers wrote their names here on a kind of nature-provided chalkboard that acted as a checkpoint.

03
Columbia River Gorge National Scenic Area, Oregon

The Columbia River Gorge in Oregon and Washington was the country's second National Scenic Area, an 80-mile stretch of the river that is not only physically stunning but has played a central role in the history of the West. The Oregon Trail ran on its southern bank, now in the state of Oregon, and culminated with one of the most difficult portions of the route. Before the construction of the Barlow Rd in 1846, pioneers turned their wagons into rafts to navigate a series of falls, known as The Dalles, before arriving in Willamette Valley.

Today numerous state parks, recreation areas, viewpoints and trailheads can be found on both sides of the river. The most popular highlight is Oregon's Multnomah Falls, which plunges from a height of 620ft. Hikers flock to the Historic Columbia River Highway State Trail (HCRHST), especially at Bridge of the Gods trailhead, Tooth Rock trailhead and Starvation Creek trailhead. When done, the 73-mile HCRHST will trace the length of the entire gorge.

42

Overmountain Victory National Historic Trail

Sunset view from Roan Mountain. Right: Kings Mountain National Military Park, Blacksburg, SC

Patriot frontiersmen crossed the Great Smoky Mountains from East Tennessee to help win a critical Revolutionary War battle. This trail follows their brave footsteps.

In 1780 it was five years into the Revolutionary War, and things had not been going well lately for the Patriots. After a six-week siege, the port city of Charleston had fallen to the British. Then the Patriots lost the Battle of Camden, in South Carolina, despite having double the troops of their foe. The British killed or wounded nearly 1000 Americans and captured another 1000. The British planned to sweep up the rest of the South and then head north to recapture the rest of their colonies. Patriot morale was low.

Scottish-born Major Patrick Ferguson, despised by the Patriots, was leading troops into North Carolina and attempting to recruit local Loyalists. There his men were repeatedly attacked by bands of rough-looking Patriots who would whoop and cry as they fought, imitating Indians. These were the so-called Overmountain Men, settlers from the western side of the Blue Ridge Mountains who scorned British rule.

Ferguson sent a message across the mountains. Surrender now, or he would come west and 'lay waste to their country with fire and sword.' Just imagine him twirling his mustache.

What do you think happened? The ornery Patriot frontiersmen mustered a force more than 1000 strong, marched over the mountains for nearly two weeks and caught Ferguson unprepared. Ferguson was killed and his Loyalist army subdued in barely over an hour. Thomas Jefferson would call the Battle of Kings Mountain in South Carolina 'the turn of the tide of success' in the American Revolution.

Yeah, okay, enough of a history lesson. All this background is to explain the significance of the Overmountain Victory Trail – the route taken by the Overmountain

Sleep here...

You'll find the full range of accommodations in the South. In general, nicer hotels often flaunt a sort of historic-chic style, especially in cities with preserved historical neighborhoods, such as New Orleans, Charleston and Savannah. Larger cities also boast contemporary design hotels. In smaller towns you'll often find a mix of chain highway hotels and frilly B&Bs that invariably occupy older homes.

 Martha Washington Inn and Spa, Virginia

This is no humble inn but a splendiferous brick mansion built in 1832. In Abingdon, Virginia, it served as a women's college and a Civil War hospital before becoming a hotel in the 1930s.

 Watauga River Cabins, Tennessee

The Overmountain Men would have approved of these rustic-chic cabins a stone's throw from the Sycamore Shoals rendezvous point in Elizabethton, Tennessee. Kitchens and multiple beds make the cabins ideal for families.

 Roan Mountain State Park, Tennessee

Camp near the trail's highest point at this large, family-friendly campground in Tennessee. It's one of many campgrounds throughout the mountains; you can camp virtually the entire trail if you want.

 Firehouse Inn, North Carolina

In, yes, an old firehouse, the brick B&B is in Rutherfordton, North Carolina, near the site of one of the trail's encampments. Rooms are plush, and breakfasts are hearty and satisfying.

Toolbox

 **When to go**

Autumn is the most glorious season in the Appalachians, and spring brings fields and riverbanks painted with wildflowers. The Overmountain Victory Trail Association (OVTA) sponsors a costumed reenactment march and associated activities each September.

Getting there

The trail starts in Abingdon, in southwestern Virginia. The small Tri-Cities Airport is 35 miles away in Tennessee. End your trail visit at Kings Mountain National Military Park near Blacksburg, South Carolina. Charlotte's major international airport is a 40-minute drive.

Practicalities

Length in miles: 330
Start: Abingdon, VA
End: Kings Mountain National Military Park, SC
Dog friendly: Yes
Bike friendly: No
Permit needed: No
States covered: Virginia, Tennessee, North Carolina, South Carolina

Kings Mountain National Military Park.

Men as they headed to battle the Loyalists. Traveling the trail today means encountering important Revolutionary-era historic sites, but it also means passing through some of the most enticing mountain scenery in the country: the cloud-shrouded Blue Ridge, the waterfalls and enticing swimming holes of the Pisgah and Cherokee National Forests, and the rolling, photogenic farmland of Central Appalachia in southwestern Virginia.

The trail consists of 87 miles of noncontiguous walkable footpaths, a 330-mile car route marked by special highway signs, and a number of affiliated historic sites, museums and exhibits. How do you want to travel? It's up to you. If you're a history nut, simply drive from muster site to battlefield to encampment spot. If you're in it for the outdoors, string together a handful of trails in the same area.

The place to start is Abingdon, a charming Virginia town known for its playhouse and its 18th-century brick downtown. This was where the Virginia Patriot Militia mustered on September 23, 1780, and then headed south to meet their Tennessee and North Carolina brethren. If you'd like some exercise before you hop in the car, the town is the starting point for the 35-mile Virginia Creeper Trail, a bike path that follows an old logging railroad. It's a half-day ride down densely forested mountainside blooming with mountain laurel and rhododendron.

On September 25, several hundred frontiersmen mustered at the Sycamore Shoals stretch of the Watauga River in Tennessee. Today it's the 70-acre Sycamore Shoals State Historic Park in the city of Elizabethton. Check out displays on Revolutionary War history and the reconstructed 18th-century Fort Watauga, surrounded by a rough-hewn palisade fence. The nearby Mountain River Trail is a pleasant 2-mile loop with interpretive signs.

The Overmountain Victory Trail's highest point is Roan Mountain, on the Tennessee–North Carolina border. The Overmountain Men crossed via an old Indian footpath at Yellow Mountain Gap. It had rained the night before, and the muddy ground made for hard going. If you're lucky enough to get a pleasant day, this is an ideal spot for a longer hike. The trail connects with the Appalachian Trail, where you can walk for as long as you please through fields of yarrow and blackberries and across windy mountain balds, the emerald valleys far below.

From Roan Mountain the men descended to Bright's Settlement, now the sleepy town of Spruce Pine, North Carolina. By October 4 they'd reached Gilbert Town, now Rutherfordton. Two days later, at Cowpens, South Carolina, the Overmountain Men met up with another 400 Patriots. On October 7, the Battle of Kings Mountain began and ended.

Today the lovely, leafy Kings Mountain National Military Park shows no sign of the bloody events of that fall afternoon. Military history aficionados can geek out all day, imagining the sneak approach, the Patriots hiding behind trees, the Loyalists backing down the wooded hillsides. The adjacent Kings Mountain State Park offers more peaceful activities: hiking, fishing for bass and bream, or paddling a canoe across the dark waters of Lake Crawford.

The next time you spot an American flag waving in the breeze, just think: if it wasn't for the actions of the Overmountain Men, you might just be looking at a Union Jack in its place.

Highlights

The Cherokee Nation once roamed these mountain foothills, which they called the 'Great Blue Hills of God,' or Sahkanaga. Trace your way from Virginia to South Carolina's Upcountry as the Blue Ridge Mountains drop dramatically to meet the Piedmont.

ROAN HIGHLANDS
These spruce- and fir-covered mountains are known for their balds, basically high-altitude meadows, which offer panoramic views across North Carolina and Tennessee.

COWPENS NATIONAL BATTLEFIELD
In early 1781, the Battle of Cowpens would be another Patriot victory. The battlefield memorial is a half-hour drive west of Kings Mountain.

BARTER THEATRE
Abingdon, Virginia, is home to America's longest-running professional theater, with reliably great shows. Produce could originally be bartered for tickets, hence the name.

PISGAH NATIONAL FOREST
At more than a half-million acres, this North Carolina forest is a wonderland of wooded gorges and silvery creeks. It's prime waterfall territory.

OVERMOUNTAIN VINEYARDS
Sample French-style southern wines at the photogenic vineyard in Tryon, in the Tryon Foothills of North Carolina. The winery offers farm tours and samples in a relaxed, cottage-style tasting room.

4.3

Ozark Highlands Trail

Spanning 270 miles across the Ozark wilderness, this trail is simply one of the most impressive walking tracks in the southern United States.

→ Haw Creek Falls, Ozark National Forest, Arkansas. Right: Entrance to Ozark National Forest.

The dominating natural feature of Northwest Arkansas – and some might argue, the entire state – are the Ozark Mountains. This extensive highland region, the largest between the Rockies and the Appalachians, is a wrinkled, forested dream of rock gullies, flinty valleys and ice-cold springs. The steady drip of water as it trickles down soaring, moss-covered bluffs to a stream below provides some of the soundtrack along the narrow path that peeks out from the underbrush surrounding it. The Ozark Highlands Trail (OHT) takes hikers along open ridges and into secluded hollows that hide waterfalls and remnants of homesteads from bygone eras as it roams some of the most remote forests and rugged landscapes in Arkansas. At nearly 270 completed miles between Lake Fort Smith and Lake Norfork near the Missouri state line, the OHT is also a testament to the volunteers who built it and the work that still needs to be done to connect the dots into a continuous line.

The OHT is made up of four major segments. At 164 miles, the Boston Mountains segment is the longest and stretches along the entire length of the Ozark National Forest from Lake Fort Smith east to Woolum Ford, where Richland Creek meets the Buffalo River. Completed in 1989, this segment was once regarded as the whole trail. The US Forest Service began putting down portions of the route in the 1970s, and when government funding ran out, volunteers stepped in to finish the project. They were led by wilderness photographer and longtime outdoorsman Tim Ernst, who founded the Ozark Highlands Trail Association (OHTA) in 1981. The OHTA advocates for the trail and continues to build portions of it while

Sleep here...

Typically, you may camp anywhere on this route so long as you go 200 feet off the trail and any water sources, no permit required. There are some unofficial campsites as well as established public ones along the course of the trail. Do sign the registration boxes along the trail as you go. Lovers of the Civilian Conservation Corps (CCC) will want to make a reservation at White Rock where the lodge and cabins were recently restored.

Camping on the Trail
While there are no official campsites along the OHT other than at the designated campgrounds, there are dozens of well-used camping areas that have been created by hikers over the past few decades.

Designated Campgrounds
The designated campgrounds along the OHT include Ozone, Haw Creek, Fairview, Richland Creek, Woolum Ford, Tyler Bend and Camp Matney. Most have primitive campsites with few amenities other than tables and fire rings.

White Rock Lodge & Cabins
White Rock Mountain is home to three CCC cabins and a lodge along Shores Lake. All were built of natural stone in the 1930s and have a fireplace and original wooden furniture. Nine primitive campsites are also available.

Norfork Lake Camping & Resorts
Along the Norfork Lake segment of the OHT, hikers can stay at campgrounds near Norfork Dam and Robinson Point. There are also numerous resorts and RV parks up and down the lake.

Toolbox

When to go
Seasoned hikers recommend trekking the Ozark Highlands Trail (OHT) between November and March, before the rain and heat of spring and summer turn the Ozarks into an overgrown jungle perfect for ticks, chiggers and mosquitoes. Because of the area's generally (though not always) snow-free winters, the trail is also a perfect destination during colder months.

Getting there
For hikers wanting to start their journey at the western terminus, both the Fort Smith Regional Airport and the Northwest Arkansas Regional Airport near Fayetteville are about an hour's drive from Lake Fort Smith.

Practicalities
Length in miles: 320 total, with 270 on designated trail
Start: Lake Fort Smith, AR
End: Norfork Lake, AR
Dog friendly: Yes, dogs allowed except on Buffalo River segment
Bike friendly: No
Permit needed: No
States covered: Arkansas

➡ Lake Fort Smith nestled in the Boston Mountains, Fort Smith, Arkansas.

maintaining existing sections.

The Boston Mountains segment is characterized by a 2ft-wide trail that skirts emerald creeks, winds down rocky descents and runs along jagged sandstone and limestone outcroppings. By spring it can be overgrown on either side with wild grasses; oak, hickory and scattered pine trees block out the sky above, and the forest fills out with blooming dogwoods, redbuds and witch hazel. In the fall, the leaves put on a brilliant display of oranges, yellows and reds before falling to the ground and turning the landscape into a black-and-white photograph as winter settles in.

This portion of the hike was formed hundreds of thousands of years ago. The Boston Mountains are actually plateaus that slowly rose out of the ground. Since then, they have been shaped by erosion caused by the rivers and creeks that still rush down their slopes into narrow valleys. Depending on the time of year, hikers are likely to cross dozens of rock-bottomed streams bubbling with cool water. And in the Ozarks, where there is a creek, there is likely a waterfall nearby. The falls range from 5ft to over 70ft and go by names like Bear Skull, Punchbowl and Fuzzybutt. These watering holes are a reminder to take a breather, but also to replenish drinking supplies. Campgrounds with faucets are few and far between on this stretch of the hike, as are places for other supplies, so caching food at major road crossings is recommended for thru-hikers.

The second segment of the OHT picks up at Woolum Ford where it overlaps with the Buffalo River Trail (BRT). As the name suggests, the trail follows the curvature of the Buffalo River, the country's first

National River, designated in 1972. The Buffalo flows freely for 150 miles and is one of the few remaining undammed rivers in the contiguous US. This section of the OHT/BRT stays with the river for 43 of those 150 miles, and for the first time there is a noticeable change in the landscape. The trail alternates between low creek crossings and the tops of dramatic bluffs that stare down at the turquoise river below. Aside from expansive views of undulating waves of trees, hikers will come across Native American bluff shelters and abandoned homesteads that serve as reminders of lives lived on the Buffalo generations ago.

At Dillard's Ferry near Hwy 14, the trail comes to a stop. From that point to the Spring Creek trailhead in the Sylamore area, which is the third segment of the OHT, there is a 15-mile gap. For now, the NPS is not allowing the OHTA to build a trail in the Lower Buffalo Wilderness, but a series of old roads and some light bushwhacking get hikers to the next portion of their journey. As the 32 miles of the Sylamore segment lose some of their hilliness, some of the trail's seclusion falls away too; in places, the trail skirts roads and passes by farms.

In comparison, the final segment of the OHT at Lake Norfork is still in its infancy. The trail becomes more fragmented as volunteers work to secure the proper permissions to finish building it, but the sections that have been completed provide generous views of the lake. All told, from Lake Fort Smith to Norfork Lake, volunteers have about 50 miles of dots left to connect on the trail before they cross the state line, where there are plans to link the OHT to Missouri's Ozark Trail. Together the two systems would create a 700-mile thru-hike all the way to St Louis.

Highlights

The Ozark Highlands Trail is an outdoor lover's playground, but note that trail maintenance is suspended from late spring to early fall. Tim Ernst's Ozark Highlands Trail Guide, *now in its sixth edition, includes all the trail's notable scenic sights.*

ELK
After being driven to extinction in the mid-1800s, elk were successfully reintroduced to Arkansas in the 1980s. Now, they thrive in the wilderness surrounding the Buffalo River.

BUFFALO NATIONAL RIVER
There are some 9700 miles of river in Arkansas, and the most iconic waterway, besides the Mississippi, is the Buffalo River, which coincides with the OHT for part of its length and can be explored by boat.

PAM'S GROTTO FALLS
This is one of many waterfalls along the OHT, but it is the only one in a grotto. Hikers can find the nearly 40ft waterfall tucked away in a ravine surrounded by towering bluffs.

HARE MOUNTAIN
At about 2360 feet, Hare Mountain in the Boston Mountains is the highest point on the OHT. Hikers will find expansive views and a chimney remnant from a homestead.

DAVID'S TRAIL
This is the last completed segment of the OHT at Norfork Lake. The trail honors David Floyd, who was a local outdoor enthusiast, and the contributions he made to the trail.

→ The sun sets in the San Jacinto Mountains.

44

Pacific Crest National Scenic Trail

America's finest alpine hiking through the Sierra Nevada and Cascade mountain ranges crosses seven national parks in the ultimate continuous wilderness trail experience.

Showcasing the splendor of the glacially carved Sierra Nevada and the volcanic Cascades, the majority of the Pacific Crest National Scenic Trail (PCT) hugs these mountain ranges on a pristine and remote wilderness route. Passing through seven national parks and another half-dozen national monuments, each offering exceptional scenery, the PCT is popular but rarely overcrowded. Unless hikers are near trailheads or in the national parks, they experience relative solitude.

Most of this mountainous terrain lies within 33 roadless wilderness areas and 24 national forests, with the longest unbroken stretch of trail extending more than 200 miles. The wilderness and extremes of elevation give the PCT a more rugged, exuberant character than its East Coast counterpart, the Appalachian Trail (p20).

Although the PCT's lowest point is a mere 140ft on the Columbia River's Bridge of the Gods along the Oregon–Washington border, average trail elevations exceed 6000ft in California, 5000ft in Oregon and 4500ft in Washington. The highest elevations in each state are 13,200ft, 7560ft and 7620ft, respectively. This altitudinal variation encompasses the diversity of the Pacific coast from its desert to its alpine zone. Both elevation and latitude affect temperature and precipitation, so at higher elevations or farther north, the weather is cooler and wetter.

The majority of hikers and backpackers enjoy short trail segments, yet others tackle longer and well-traveled routes such as the John Muir Trail (p138) in California, the Mt Jefferson Wilderness in Oregon or the Alpine Lakes Wilderness in Washington.

Credit the idea of a border-to-border mountain trail between Mexico and Canada

Sleep here...

Most pack a tent, sleeping bag and sleeping pad for protection from weather and the environment as they camp trailside. Yet hikers will cross a road or highway weekly, where it is possible to hitchhike into a town to stay at a hotel or hostel for the night. Be advised, however: most towns rarely have more than a grocery store and gas station. And while it's common practice in the region around the trail, hitchhiking is never entirely safe and we don't recommend it. Those who hitch should understand that they are taking a small but potentially serious risk.

Backcountry Camping
Hikers and backpackers must follow the rules on their wilderness permit and be self-sufficient, carrying all of their own food as well as cooking and camping gear. A basic knowledge of camping and backpacking gear is really all you need, so long as you follow the principle to travel and camp on durable surfaces (at least 200ft away from the PCT and water sources). Avoid soil damage by planning ahead and choosing a site wisely, and don't wait to set up camp in the dark.

Timberline Lodge, Oregon
The historic grand lodge, whose setting and architecture have attracted the motion picture industry since the 1940s, lies on the flanks of Oregon's Mt Hood at 6000ft.

North Cascades Lodge at Stehekin, Washington
This idyllic, isolated community, which serves as the gateway to Washington's North Cascades, is accessible only by foot, horseback, ferry or seaplane; there is no road access.

Toolbox

When to go
Southern California's deserts are pleasant in April and May. Higher-elevation mountains are typically snow-free between July and September in California and Oregon, and from August to September in Washington. Thru-hikers typically start in April and end by October.

Getting there
Most trailheads are between two and five hours' drive from major airports. The primary north–south interstate along the West Coast, I-5 connects with many east–west roads leading to western trailheads. US 395 accesses many roads leading to eastern trailheads.

Practicalities
Length in miles: 2650
Start: Campo, CA
End: Near the US–Canada border in EC Manning Provincial Park, British Columbia, Canada
Dog friendly: Yes, in sections (pets not allowed in national parks)
Bike friendly: No
Permit needed: Yes
States covered: California, Oregon, Washington

A trailside stream transforms into a gushing waterfall along the Pacific Crest Trail. Left: Sunrise on the top of Mt Whitney.

➡ The Pacific Crest Trail
through the mountains.

to Clinton C Clarke of Pasadena, California, who formed the Pacific Crest Trail System Conference in 1932. This group of hiking and horseback-riding clubs worked to link existing long-distance trails, such as the John Muir Trail, the Oregon Skyline Trail and Washington's Cascade Crest Trail into one continuous wilderness trail. In 1948 the USDA Forest Service took responsibility for trail oversight. The PCT was designated a National Scenic Trail in 1968 and saw its first thru-hiker in 1972. Its segments through Oregon and Washington were completed in 1987, and by 1993 the route was formally declared complete. Today only a handful of miles in California remain unprotected, or still follow roads or detour around private land.

Each of the trail's five segments offers a unique experience: Southern California (648 miles), Central California (505 miles), Northern California (567 miles), Oregon (430 miles) and Washington (500 miles).

Southern California's Sonoran and Mojave Deserts, with their chollas, barrel cacti, yuccas and Joshua trees, contrast starkly with the mountains to come. As the trail winds through chaparral into the oak woodlands of the Laguna Mountains, it skirts the Anza-Borrego Desert State Park and enters the San Jacinto Mountains west of Palm Springs. The pine-forested San Bernardino Mountains east of Los Angeles offer a quick getaway from urban sprawl, so day hikes and overnight trips are popular here. Paralleling the San Andreas Fault and skirting the Mojave Desert along the Tehachapi Range, the PCT enters the southern Sierra Nevada.

In Central California, only five roads bisect the Sierra Nevada's wilderness between Walker Pass at Hwy 178 and

Donner Summit at I-80, a distance of more than 275 miles as the crow flies or more than 500 trail miles. Many consider this High Sierra traverse through Sequoia, Kings Canyon and Yosemite National Parks to offer the most outstanding mountain hiking in the US, with highlights of 14,000ft summits, a sea of granite peaks, sparkling lakes and streams and flowery meadows.

Undulating through Northern California's deep river valleys and past granite outcrops and domes, the PCT reaches the southern extent of the Cascade Range at Lassen Volcanic National Park. As the trail swings away from the Cascades and closer to the coast, snowcapped Mt Shasta (14,162ft) dominates the horizon as the route traverses the rugged Trinity Alps and the forested Marble and Siskiyou Mountains.

Southern Oregon's drier terrain yields to lake-filled wilderness near Crater Lake National Park. Skirting glacier-clad extinct volcanoes through the spectacular Three Sisters Wilderness and Mt Jefferson Wilderness, this segment culminates in the timberline traverse of dormant Mt Hood (11,240ft), Oregon's highest summit, before descending to the Columbia River.

In Washington the PCT climbs through forest to the Cascades' crest, passing west of Mt Adams before crossing the enchanting Goat Rocks Wilderness. Heading north, the trail passes along the eastern edge of Mt Rainier National Park. Beyond Norse Peak Wilderness, it continues through the southeastern corner of North Cascades National Park, with more glaciers than any US park outside of Alaska. A final segment through the vast Pasayten Wilderness leads to the US–Canada border and the northern terminus.

Highlights

The Pacific Crest Trail covers everything from the heat of the Mojave Desert in California to the high-altitude granite peaks of the Sierras, volcano-hopping in the central regions of Oregon before traversing the Cascade Mountains in Washington up to Canada.

JOHN MUIR TRAIL
The iconic 211-mile trail (p138) through continuous wilderness links Mt Whitney and Yosemite Valley, traversing 11 passes through stunning national parks.

LASSEN VOLCANIC NATIONAL PARK
California's Lassen Peak (10,457ft), a recently active volcano, is a 5-mile round trip; it towers above the park's geysers, fumaroles, mud pots and hot springs.

CRATER LAKE NATIONAL PARK
The pristine blue waters of the country's deepest lake fill the 6-mile-wide caldera formed by the volcanic eruption and collapse of Oregon's Mt Mazama.

MT RAINIER NATIONAL PARK
An active volcano, Mt Rainier is the most glaciated peak in the contiguous US and the highest peak in Washington and the Cascade Range.

NORTH CASCADES NATIONAL PARK
Hundreds of glaciers descend from jagged peaks into lake-filled cirques in this Washington park with diverse habitats, flora and fauna.

Resources

01 Pacific Crest National Scenic Trail

www.fs.usda.gov/pct
The USDA Forest Service and its partners manage and maintain the PCT.

02 Pacific Crest Trail Association

www.pcta.org
Founded in 1977, the Pacific Crest Trail Association protects the PCT and promotes it as a world-class experience. It sells books and maps for state segments and shorter hikes. The Pacific Crest Trail Data Book by Benedict Go and The PCT Hiker's Handbook by Ray Jardine appeal to thru-hikers.

03 *Wild: From Lost to Found on the Pacific Crest Trail*

Cheryl's Strayed's 2012 memoir is mandatory reading for aspiring PCT thru-hikers.

Mt Hood towering over the vineyards of the Columbia River Valley.

Hike this...

This National Scenic Trail includes stunning deserts, shady woodlands, volcanic peaks and breathtaking views of the glaciated tips of the Sierra Nevada. The sheer size of the trail means that some hikers only do a portion of it, while others choose to take it in sections according to the season. These are popular options.

➡ Flowers of the Pacific Crest Trail.

01
Mt Whitney, California

The highest peak in the contiguous US, Mt Whitney (14,505ft), named for Josiah Whitney who headed the California Geological Survey from 1860–1874, is an object of desire for almost all thru-hikers and anyone else who finds themselves in Sequoia National Park. Nearby, five other southern Sierra peaks soar higher than 14,000ft. The trail to Whitney leaves the PCT near Crabtree Meadow and follows the John Muir Trail past Timberline and Guitar Lakes to the crest of the Sierra, where it joins the trail coming from Whitney Portal far below on the eastern side of the Sierra. The final push as the trail wends through talus blocks takes you to the broad summit plateau with its awesome vistas. Due to huge demand, wilderness permits for the Mt Whitney Trail are distributed via the online Mt Whitney lottery between May 1 and November 1. Applications are accepted from February to mid-March. Those with the expertise and snow gear can hike out of season.

02
Devils Postpile National Monument, California

Symmetrical columns of polished blue-gray basalt between 40ft and 60ft tall testify to a history of now-dormant volcanic activity near Mammoth Lakes, a year-round resort in California. Although the area was originally included in 1890 as part of Yosemite National Park, mining interests lobbied to exclude Devils Postpile from the park; in 1905 Congress removed it. By 1910 mining operations wanted to dynamite it to create a dam on the Middle Fork San Joaquin River to generate electricity. Alarmed, the Sierra Club and others wrote to the US president, urging the area's preservation.

In 1911 President Taft declared Devils Postpile a national monument, restoring its federal protection. Less than a mile from the PCT near Reds Meadow, a trail follows the base of this geologic wonder. This honeycomb design is best appreciated from atop the columns, reached by a short trail. The columns are an easy half-mile hike from the Devils Postpile Ranger Station.

03
Goat Rocks Wilderness, Washington

Named for the Goat Rocks, which are remnants of an extinct volcano from two million years ago, this wilderness area nestles between Washington's Mt Rainier and Mt Adams. Observant hikers may spot mountain goats on its rocky ridges, where snow frequently lingers into late summer. Although all of its trails are lower than 8000ft, this rugged wilderness awes with glorious views of the Cascades' volcanoes and snow-clad peaks. Panoramic views of Mt Rainier (14,411ft) dominate many trail miles.

Much of the trail follows ridgelines at or higher than timberline, yet below these ridges are wildflower-filled alpine meadows dotted by turquoise glacial lakes. Old Snowy Mountain (7930ft), flanked by glaciers on two sides, is a popular summit. You can access the Packwood Glacier section of the PCT at Hwy 12 near the White Pass ski area. This is considered some of the northern trail's best scenery, but snow can interfere starting in late September and often lingers on the ground until August.

Bowman Lake, Glacier National Park.

45

Pacific Northwest National Scenic Trail

From 'crown to coast,' this journey is 1200 miles westward from Montana's glacial Rockies to the Pacific Ocean. Expect all manner of contrasts in between.

Imagine, if you will, the distinct weight of ocean air: its dank, salty fragrance and rhythmic, overwhelming shush. Feel the sandy sinking of each footstep, and breezes kicking up your hair. Scan the rippling horizon for great blue herons or sea lions perched on sea stacks, but don't forget to look closely at the rocks on shore. You may see petroglyphs marking the longtime human affinity for and attraction to this westernmost headland on the Pacific Ocean.

The Pacific Northwest Trail (PNT) ends appropriately at this encompassing scene after traversing three national parks and seven mountain ranges from its eastern terminus in the Rockies. But don't expect a sign: as along much of the PNT, you'll have to know where you are. Or at least pretend you do. Harvey Manning, the PNT's original visionary, conceived this moment of accomplishment and connectedness with a call to the Pacific Ocean in 1970 via a cross-Cascades trail. Luckily for us, Manning's clarion call brought into existence a trail from west of the Cascades all the way to the coast.

The PNT is one of the youngest of the National Scenic Trails, having been designated in 2009. Thanks to the tireless work of Ron Strickland, founder of the Pacific Northwest Trail Association (PNTA), the trail is protected by a core of volunteers coordinating maintenance, advocacy and communication as well as maintaining a record of those who have completed the trail end to end. Compared with elder National Scenic Trails, the PNT still has relatively few thru-hikers, though the number is steadily increasing to well over 30 per year. For those willing to commit time and adopt a flexible,

Sleep here...

Per National Park Service regulations, 'in the three National Parks along the PNT, backcountry camping is only allowed in designated sites. Backcountry visitors are required to obtain a permit from the NPS in advance of their trip.' National Forests are more lax, and dispersed camping is allowed at the appropriate distance from the trail and water sources. Leave No Trace is always the operating rule.

 Polebridge, Montana
The unincorporated, solar-powered town on the western edge of Glacier offers huckleberry bear claws at the Mercantile and stiff drinks at Northern Lights Saloon, as well as the North Fork Hostel and cabins for rent. Try live music for a nightcap!

 Webb and Garver Lookouts, Montana
These retired and renovated fire observation posts in Montana's Kootenai National Forest are available by reservation. They have minimal amenities but stellar panoramic views.

 Ross Lake Resort, Washington
Located in North Cascades National Park, this remote resort is an angler's haven. Originally built for loggers in the 1950s, the 13 floating cabins and three bunkhouses are often booked, but hosts accept resupply shipments.

Park Butte, Washington
Available first come, first served, the historic fire lookout is a lucky stay for day trekkers and thru-hikers. Views of glacial Mt Baker and wisps of Pacific blue-gray on the horizon may inspire introspection. No worries; there's a poetry register for that.

© davidmarxphoto / Shutterstock; © Velimir Isaevich / Shutterstock

Toolbox
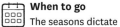

When to go
The seasons dictate the window of opportunity. From Glacier National Park, a June–September thru-hike is most common. Be wary of snow on Glacier and Olympic peaks as late as July and possible wildfires in August.

Getting there
The eastern terminus is the Chief Mountain Customs parking area in Glacier National Park in Montana. The western terminus at Cape Alava is 3 miles from Ozette Ranger Station on Washington's Olympic Peninsula.

Practicalities
Distance: 1200 miles
Start: Glacier National Park, MT
End: Cape Alava, Olympic National Park, WA
Dog friendly: Yes, for section hiking. Leash required in some areas; no dogs allowed in national parks and Loomis NRCA.
Bike friendly: Yes, some areas. No bikes in wilderness-designated areas. Bikers love sections in Colville National Forest and Puget Sound.
Permit required: No thru-hike permitting required
States covered: Montana, Idaho, Washington

→ Bridge in Deception Pass State Park, Washington. Left: Camping in Polebridge, Montana.

→ The deep valley views from Hannegan Pass in Mt Baker-Snoqualmie National Forest.

patient attitude to navigate the trail's challenges, the PNTA is there to support the journey, well aware that the trail is a work in progress. Wildfires, weather, and wildlife wrench unpredictable navigational complications in planning and executing an end-to-end walk, twisting and turning sojourns into convoluted alternatives and rerouting.

After a breezy walk through Glacier National Park, you might expect a certain level of regulated tameness to accompany all wilderness experience. Organized campsites and wide, marked trails facilitate the national park journey. Just outside the park's perimeter, however, the PNT has its first surprise. Montana's northwest corner and Idaho's panhandle impose a tangle of unpeopled wildlands. Relentless backcountry bushwhacking and craggy rock scrambling demand a whole new level of self-reliance. On the plus side, there are abundant photo ops undisturbed by tourists with selfie sticks. Elsewhere, the miles of trail are supplemented by road walking that stitches together the route.

Yet even more twists lie in wait. While you're watching the sunset atop Stahl Peak's fire lookout a handful of miles outside Eureka, Montana, the tough moments will seem to shrink amid the panoramic views of your cozy shelter. With forehead pressed to a windowpane overlooking mountain upon mountain, you may even be able to laugh at yourself. Were you really so childish to think throwing the 'stupid rock' that tripped you during a creek crossing would shame it? And remember that fear-induced moment you spent flailing your arms and screaming at the deer you thought was a cougar? That was funny. At least it will be with a

little more distance in the rearview mirror. Perspective is one of many gifts of the trail.

All in all, the 1200-mile corridor bills itself among the 'most scenic, rugged and wild trails in the world,' according to the PNTA, and its contrasts are intensely interesting. From end to end, each of its 10 sections builds appreciation for the unique terrain, flora, fauna and weather – from moose to otters, arid highlands to rainforest, road walking to trailblazing. It's the contradictions that keep you walking with your curiosity piqued.

Take, for example, a section in the middle that happens to be the longest stretch between resupply points (150 miles). The Pasayten Wilderness connects the grasslands of eastern Washington to the glacial peaks of the Cascades, but it will leave you disconnected from modern conveniences for many, many days. Here, though, you can take a short detour to rifle through remnants of a WWI-era mining site. The area was originally opened for wolframite and tungsten mining in 1908, and it was precisely the prospect of extracting minerals from this land that led to the establishment of paths into this remote spot. The irony is palpable.

As you swing a sweaty pack off your shoulders and lay it next to thick-cut timber, you may gawk at the Herculean effort it took to get this stuff here, including an iron bathtub lugged through the wilderness on a donkey named Jack. If the angels of the PNT shine upon you, you might even discover a jar of peanut butter fortuitously stored inside an abandoned cabin. You are days away from resupply – and hungry. You'll dip your spoon into that. In renewed spirits, you get back to walking. The Pacific Ocean awaits.

Highlights

The Pacific Northwest Trail offers an endless list of gorgeous panoramas, including stunning ocean coastlines, verdant forests dotted with pristine lakes and snowy volcanoes silhouetted against blue skies. Don't forget its national parks and national forests either.

MT BAKER-SNOQUALMIE
Hikers in Mt Baker-Snoqualmie National Forest delight in some of the trail's best scenery, sometimes called the American Alps and where the first PNT miles were blazed.

CONTINENTAL DIVIDE TRAIL
Another epic thru-hike, the Continental Divide Trail (p68) travels with the PNT for 19 miles in section 1 of the trail as it gets its start in Glacier National Park.

PRIEST LAKE
From Idaho's Bonners Ferry and the Kootenai River, the trail bushwhacks north along Lion's Head Ridge leading into Priest Lake. Avid orienteers will love this challenge.

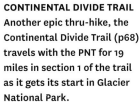

ROSS LAKE, NORTH CASCADES
Ross Lake and its welcoming resort receive weary hikers who've finished section 6 through the Pasayten Wilderness, 121 miles from the last resupply town to the east.

OLYMPIC NATIONAL PARK
Declared a national park in 1938, 1406-sq-mile Olympic National Park has a unique rainforest, glaciated mountain peaks and a 57-mile strip of Pacific coastal wilderness.

Resources

O1 Pacific Northwest Trail Association
www.pnt.org
This should be your primary resource for the PNT. In partnership with the US Forest Service and National Park Service, PNTA is the coordinating organization for maintenance, advocacy and communication.

O2 *Pacific Northwest Trail Digest*
Tim Youngbluth updates this digest yearly with thru-hiker input. It includes practical details for navigational planning, camping, water and food resupply.

O3 *Pacific Northwest Trail Town Guide*
Trailside services, lodging information and resupply tips are covered in this guide by Melanie Simmerman.

⬆ Mt Shuksan and Picture Lake in Washington. Left: Driftwood on Tskawahyah Island, Flattery Rocks area, seen from Cape Alava in Olympic National Park.

Hike this...

In the Pacific Northwest, it's hard to throw a rock without hitting a hiking trail. Starting in Glacier National Park, these sections of the PNT are some of the gems available to get a taste of the region's grandeur.

 Hiking Cape Alava's temperate rainforest.

01
Bowman Lake, Montana

Day hikers with a taste for adventure can appreciate the placid, reflective waters and remote beauty of Bowman Lake in the less-traveled northwestern corner of Glacier National Park in Montana. Accessible 6.3 miles northeast of Polebridge via bumpy, unpaved road (4WD recommended), the Bowman Lake trails in section 1 of the PNT offer a serene experience of Glacier. On the western side of the Continental Divide, multiday hikes create chances to spot eagles, loons and ospreys, black bears, grizzly bears, elks and moose. Numa Lookout (12 miles round trip) has some challenging elevation gain but offers the most expansive views. Bowman Lake trail follows the actual PNT, and hikers can choose their distance along the hills hugging the lake's edge; it's 7.1 miles to the end of the lake. Plan to camp at Bowman Campground for a more leisurely time frame. After Bowman Lake, the trail joins the road on its way to the town of Polebridge.

02
Kettle Crest Trail, Washington

Popular for mountain biking and a great primer for thru-hiking (though a few trailheads allow for shorter routes), section 4 in the Kettle River Range showcases the arid beauty of northeastern Washington along 44 miles of trail. Along the spine of the Kettle Range, you'll enjoy big vistas onto rolling, open meadows colored with the orange-red flame of Indian paintbrush, purple lupines, and white and pink asters buttoned in yellow. Opportunities for rare wildlife viewing include gray wolves and bighorn sheep. In addition to a reservable cabin at Snow Peak and camping at Sherman Overlook, the town of Republic, nestled close by, has cozy inns and retains much of its original gold rush–era charms. Fossils, longhorn burgers and a friendly-neighbor demeanor make it a pleasant base camp for adventure in Colville National Forest, especially as the town can be reached via three different trail entrances: Hwy 20 at Sweat Creek, Hwy 21 at Thirteen Mile and Sherman Pass on the Kettle Crest Trail.

03
Ozette to Cape Alava, Washington

Lake Ozette, in the northwest region of Washington's Olympic Peninsula, is the launching point for an out-and-back 6.2-mile walk to Cape Alava, the PNT's western terminus. Adhering to tides, you may be able to complete the Ozette Loop, 9.2 miles that connect Cape Alava to Sand Point. The southern Sand Point Trail from Lake Ozette Ranger Station leads 3 miles to beaches below a low bluff; whale-watchers often come here in the migration season. Between vestiges of farmstead life at Ahlstrom's Prairie and petroglyphs at Wedding Rocks, there are reasons to take it slow.

Add in ferns, evergreens and western red cedars along the forested boardwalks, plus sea stacks, gulls and marine life dotting the Pacific shoreline, and it is easy to appreciate the ecological diversity in such a (relatively) short walk. Before you go, stop at the Makah Museum in Neah Bay on the Makah Indian Reservation to witness the area's rich history: archaeological discoveries of life from 2000 years ago.

4.6

Pony Express National Historic Trail

➡ Wheeler Peak grove in Great Basin National Park, Nevada. Right: Clan Alpine Herd Management Area, Nevada.

Pony Express riders and their galloping steeds lead the way on this multistate adventure that traces the Wild West's most audacious commercial venture.

As he galloped into the Cold Springs station on a spring afternoon in 1860, ready to climb onto a fresh horse and continue his journey, Pony Express rider Robert Haslam made a gruesome discovery: the dead body of the station keeper, who was probably killed during an attack by Paiute warriors and their allies. At the time, the scrubby high desert of what is now western Nevada was in the thick of the Pyramid Lake War, a series of deadly skirmishes between local tribes and encroaching settlers, miners and soldiers. Haslam looked around. All the horses were gone. Though he'd just finished a 30-mile ride and night was falling, he decided to push on to the Sand Springs station, some 35 miles ahead.

Haslam safely reached Sand Springs, where he convinced the station keeper to leave with him. Haslam's foresight possibly saved the man's life, because another station on the route was attacked the next day.

In operation from April 1860 to October 1861, the Pony Express was the FedEx of its day, a commercial venture relying on a fleet of brave riders and swift horses to carry mail between Missouri and California in an astounding 10 days. The route stretched 1966 miles, and riders covered 75 to 100 miles per day. The original mail pouch, called a mochila, moved with the riders as they swapped horses at relay stations along the route.

At its peak the Pony Express employed between 80 and 100 riders and relied on 420 horses. Home stations, where fresh riders began their journey, were anywhere from 60 to 100 miles apart. Relay stations, where riders switched to new horses, were 10 to 15 miles apart. The entire enterprise

Sleep here...

Since the Pony Express route often traced the path of today's modern highways, finding a place to stop is typically easy, especially at major stops like Sacramento, Reno and Salt Lake City. Some of the land is prime camping territory as well. In addition to the below choices, if you want to gussy it up in Utah, the Inn on the Hill in Salt Lake City is the place.

 Barn Anew, Nebraska
Enjoy mesmerizing views of Scotts Bluff from this Nebraska B&B in Scottsbluff, where you can sleep in the Pony Express room inside a restored barn or inside two converted sheepherders' wagons.

Camping in Great Basin National Park, Nevada
For fantastic stargazing, snag a primitive campsite along Snake Creek Rd at this International Dark Sky Park in eastern Nevada. Five developed campgrounds are also available, including lofty Wheeler Peak with impressive mountain views.

Hotel Nevada, Nevada
For the perfect mix of history and kitsch, spend the night in Ely, Nevada, at this 64-room hotel, open since 1929. Its eclectically Western lobby and funky casino are a hoot.

Whitney Peak Hotel, Nevada
Wait, is that a climbing wall in my hotel? Yep, this indie hotel in Reno, Nevada, embraces the great outdoors with a sense of fun. Spacious rooms have a youthful vibe, and staff is friendly and professional.

Toolbox

When to go
You'll avoid summer crowds and heat, and enjoy pleasant temperatures, in April, May, September and October. The Pony Express Re-Ride is held in June. Great Basin National Park in Nevada runs Saturday evening astronomy programs April through October. As this is mainly a driving route, however, most of it can be done year-round with no issue.

Getting there
The Sand Springs Pony Express Station is 90 miles east of Reno–Tahoe International Airport via I-80 and Hwy 50. From Denver International Airport it's 280 miles to Casper, Wyoming, via I-25, and 200 miles to Scottsbluff, Nebraska, traveling I-25 and US 85.

Practicalities
Length in miles: 2000
Start: St Joseph, MO
End: Sacramento, CA
Dog friendly: Varies by location
Bike friendly: Limited sections
Permit needed: No
States covered: MO, KS, NE, CO, WY, UT, NV, CA

was short-lived, however, terminating when the first transcontinental telegraph message was successfully sent between New York City and San Francisco – a mere 18 months after the Pony Express began.

Today visitors can revisit Haslam's route on the Pony Express National Historic Trail. The stretch of the trail that parallels Hwy 50 in Nevada is one of the easiest places to delve into its history up close. Since the scenery here is much unchanged from the early 1860s, it's also easy to visualize the epic rides of the horse-riding couriers.

Stretching east–west across the state, Hwy 50 has been dubbed the 'Loneliest Road in America.' It crosses the Great Basin, a series of high desert depressions between the Sierra Nevada to the west and the Wasatch Range in Utah to the east. Numerous mountain ranges and lowland valleys run north–south across this basin. The road also follows the route of the Overland Stage Line as well as the first transcontinental telegraph line and the coast-to-coast Lincoln Highway.

Some modern historians say that Haslam, affectionately known as 'Pony Bob,' and other riders exaggerated their exploits. But records do indicate that four Pony Express riders and numerous station keepers were killed by Native American warriors. As you drive the vast desert between Sand Springs and Cold Springs, the vulnerability of the lone rider and the isolated stations hits home. The desert is empty and exposed, with the Desatoya Mountains foothills looming to the south.

A good place to start a Pony Express day trip is Sand Mountain Recreation Area, 20 miles east of Fallon, Nevada. The prime attraction here is a 600ft-high sand dune, a popular destination for ATV riders. The dune sometimes 'sings' at night, when vibrating sand produces a low-pitched boom. Sand Springs station, or what's left of it, is also here.

Covered by sand for a century, the building was 'discovered' by archaeologists in 1976. Sand Springs was an unpleasant place, at least as described by British explorer Richard Burton, who visited this expanse of volcanic rock in 1860. It was, he said, 'roofless and chairless, filthy and squalid, with a smoky fire in one corner and a table in the center of an impure floor, the walls open to every wind and the interior full of dust.'

About 21 miles east, at the Hwy 50 and NV 361 junction, sits Middlegate station. The original Pony Express building is gone, but you can enjoy lunch at the well-weathered restaurant here. As you approach, check the hand-painted sign for the current population of Middlegate, which fluctuates between 17 and 22 depending on who has died or moved in. Navy SEALs sometimes drop in by helicopter after training exercises to scarf down the famous Middlegate Monster, a hefty burger well over 1lb.

Back on Hwy 50, heading east, you'll pass the Shoe Tree, a tall cottonwood draped with knotted pairs of shoes. Next up is Cold Springs station, where Pony Bob discovered the body of the slain station keeper. A roadside exhibit shares Pony Express history, and a trail leads to the well-preserved remains of the station. The ruins just north of the parking area are those of an Overland Stagecoach station and a transcontinental telegraph office. And the pit toilet at Cold Springs? The Bureau of Land Management calls it the 'Loneliest Rest Stop on the Loneliest Road.'

Highlights

Follow the original route that horse-and-rider mail delivery took on the Pony Express Trail, the FedEx of its day, between Missouri and California, across the breadth of Nevada, as riders delivered mail in an astounding 10 days in its brief heyday.

PONY EXPRESS NATIONAL BACKCOUNTRY BYWAY
This 133-mile byway across western Utah rangelands begins near Fairfield and passes several former Pony Express station sites.

GOTHENBURG PONY EXPRESS STATION
Step into an original Pony Express station in Gothenburg, Nebraska, one of only a few still in existence. On display is a replica mochila, the mail saddlebag.

HWY 50
Stretching east from Fallon, NV, to Great Basin National Park and the Nevada state line, remote, lonely Hwy 50 follows the Pony Express across the heart of the state.

PONY EXPRESS RE-RIDE
Each June the National Pony Express Association organizes a rerunning of the eight-state Pony Express route. Watch a mail exchange in person or track the riders online.

NATIONAL HISTORIC TRAILS INTERPRETIVE CENTER
This Casper, Wyoming, center explores the Pony Express, Oregon, Mormon and California Trails, with talks and guided hikes available.

Resources

01 **Pony Express National Historic Trail**
www.nps.gov/poex
The National Park Service website provides current information plus links to an auto tour interpretive guide and maps.

02 **National Pony Express Association**
www.nationalpony express.org
The association keeps a calendar of Pony Express–related events and shares history about the venture. It also organizes and promotes the annual Pony Express Re-Ride.

03 *West Like Lightning: The Brief, Legendary Ride of the Pony Express*
This 2018 history of the Pony Express by Jim DeFelice separates tall tales from the truth – or tries to.

Wheeler Peak grove in Great Basin National Park. Left: Sunset at Rhyolite, Nevada along the trail.

Hike this...

Although the Pony Express National Historic Trail is mainly a driving route, there are several opportunities to walk along the route used for this brief but legendary service. Some even follow the path on horseback at points.

➡️ A sign shows the old Pony Express Route off of Hwy 50, Nevada.

01
Cold Springs Station, Nevada

A trail leads to the well-preserved ruins of the Cold Springs station in Nevada, where you'll find several rooms within one stone-walled building. The high desert surroundings have remained undeveloped, so this is a good place to experience the landscape much as it was during the Paiute conflict in the early 1860s. The station itself was roofless, so occupants were at the mercy of the weather and their enemies. Mortally wounded during a Paiute ambush at a nearby creek, rider Jose Zowgaltz perished here in 1860, just a few weeks after Robert Haslam found the slain station keeper.

In the spring, wildflowers bloom along the trail, which gently ascends from the parking lot. There is no shade, but there are large rocks along the trail where you can rest. Bring water; the trail length is 1.5 miles out, and 3 miles round trip in the desert can be grueling for those who aren't properly prepared. Always be mindful of the symptoms of heat exhaustion.

02
Saddle Rock & South Overlook Trails, Nebraska

Pioneers traveling on the Oregon Trail and Pony Express riders racing through Nebraska rode through Mitchell Pass at Scotts Bluff. For a bird's-eye view of their route through the sandstone bluffs flanking the pass, take this 3.8-mile round-trip hike that begins near the Scotts Bluff National Monument visitors center. The Saddle Rock Trail passes through a wash and a tunnel on its way to the top of the bluff, where views open up of the expanse traveled by pioneers and Pony Express riders alike.

From the summit, the paved South Overlook Trail leads to views of the pass. Pioneers reaching this landmark on the Oregon Trail had completed one-third of their journey west. From a stagecoach not far from Scotts Bluff, author Mark Twain witnessed a Pony Express rider and his horse burst past 'and go swinging away like a belated fragment of a storm!' Each horseman rode full-bore for almost six hours – changing horses every 10 miles – before passing the mail to the next rider.

03
Great Basin National Park, Nevada

Pony Express riders swung well north of what is now Great Basin National Park in Nevada, near the Utah border. Today Hwy 50 is the main road through these parts. It rolls right past the park, where hiking is superb, with a range of options for scenery. The Sky Islands Forest Trail is a wheelchair-accessible trail through a high-alpine conifer forest. The 0.4-mile round-trip trail has interpretive signage. The aply named Bristlecone & Glacier Trail, a 4.6-mile round-trip hike, passes bristlecone pine trees that have been growing for millennia, as well as the state's only glacier, Wheeler Peak Glacier – melting fast! Wheeler Peak Summit Trail ends at the roof of the park, offering stunning views of the Snake Range; it's 8.6 miles round-trip and the highlight of many visits to Great Basin National Park. And if you want to visit the summit but can't spare time or energy for the hike, plan your visit carefully, as the peak's scenic drive is open only during summer, usually from July through October.

47

Potomac Heritage National Scenic Trail

Linking the Chesapeake Bay estuary to western Pennsylvania's Allegheny Plateau, this historic trail and waterway has something for everyone.

→ Harpers Ferry National Historical Park. Right: Point Lookout Lighthouse on the Chesapeake, Maryland.

Whatever mode of self-powered travel you enjoy – hiking, bicycling, paddling or cross-country skiing – at whatever pace you choose, you can explore the nature, history and cultural heritage of the Potomac River corridor for a few hours, days or weeks at a time on the Potomac Heritage National Scenic Trail (PHT). This is the only National Scenic Trail that passes through a major metropolitan area, Washington, DC; with trails on both the Virginia and Maryland sides of the Potomac River, it is deservedly popular.

The Potomac River, which forms the Virginia–Maryland border, is steeped in the history of westward movement and the Civil War. It was a corridor into the mountains for indigenous and Colonial peoples and a path for the Underground Railroad. George Washington envisioned the river as a transportation corridor, and his Patowmack Company linked the mountains to the Chesapeake seaports, building canals to bypass its rapids.

The 19th century brought a new vision of a continuous canal linking the Chesapeake Bay with the Ohio River. Construction of the Chesapeake & Ohio (C&O) Canal began in 1828; it reached Cumberland, Maryland, by 1850 and operated commercially until 1924 when railroads rendered the canal obsolete. The C&O Canal languished until Supreme Court Justice William O Douglas organized efforts to save it, leading a walk of its entire length in 1954. When the railways were abandoned in the late 20th century, a rail-to-trail movement began, culminating in the Great Allegheny Passage, a 150-mile recreational trail between Cumberland and Pittsburgh. The Potomac corridor was officially designated

Sleep here...

Virginia's Chesapeake shore and Washington, DC's vibrant neighborhoods offer many conventional lodging opportunities from hotels to quaint B&Bs and inns, but treat yourself to the more historic overnight options of trail shelters and lockhouses. They're unique places to spend an evening and carry over the day's adventures into your slumber.

 C&O Canal Campsites, Maryland
In Maryland's C&O Canal National Historical Park (p60), camping is allowed in designated sites approximately every 5 miles (starting at mile 16), including sites specifically for hikers and cyclists.

 Canal Quarters Lockhouses, Maryland
Maryland's seven historical lockhouses, in peaceful settings between mile 5.4 and mile 108.7, are furnished with period pieces from the C&O Canal's development. They sleep up to eight people and offer amenities.

 Allegheny Trail House, Maryland
Just a half mile from the Great Allegheny Passage, this historic B&B in Frostburg, Maryland, built in 1865, offers a farm-to-table breakfast and oozes charm.

Laurel Highlands Hiking Trail Shelters, Pennsylvania
Camping requires reservations and a fee, and is allowed in eight sites every 6–12 miles. Each site has five shelters, space for 30 tents and a one-night maximum.

Toolbox

When to go
The mountain highlands offer a respite from the hot, humid summers of coastal areas. April to June and September to November are pleasant, mild months for exploring. Winters are cold, and precipitation occurs in any season.

Getting there
The nearest airports are in Washington, DC, Baltimore and Pittsburgh. Amtrak has service to Harpers Ferry, West Virginia, and Cumberland, Maryland. In Washington, DC, local buses and the Metro serve several points along the George Washington Memorial Parkway and Theodore Roosevelt Island.

Practicalities
Length in miles: 924 (833 existing, 91 planned)
Start: Point Lookout, MD, and Smith Point, VA
End: Seward, PA
Dog friendly: Yes
Bike friendly: Yes
Permit needed: No
States covered: Washington, D.C., Virginia, Maryland, Pennsylvania

A country road crossing a steel trestle bridge at Perryopolis, Pennsylvania.

the PHT in 1983, bringing new life to the historic canals and railways.

The trail's natural beauty brings a welcome change from urban bustle. Its tidewater cattail marshes are home to muskrats and hundreds of bird species. Along the C&O Canal, broad-leaved trees provide summer shade and autumn color. Deer, partridges and grouse live in the Piedmont of Maryland and the Allegheny Mountains, where a few black bears roam. Fragrant mountain laurels bloom in early June, and rhododendrons in summer.

Tidewater Virginia's portion of the trail follows the Northern Neck Heritage Trail along mostly lightly traveled roads. Near the trail's eastern terminus at Smith Point overlooking the Chesapeake Bay, the active fishing village of Reedville has a museum showcasing 400 years of maritime history. Along the route are tidal marshes, blue heron rookeries, parks, beaches, wineries and the birthplaces of two US presidents. Closer to Washington, DC, the paved Mt Vernon Trail offers excellent hiking and biking for 17 miles through parks, wetlands and the historic town of Alexandria to Theodore Roosevelt Island, passing within sight of the Jefferson and Lincoln Memorials and the Washington Monument. The PHT continues through Great Falls Park to the White's Ferry river crossing.

Maryland's Point Lookout marks the confluence of the Potomac with the Chesapeake Bay and the start of the Southern Maryland Potomac Heritage Trail Bicycling Route, which runs almost 300 miles to Washington, DC. The rural route passes Maryland's first capital, St Mary's City, as well as historic sites and state parks. Paddling opportunities abound.

From Georgetown Visitor Center in Washington, DC, the 12ft-wide, unpaved C&O Canal towpath rises about 600ft along its 185 miles to Cumberland. The first 14 miles to Great Falls are heavily visited year-round, yet beyond the cascades, the trail brings quiet and solitude. The canal holds water only as far as Violettes Lock (mile 22), although some upstream segments have water. Near Harpers Ferry, the Appalachian Trail briefly joins the towpath. Near Cumberland, the Paw Paw Tunnel, an engineering marvel, carries the canal and towpath 3118ft through the hillside, with a hiking trail going over the top.

From Cumberland, the PHT follows the gentle Great Allegheny Passage along the former Western Maryland Railroad line. Touching historic, lively Frostburg, Maryland, and continuing through renovated railroad tunnels, the trail crosses the historic Mason-Dixon Line, which marks the Maryland–Pennsylvania border. After the 3294ft-long Big Savage Tunnel, it reaches its highest elevation (2392ft) at the Eastern Continental Divide and enters the Ohio River's watershed. The Great Allegheny Passage crosses several long and level paved viaducts, including the curving Keystone Viaduct, and visits charming towns along the Casselman River. From the aptly named town of Confluence, Pennsylvania, where the Casselman joins the Youghiogheny River, the PHT follows the Youghiogheny through Ohiopyle State Park, known for the best whitewater rafting in the eastern US. As you near the end, the 70-mile Laurel Highlands Hiking Trail heads east from Ohiopyle through forested state parks along a scenic ridge of the Allegheny Mountains. The trail leads to the PHT terminus in Seward on the Conemaugh River, many a mile from your start.

Highlights

Trace up through lovely Chesapeake country into the historic center of Mount Vernon and Georgetown, then travel all the way up to the Great Allegheny Passage on this gentle, varied mid-Atlantic journey.

CHERRY BLOSSOMS IN DC
Thousands of cherry trees surrounding Washington, DC's Tidal Basin blossom for a few days between late March and early April in a world-renowned floral display.

GEORGE WASHINGTON'S MOUNT VERNON
Visiting George and Martha Washington's stately home in Virginia brings you into the world of 18th-century America and the life of this Founding Father.

LAUREL HIGHLANDS
In Pennsylvania, the hardwood forests' annual display of vibrant colors for a week around mid-October elates most avid leaf peepers, especially along the Laurel Highlands Trail.

UNDERGROUND RAILROAD
The Potomac corridor formed an important though lesser-known part of the Underground Railroad, which allowed escaped slaves to stay out of sight and reach freedom.

HARPERS FERRY NATIONAL HISTORICAL PARK
Across the Potomac from Maryland in West Virginia is Harpers Ferry, a historic community that played a pivotal role in the Civil War.

48

Resurrection Pass Trail

Trek this locals' favorite trail on Alaska's Kenai Peninsula, spending a night or three in a public use cabin and letting your soul feast on the grandeur around you.

Hiking in Chugach State Park near Anchorage, Alaska. Right: Sign welcomes visitors to the small town of Hope on Alaska's Kenai Peninsula.

The Resurrection Pass Trail stretches 39 mountainous miles through the Chugach National Forest from the tiny town of Hope to the bustling summer hub of Cooper Landing. The south central Alaska trail is well connected to the road system and less than a two-hour drive to either trailhead from Anchorage on the Kenai Peninsula, making it a popular recreation site for locals. In summer, hikers and mountain bikers flock for day trips or multiday treks across the pass, and cross-country skiers brave it in winter. The trail is well maintained, has eight public-use cabins and plenty of official campsites, and is an excellent introduction to the plants and wildlife of the region.

The route, like many in south central Alaska, was first put on the map by gold miners who used it in the late 1800s to reach claims along Resurrection Creek and other streams. Like many routes in the region, though, it was used by the local Dena'ina people long before that. Dena'ina walked the route to access Resurrection Bay; indeed the trail system continues another 30 miles from Cooper Landing to Exit Glacier outside of Seward, though the trail is primitive in places.

The trail climbs from 600ft elevation to 2600ft in a mostly gentle ascent, following a long alpine valley. Most hikers and bikers begin in Hope, since the gradient is easier at this end. The trail starts 4 miles from this tiny Gold Rush–era town with a current population of fewer than 200. It boasts a hopping bar, creekside tent sites and dramatic views of Turnagain Arm, a narrow branch of Cook Inlet with the Chugach Mountains behind and a hiking destination in its own right. Hope is a good place to

Sleep here...

Sleeping options on the Kenai Peninsula are plentiful. However, during peak summer season everything can fill, so book in advance if you're visiting in June, July or August. The Kenai Peninsula B&B Association (kpbba.net) can help you find a room. On the trail, there are designated backcountry campsites at mile 4, Wolf Creek (mile 5.3), Caribou Creek (mile 7), mile 9.6, mile 12.6, and East Creek (mile 14.6).

Trail Campsites
You can camp anywhere along the trail, though designated campsites usually include flat and clear tent sites as well as a rustic toilet or outhouse.

Public-Use Cabins
Eight public-use cabins dot the trail, offering a respite from bugs and bad weather. These book up months in advance, so you'll want to plan ahead and book at www.recreation.gov.

Lodgings in Hope
Tent sites, cabins and B&Bs make up the accommodations in Hope. Much of this can be rustic, but there are some cozy and modern options, plus a couple of restaurants.

Lodgings in Cooper Landing
Thanks to the Kenai River, on which Cooper Landing is built, fishing lodges are king here. The area has large public campgrounds and a couple of B&Bs as well.

Toolbox

When to go
Late June, July and August are the best times to traverse Resurrection Pass on foot or by bike. This is Alaska, and you risk snow and cold temperatures any earlier or later than that. In winter, hardy beings will ski the trail over several days.

Getting there
Both trailheads are on Alaska's road system and have parking. Hope is 1¼ hours south of Anchorage and 16.5 miles down the Hope Hwy; Cooper Landing is 100 miles south of Anchorage and 1½ hours away. It's 30 miles from Seward.

Practicalities
Length in miles: 39
Start: Hope, AK
End: Cooper Landing, AK
Dog friendly: Yes; must be leashed at all times
Bike friendly: Yes
Permit needed: No
States covered: Alaska

→ Mist on the Russian River in Alaska.

stay for a night or two to catch a local band or explore one of the many other trails in the area. Resurrection Creek in downtown Hope is also one of the best places in the world to fish pink salmon during Alaska's late summer run.

From the trailhead outside Hope you'll follow Resurrection Creek as it churns through birch and spruce forest before it opens up to meadows in the long glacial valley. The trail skirts several small lakes, where you can drop a line and fish for grayling or rainbow trout. At mile 29.3 from Hope (9.5 miles from Cooper Landing), Juneau Lake is a popular spot, and every now and then you'll catch sight of a floatplane dramatically landing or taking off from the forest-ringed waters.

In the final miles of trail, Juneau Creek Falls announces itself by the sound of the water long before you see it. The namesake Juneau Creek trundles along from Juneau Lake before crashing suddenly into a small gorge. The falls are only 4 miles from Cooper Landing (though they're fairly steep miles), so it makes a pleasant day hike. There are also several official campsites next to it, complete with bear bins to store your food.

The trail has a third access point, the Devil's Pass trailhead, which starts at mile 39 of Seward Hwy. Devil's Pass to Cooper Landing covers 27 miles that you can bike in a day or hike in two. The 10 miles from the Devil's Pass trailhead to its meeting point with the Resurrection Pass Trail are steep and beautiful, ringed by rocky alpine peaks. The trail winds through a mossy forest for the first few miles and then quickly climbs above the tree line in a steep, rocky and gorgeous valley. At mile 9 is quiet Devil's Pass Lake, and a mile

beyond that is Devil's Pass Cabin and the main trail, which leads to scenic Cooper Landing. This picturesque outpost – named for Joseph Cooper, a miner who worked the area in the 1880s – is best known for its rich and brutal combat salmon fishing along the Russian and Kenai Rivers. While rustic log-cabin lodges featuring giant fish freezers are still the lifeblood of this town, the trails, rafting and kayaking opportunities attract avid outdoors lovers.

In July the valleys are full of wildflowers such as bright pink fireweed and purple lupines. The tundra around the area where the two trails meet has excellent lowbush blueberry picking in mid- to late August. Potential wildlife you may spot includes bears, moose, lynx, marmots and ptarmigan. If you've holed up at one spot for a couple of nights, a popular side trip is up the western ridgeline. The climb will gain you roughly 1600ft, but the views are absolutely worth it. On a clear day you can see the Harding Icefield, Denali, and row upon row of other ridgelines.

Because this is Alaska, the high elevation ridgelines sometimes have snow until mid-June, and muddy conditions mean the trail is closed to equestrian travel from June 1st to June 30th. Every other year, snowmobile access is allowed during the winter season. And for bikers, the Resurrection Pass, Russian River and Johnson Pass Trails in the Chugach National Forest are all popular among off-road cyclists in the Kenai Peninsula. Just be mindful that the last mile of the road to the trailhead outside Hope doesn't get plowed in winter. And no matter the time of year, bring a fleece pullover (it can get cold at night, even in July) and rain gear – both pants and parka to be on the safe side.

Highlights

Majestic Chugach National Forest is the size of New Hampshire, and one of Alaska's greatest natural resources. The mountains, lakes and rivers on this trail are what make Alaska wild; in fact, wild salmon swim in droves up Resurrection Creek each year.

JUNEAU CREEK FALLS
Thundering into a narrow gorge, Juneau Creek Falls makes a great day hike from Cooper Landing (it's a somewhat steep 4-mile hike) or an overnight stop at the creekside campground.

DEVIL'S PASS LAKE
Ten miles from the Devil's Pass trailhead, a mile from where this trail meets the main one, sits a clear blue alpine lake hugged by mountains.

HOPE
With a bawdy bar, a rushing creek filled with salmon during the run, steep mountains and the northern trailhead, Gold Rush–era Hope is worth a night or two of your time.

COOPER LANDING
The Kenai River, turquoise and serpentine, calls paddlers, fisherfolk and wildlife watchers to its waters. Cooper Landing is the jumping-off point.

JUNEAU LAKE
The largest lake on the Resurrection Pass Trail often sees floatplanes skimming its surface. The public-use cabin in the forest here sleeps eight.

49

Rim-to-Rim Trail

During a 24-mile trek across one of the natural wonders of the world, two billion years of miraculous geologic history are on display from rim to rim, ample reward for the challenging descent and ascent.

The Grand Canyon in Arizona is one of the most iconic natural landmarks in the US. Defined by steep plateau walls stained a multitude of colors and reaching over a mile high – with the emerald waters of the Colorado River flowing below – this truly is one of the Earth's most beautiful landscapes. Believed to have been carved by snow-fed river waters 70 million years ago, its eroded walls unveiling two billion years of geologic history, the Grand Canyon stands as a testament to the incredible works of Mother Nature.

Grand Canyon National Park draws over six million visitors annually to witness its immeasurable beauty. Overwhelming in size at 277 miles long and 18 miles wide, the canyon does more than delight the senses – it engulfs them. Photographs capture only a sliver of its grandeur; it is only through firsthand experience that you can fully comprehend this supreme earthly phenomenon. From the sounds of soft winds rustling through the trees of its forested rims, to the 40-some layers of rock washed red and purple by the rising sun, the Grand Canyon is a feast for the senses. It astonishes the naked eye, leaving you to stand in awe.

A visit to the canyon is a bucket-list given. For many hikers, it's an essential adventure. Trails, lookouts and viewpoints allow visitors of all levels to experience the canyon; this natural wonder neither rejects nor excludes, but rather calls with open arms. More seasoned hikers can get up close and personal with the Grand Canyon by diving right in...from rim to rim.

Crossing the Grand Canyon is no easy feat; the legendary Rim-to-Rim Trail, built in 1928 by the National Park Service,

Sleep here...

Accommodations in the park range from historic lodges to rustic cabins to standard motel rooms (book 13 months in advance). There are developed campgrounds as well as backcountry campsites, where you can roll out your sleeping bag under the stars to experience an unforgettable inner-canyon sunrise. Casting a wider net opens up any number of accommodation options in nearby towns.

Grand Canyon Lodge
Built in 1937 out of Kaibab limestone, the lodge features spacious rimside dining rooms and porches with Adirondack chairs. A National Historic Landmark and an architectural delight, the lodge's natural materials blend unobtrusively into the landscape.

Camping
Camp in the North Rim or outside the national park at Jacob Lake. For a starlit canopy along the trail, reserve a spot at Cottonwood, Bright Angel or Indian Garden (permit required).

Phantom Ranch
Spend the night at the famous Phantom Ranch, a rare desert oasis with beds, showers, hot meals and unbeatable stargazing opportunities from the floor of the Grand Canyon.

El Tovar Hotel
Built in 1905, this lodge in the national park is a historical gem with cabin-style charm reminiscent of a rural Swiss chalet. It has played host to famous guests such as Theodore Roosevelt and Albert Einstein.

Toolbox

When to go
The North Rim season runs from May 15 to October 15. Plan for a mid-May or late-September hike to beat Arizona's heat and the summer crowds.

Getting there
The North Rim of Grand Canyon National Park can be reached via car from Flagstaff, Arizona (207 miles), Phoenix, Arizona (351 miles), or Las Vegas, Nevada (275 miles). Shuttles depart daily from Grand Canyon Lodge to the North Kaibab trailhead.

Practicalities
Length in miles: 24 to Bright Angel trailhead; 21 to South Kaibab trailhead
Start: North Rim, North Kaibab trailhead, AZ
End: South Rim, Bright Angel trailhead. For the shorter version, opt for the South Kaibab route.
Dog friendly: Only above the rim; not allowed on the Rim-to-Rim hike
Bike friendly: No
Permit needed: Required only for backcountry camping outside Mather, Desert View and North Rim Campgrounds
States covered: Arizona

requires planning and preparation, good physical conditioning and some hiking experience. The route is 24 miles one-way from the North Kaibab trailhead to the Bright Angel trailhead – a challenging backcountry trail through varying landscapes, steep elevations, semiarid desert lands with limited water resources and temperature extremes, all under the Arizona sun. Descend 14.2 miles and over 5500ft in elevation and cross the banks of the Colorado River; then climb 7.8 miles and over 4400ft in elevation up the South Rim. Bright Angel is a steeper, longer and more difficult climb but has ample shade and water sources; South Kaibab, the shorter route up the South Rim, travels along an exposed ridgeline with breathtaking views of the canyon, but it lacks shade and water. Hikers should be comfortable with the ruggedness and challenges of backcountry thru-hiking; familiarity with the hazards of desert hiking (dehydration, heat exhaustion, sun exposure) is highly recommended. While the trek can be completed in one day by well-versed thru-hikers, the journey is best covered over several days, allowing time to explore and soak in the surroundings

Arrive at the Grand Canyon Lodge for dinner with a view and a good night's rest. The sweeping canyon views at sunset from Bright Angel Point should not be missed. Day 1 begins before sunrise; embark from the North Kaibab Trail, with tall aspens and ponderosa pines guiding you down red canyon switchbacks. The forested North Rim is especially magical in early October when hints of fall color begin to appear on nearby foliage. Walk through Supai Tunnel, blasted by trail workers in the 1920s, before reaching Roaring Springs,

its waters a cool relief from the sun. One of the most incredible stop-offs along the route lies ahead: Ribbon Falls, hidden in a side canyon a mile off the trail. Encounter waters thundering down on mossy rock from 100ft in the air.

Some of the greatest moments along the route await you deeper into the canyon. Walk the canyon floor along a winding trail, tightly hugging nearby cliffs with glimmers of flora and fauna. Stop and stare as colorful buttes and purple-stained rock formations jut into the desert sky, canyon walls holding thousands of years of ancient Puebloan history seemingly within grasp. 'The Box,' a narrow inner gorge carved by Bright Angel Creek, is the hottest part of the canyon, so plan accordingly: water is available at Cottonwood Campground, Roaring Springs and Supai Tunnel. Cross the malt-hued waters of the Colorado River, which turn emerald green during winter, and begin your ascent. Along this strenuous stretch, rejoice in the many viewpoints; Plateau Point reveals boundless panoramas of the naked canyon rock along a striking series of switchbacks, the myriad shades and textures captivating the eye.

Be met with junipers and ponderosa pines, and know that you have reached the peak of the South Rim. Sore feet and a sense of accomplishment intact, complete this epic tour of the Grand Canyon with dinner at the historic Arizona Room at Bright Angel Lodge, bringing with you memories of sun-splashed canyon walls and dark night skies marked by nothing more than the faded light of nearby stars and the occasional passing cloud. Experiencing this seemingly immovable, water-carved landmark is unforgettable.

Highlights

As the crow flies, it's only 11 miles from the South Rim's Bright Angel Lodge to the North Rim's Grand Canyon Lodge, but it'll take you at least two days by foot on the challenging trails that descend into the canyon, revealing its full majesty.

CAVERNS
Go off the beaten path and explore the Grand Canyon's dry caverns – the largest in the US and located 200–300ft belowground.

GRAND CANYON HISTORY
Delve into the history of the Grand Canyon at one of the park's museums or visitors centers. See 4000-year-old artifacts on display at the Tusayan Museum.

DESERT VIEW WATCHTOWER
Climb atop the 70ft stone watchtower at Desert View Point for panoramic views of the canyon extending 100 miles into the distance.

COLORADO RIVER RAFTING
Book a rafting trip down the Colorado River, its waters spilling over millions of years of history. Adventures range from 3 to 21 days.

WEST RIM CANYONS
Experience the psychedelic pools at Havasupai and Mooney Falls on a four-day backpacking trip through the beautifully carved canyons of the West Rim.

→ Viewing the Colorado River as it winds through the Grand Canyon.

Resources

01 Grand Canyon National Park
www.nps.gov/grca
The National Park Service (NPS) protects, manages and preserves Grand Canyon National Park, ensuring public access is available and enjoyable.

02 Grand Canyon Conservancy
www.grandcanyon.org
The Grand Canyon Conservancy's mission is to protect the site, raise funds and provide educational programs about the history of the region.

03 *Into the Canyon*
This must-see 2016 documentary is about two journalists who travel 750 miles across the length of the Grand Canyon by foot, raising awareness of threats to this treasure.

↑ Cloud-filled Grand Canyon at sunrise. Left: Photographing from Cape Royal at the North Rim of Grand Canyon National Park.

Hike this...

The best way to truly experience the Grand Canyon is to take a hike, whether you tackle the Rim-to-Rim gauntlet or no. If you think the view from the rim is exhilarating, wait until you see how it looks while standing on top of the Redwall, or when you become a tiny speck walking the Tonto Trail.

➔ Hiking on the South Kaibab Trail at the Grand Canyon.

01
West Rim Skywalk

Take a drive to the West Rim, on the Hualapai Reservation, and experience the Grand Canyon from another angle. The Skywalk is a sought-after destination here for good reason. A glass structure extends 70ft over the canyon's edge – 4000ft of only desert air between visitors' feet and the canyon floor. Step out onto the glass floors and enter another world, with miles upon miles of sprawling canyon views in every direction (and no cameras permitted). Another stop,

Guano Point (named after a former bat guano mine), offers fantastic canyon and river views. Post-Skywalk, explore the historic Native American village at Eagle Point, a place where history and heritage are preserved through ancient dwellings and Indigenous songs and dances. The Hualapai Nation administers this part of the canyon, running the shuttle rides and all cultural activities. Short helicopter tours are also offered (for a price). It's a common choice for the time-pressed.

02
Hermit's Rest Route

For visitors looking to connect with the Grand Canyon without the commitment, embark along the South Rim's Hermit's Rest Route – a 7-mile path studded with nine spectacular canyon overlooks, each one more beautiful than the last. During peak season the route must be traveled by foot or on a shuttle bus; the road opens to private vehicles during winter. For a quick jaunt, visit Maricopa Point for stunning canyon views just a little over a mile from Grand Canyon Village.

Sunrises and sunsets are best seen from Hopi Point and Mojave Point, a 3-mile hike to expansive panoramas of the canyon. Pause at the Abyss for vertical vistas plunging 3000ft below. Pima Point offers the best angle to view the Colorado River carving through ancient rock. Equally appealing to both day hikers and backcountry adventurers, parts are quite treacherous, but even just a few minutes' meander down offers a marvelously accessible opportunity to stretch out, relax, and enjoy the canyon in quiet solitude.

03
South Kaibab Trail

Though it's part of the Rim-to-Rim Trail, the South Kaibab Trail isn't just for skilled backcountry hikers. A pretty, well-maintained trail, its trailhead is served by shuttles and it can be walked as a day hike from the South Rim, a fact that can sometimes make it feel like a superhighway in summer. Several viewpoints along this route to the canyon floor provide opportunities for day hikers to experience parts of the Rim-to-Rim Trail that make the journey so special, with short options ideal for hot

summer days.

Ooh-Aah Point, a turnaround and overlook less than a mile from the trailhead, is ideal for escaping the crowds on the South Rim; you may see wildlife along this pathway before reaching the lookout point. For a more strenuous hike, visitors can trek to Cedar Ridge (1.5 miles one-way) or Skeleton Point (3 miles one-way) along a wildflower-studded trail with unforgettable views. Hikers be warned: there is no water access or shade along this hike.

50.

Santa Fe National Historic Trail

The original American highway, this 900-mile trail was traveled by cowboys, traders, soldiers and pioneers in the wild days before the railroad came west.

→ Bent's Old Fort National Historic Site, Colorado.
Right: A horned lark perches on top of a fence in
the Cimarron National Grassland of Kansas.

America hadn't been a country for even 50 years when a debt-riddled trader named William Becknell left Missouri in 1821 to peddle his wares in the northern Mexican province of New Mexico. His trip was so lucrative that he began mapping a better route, using portions of old Indian and Spanish paths. For his troubles Becknell is considered the father of the Santa Fe Trail.

Scores of traders – and later, soldiers, stagecoach travelers, missionaries, gold seekers and others – would follow Becknell. Today you can too. The Santa Fe Trail is a journey into the history of the American West. You'll cross wind-whipped prairie and high desert. You'll sidestep rattlesnakes by day and hear coyotes baying at the stars by night. You'll stop at haunted trading posts and sip coffee at diners alongside working cowboys. You'll see tumbleweeds literally tumbling.

Start your journey in Franklin, Missouri, where Becknell first set out in 1821. There's nothing much to see here, so move along to Boone's Lick State Historic Site, on the bluffs of the Missouri River. It's home to a salt lick – a natural saltwater spring – that supplied salt to settlers in the region in the early 1800s. You can still see an old iron kettle and other artifacts from the salt industry that was once based here.

Cross the wide brown Missouri River and head 70 miles west to Fort Osage, which trail travelers would reach via the old Osage Trace, a Native American footpath. You'll be traveling by highway. On a bluff overlooking the Missouri, the fort was built in 1808 for the protection of the Osage tribes in exchange for some of their lands. It became a major frontier trading post for Native Americans, fur trappers and

Sleep here...

No backcountry camping considerations need plague the Santa Fe National Historic Trail traveler. As it crosses the states of New Mexico, Oklahoma, Colorado, Kansas and Missouri, this auto route passes National Grassland campgrounds, historic hotels, simple cabins and the occasional ranch property. If you're road-tripping, you'll have no trouble finding options in even the smallest towns.

 Silver Heart Inn, Missouri
In the pioneer jumping-off hot spot of Independence, Missouri, this 1856 house saw some of the trail's original travelers embark on their journeys. The B&B's rooms are agreeably old-fashioned, with floral wallpaper and canopy beds.

 Santa Fe Trail Campground, Kansas
You'll find a number of state- and privately-run campsites near the trail, including this pleasant 35-site spot on the forested banks of Council Grove Lake in eastern Kansas.

 Raton Pass Motor Inn, New Mexico
Near the trail's high point amid the Sangre de Cristo Mountains, this welcoming motel in New Mexico works a vintage '50s theme, with cool touches like old typewriters, a jukebox and antler lamps.

 La Fonda on the Plaza, New Mexico
An inn on this site in Santa Fe's Plaza has welcomed road-weary travelers for 400 years. The luxurious Pueblo Revival–style building was built in the 1920s. Expect excellent food and authentic historical details.

mountain men. The wooden buildings are replicas built in the 20th century. Inside are exhibits on the site's frontier past, including information on the Hopewell and Osage cultures.

Driving another 20 minutes takes you to Independence, Missouri, home to the excellent National Frontier Trails Museum. Independence was a major jumping-off point for pioneers headed to Oregon, New Mexico and California; the museum tells their stories with artifacts like calico dresses, worn Bibles and a real covered wagon.

Travel west over the windy prairies, stopping to see historic homes, preserved wagon wheel ruts and other minor trail sites. Cross into Kansas and stop at the redbrick Shawnee Indian Mission State Historic Site, once a trade school for Native American children. The trail's Kansas section has dozens of charmingly creaky small-town museums, old roadhouses, 19th-century saloons and trail-era trading posts. Stop at as many or as few as you like before hitting Cimarron National Grassland in Kansas. Here you'll have a choice to make, just as the original trail travelers did. They could take the Mountain Route north through Colorado, which had dangerous mountain passes but dependable water sources. Or they could go south along New Mexico's shorter Cimarron Cutoff, which had little water and was subject to occasional Indian raids.

For scenery, we recommend the Mountain Route, where you'll cut through the Comanche National Grassland and breathe in the thin air atop Raton Pass in the Sangre de Cristo Mountains on the Colorado–New Mexico border. Descending into New Mexico, you'll explore Wild West

towns like Cimarron and Las Vegas (not the Vegas in Nevada, though!) and skirt the fir and spruce forests of the Pecos Wilderness. Stop for a stretch, a hike or a lungful of cool mountain air. Note that doing the trail via the Mountain Route skips Oklahoma, but the trail cuts through only a small slice of the Panhandle anyway.

Finally you reach Santa Fe, the pot of gold at the end of the rainbow. With its adobe houses, bewitching golden light, and air perfumed by roasted chiles, it's America's oldest and loveliest state capital. Head directly to the Spanish-style central plaza, the trail's official end, where locals have been taking evening strolls since the early 1600s. Order a margarita at one of the surrounding cafes and sip it with satisfaction. Missouri is a memory now, 900 miles behind you.

The Santa Fe Trail irrevocably changed this part of the world. Settlers filled the plains and deserts, building towns and fencing the wilds into private ranches. Native tribes, including the Pawnee, Comanche, Cheyenne, Kiowa and Arapaho, would be displaced, both by force and by the decimation of their food sources, including bison. Borders would change. The trail gave US soldiers a quick route to New Mexico, which was claimed as a US territory in the Mexican-American War of 1846–48. Kansas achieved statehood in 1861.

As the Civil War ended, America turned its energies to railroad expansion. By the early 1870s, three railroad companies were in hot competition to get rail lines over Raton Pass. The winner reached the top in the winter of 1878. By 1880 the railroad reached all the way to Santa Fe. The 'iron horses' replaced the real ones, and the Santa Fe Trail ended for good.

Highlights

For those who like to walk along the old wagon ruts of history, back to a time when finding yourself in this part of the world meant facing a daily fight for survival, driving the Santa Fe Trail is a rewarding opportunity for reflection and contemplation.

ARROW ROCK
This sweet Missouri village was once a thriving river port, one of the launch points for westbound settlers. The entire place is a National Historic Landmark with well-preserved buildings.

SANTA FE
New Mexico's delightful capital is good for days of eating, museum going, gallery visits, hikes and spas. Be sure to try the famous green chile, which locals put on everything.

BENT'S OLD FORT NATIONAL HISTORIC SITE
Natives and settlers came together to trade at this 1833 Colorado post. The reconstructed adobe building gives a taste of the frontier era, and hosts lively events bringing the age to life.

MAHAFFIE STAGECOACH STOP & FARM HISTORIC SITE
In Olathe, Kansas, this homestead once hosted trail travelers, and now holds historical reenactments.

RATON PASS
Crossing this nearly 8000ft pass was the most dangerous part of the trail for travelers on the Mountain Route. Today, thanks to paved roads and a rail line, it's the most scenic.

➡ Picture Canyon, part of the Comanche National Grassland in southeast Colorado.

Resources

O1 **Santa Fe National Historic Trail**
www.nps.gov/safe
The National Park Service's useful website has suggested itineraries and detailed descriptions of trail stops.

O2 **Santa Fe Trail Association**
www.santafetrail.org
This nonprofit is dedicated to protecting and preserving the trail; its website has excellent interactive maps and lots of suggested readings.

O3 *The Santa Fe Trail: Its History, Legends, and Lore*
Historian David Dary brings the trail to life in this 2000 book with first-person accounts from traders, trappers, pioneers and others.

⬆ The Amtrak Southwest Chief near Raton Pass, New Mexico. Left: Trinidad city landmark sign.

Hike this...

From the wild, sun-drenched prairie around Bent's Fort to the high mesas and billowing clouds outside Trinidad on the New Mexico border and the ancient volcanic walls of the twin Spanish Peaks near La Veta, this long-traveled route provides a good mix of history and natural wonder.

➜ Santa Fe's downtown skyline.

01
Kansas City to Council Grove, Kansas

This 125-mile stretch of east Kansas is extremely flat and has little scenic variation, but it's home to some of the most fun and quirky historic sites on the trail. Start in Kansas City, Kansas, adjacent to but separate from Kansas City, Missouri. Stop to gawk at the wagon wheel ruts preserved in the earth at Harmon Park, then hit Mahaffie Stagecoach Stop & Farm Historic Site in Olathe for a quick stagecoach ride. Call it a day with a skillet-fried chicken dinner at Hays House in Council Grove,

the oldest restaurant west of the Mississippi. It was built by legendary frontiersman Daniel Boone's great-grandson in 1857. The next morning, wander Council Grove's pretty brick downtown and check out the Hermit's Cave, once home to an Italian religious mystic who wandered the West trying to convert Native Americans. It's a good place to reflect on the disconnect between the historic site's packaged story of the wild frontier and the cost these legends had on Indigenous peoples.

02
Cimarron Cutoff, Kansas to New Mexico

We've given short shrift to the southern Cimarron Cutoff route, as it's less scenic than the northern Mountain Route. But if you've got time, this route has its own rewards. There's the 108,175-acre Cimarron National Grassland of western Kansas at its start, where the land's so flat you can see storms purpling the horizon hundreds of miles away. Containing 23 miles of the Santa Fe NHT, it's the largest section on public land. Here you'll understand why the trail's other name was the Great Prairie Highway.

There's also Autograph Rock in Oklahoma, where passing travelers on other historic trails chiseled their names in the sandstone. The oldest name is T Potts, from 1806. After entering New Mexico, stop at historic McNees Crossing, a popular trail campground where wagon ruts are still visible in the reddish dirt. Then there's the Kiowa National Grassland, a vast shortgrass prairie with patches of piñon-juniper woodland and sagebrush. The southern and northern trails rejoin by the town of Watrous, New Mexico.

03
Raton Pass to Santa Fe, New Mexico

The New Mexico portion of the trail is relatively short; driving from point to point takes about 3½ hours. But it's one of the richest sections in terms of natural beauty and historic interest. Start at Raton Pass, the 7834ft mountain crossing between Colorado and New Mexico. From here, descend into the high desert of northern New Mexico, a land of silvery sagebrush and piñon, of pink-gold dawns and heart-piercing sunsets that seem to last hours. Highlights include Las Vegas, a classic Old

West town of saloons and faded hotels. The trail passed directly through the town's central plaza.

Outside Santa Fe, the Pecos National Historical Park features the remarkable ruins of Pecos Pueblo, begun by the Pecos people nearly 1000 years ago. La Cueva Mill is also in the state; the preserved 1870s adobe mill 6 miles east of Mora originally provided flour for travelers on the Santa Fe Trail. Today it's a National Historic Site, although you can only view it from the exterior.

51

Selma to Montgomery National Historic Trail

A National Historic Trail since 1996, this somber commemorative path honors the 1965 coalition of nonviolent protesters who overcame great opposition to make a highly symbolic march across Alabama.

→ Statue of Martin Luther King Jr in Kelly Ingram Park, Birmingham. Right: The Edmund Pettus Bridge in Selma, Alabama, the Bloody Sunday site.

The events of March 1965 in Selma, Alabama, galvanized public support for the civil rights movement and led to the passage of the Voting Rights Act of 1965 and its signing by President Lyndon B Johnson. It took two attempts, three weeks of negotiation and an intervention by the National Guard before thousands of peaceful protesters were able to successfully walk the 54 miles between Selma and Montgomery in support of voting rights for African Americans. As with all civil rights victories, though, the path to success was paved with loss and struggle.

Today the path of the Selma to Montgomery march is a National Historic Trail, albeit one that is better traced by car than on foot. Both cities, and the stretch of highway between them, contain landmarks and museums that are must-sees for those who want to understand how the struggles of the past have shaped the conflicts of the present. Though the 54 miles of the trail can be easily driven in an afternoon, it's best to spend at least a night in the region to allow time to visit a few museums – or even fit in a trip to neighboring Birmingham, where the 16th Street Baptist Church and Birmingham Civil Rights Institute bear witness to the many heroes of the movement.

Begin, as the marchers did, in Selma, starting point for the dramatic march to Montgomery, the state capital. The Student Nonviolent Coordinating Committee (SNCC), Southern Christian Leadership Conference (SCLC) and local activists wanted to make a statement about the need to protect voting rights, which the Civil Rights Act of 1964 failed to compel southern states to do. Thanks to poll taxes,

Sleep here...

In general, Montgomery and Selma's hotel scenes include some cheaper, solid chain options; other forms of accommodation are thinner on the ground for now (hopefully Selma's historic St James Hotel will eventually reopen). You may want to try couchsurfing or services like Airbnb to connect with local hosts and get more of an intimate sense of life here in Alabama's Black Belt.

Lattice Inn, Montgomery
Friendly hosts, lush landscaping and cozy vintage furnishings await guests at this highly recommended B&B in Montgomery, only 2 miles from downtown.

DoubleTree by Hilton Downtown Montgomery
Yes, it's a chain (as are most options in Selma and Montgomery), but this DoubleTree stands out for its attractive rooms and pet-friendly policy.

Red Bluff Cottage Bed & Breakfast, Montgomery
The well-furnished B&B in Montgomery offers a huge organic breakfast as well as comfortable rooms, each with its own theme.

Elyton Hotel, Birmingham
In a 1909 building in Birmingham, this stylishly renovated boutique hotel is a 1½-hour drive from Montgomery. The rooftop bar, Moon Shine, is one of the best places in town for a drink.

Toolbox

When to go
The trail is open year-round, although only those accustomed to extreme heat should attempt it in July and August, the height of a humid Alabama summer. Spring is the state's loveliest season: azaleas, dogwoods and forsythias begin to flower as early as March, when an annual reenactment of the 1965 march takes place.

Getting there
Selma and Montgomery are in south central Alabama, an area known as the 'Black Belt' thanks to its fertile black topsoil. Most of the trail is along US 80, which ranges from two to four lanes between the two cities. The closest major airport is in Birmingham, just over an hour's drive away.

Practicalities
Length in miles: 54
Start: Selma, AL
End: Montgomery, AL
Dog friendly: Not allowed at historic sites
Bike friendly: It's possible to bike the route; local bike groups sometimes hold rides
Permit needed: No
States covered: Alabama

literacy tests and other voter suppression strategies, only 2% of the black voters in Selma were registered to vote. The march was also in honor of activist Jimmie Lee Jackson, killed by an Alabama state trooper during a peaceful protest the month before.

The National Voting Rights Museum and Institute in Selma tells the story of how the march was organized, explores the many ways that racist laws kept black citizens from the polls, and profiles many of the movement's organizers. Plan to spend at least an hour here before you start your trip. The museum is at the foot of Edmund Pettus Bridge, where, on March 7, 1965, police armed with billy clubs and tear gas confronted the approximately 600 peaceful marchers, pushing them back into the city. The resulting violence became known as Bloody Sunday, and it was caught on video by the TV crews on-site to cover the march. Men and women were viciously beaten by police, and at least 50 people were hospitalized. When the images of bloodstained bodies and tear-streaked faces were broadcast, they outraged the nation and the world, and made it impossible to deny the terrorism directed at black citizens in their own country.

A second march, led by Dr Martin Luther King, Jr, was attempted on March 9. The nonviolent protesters were again blocked by police, and this time they turned back before law enforcement could advance. Still, tensions were so high that a group of white locals attacked three Unitarian ministers who had come to Alabama to join the march. One of them, Reverend James Reeb, died from his wounds two days later.

The marchers didn't give up. King was granted an injunction for the march, and

the federal government mobilized the National Guard to protect the nonviolent protesters. On March 21, 1965, a third, successful march was launched, one that was able to make it all the way to the state capitol in Montgomery.

Once you're outside of Selma, there's not much to see along US 80. The highway alternates between two and four lanes, and the area is sparsely populated. In 1965 there were supporters offering food and drink, as well as jeering counter-protesters, for some 8000 marchers to encounter along the way. The four nights on the road were spent at campsites on privately owned land, all prearranged by the organizers. The first three campsites are still privately owned, with only a sign to mark their significance.

About one-third of the way into the march, you'll find the Lowndes Interpretive Center. This small museum houses exhibits on the events that happened in Lowndes County at the time of the march, including the murder of Viola Liuzzo, killed for driving marchers to Selma. Just outside of Montgomery is the City of St Jude. Protesters spent their last night on the march here, revved up by the Stars for Freedom concert organized by superstar Harry Belafonte.

Finish your trip in downtown Montgomery, outside the state capitol. When the tired but exhilarated marchers reached this spot on March 25, 1965, they joined a crowd of 25,000 to hear King deliver his 'How Long, Not Long' speech from the marble steps of this Greek Revival building. Take time to visit the Dexter Avenue King Memorial Baptist Church, where King preached, and the National Memorial for Peace and Justice.

Highlights

No movement has challenged the United States to live up to its highest ideals, while tempting its worst demons, like the battle for civil rights. The fight is not one contained narrative, but a series of episodes, many of which can be found on this historic trail.

NATIONAL MEMORIAL FOR PEACE AND JUSTICE
Harrowing in its stark simplicity, this memorial in Montgomery is the first in the US to honor the 4400 known victims of lynching.

CIVIL RIGHTS MEMORIAL CENTER
Maya Lin designed the monument at the entrance to this Montgomery museum that tells the stories of 40 people who died in the struggle for civil rights. Many of the murders remain unsolved.

DEXTER PARSONAGE MUSEUM
The home of Dr Martin Luther King, Jr and Coretta Scott King during their time in Montgomery has been carefully preserved, including King's extensive library, and is near King Memorial Baptist Church.

NATIONAL VOTING RIGHTS MUSEUM AND INSTITUTE
This Selma museum contextualizes civil rights history, including the Montgomery bus boycotts led by Rosa Parks.

EDMUND PETTUS BRIDGE
This bridge in Selma, mainly used by cars, was the backdrop for the Bloody Sunday confrontation between nonviolent protesters and police armed with clubs and tear gas.

52

Sierra High Route

For a rugged, adventurous alternative to the John Muir Trail, consider this 195-mile California route above the tree line in the highest corners of the Sierra Nevada.

→ Twin Falls and Upper Twin Lake, Mammoth Mountain Lakes Basin, Inyo National Forest, California. Right: Dusy Basin and the Palisades, Kings Canyon National Park, Sierra Nevada, California.

Reach the top of the 12,000ft Potluck Pass and the peaks of the Sierra Nevada ripple away in all directions, for once no longer above you but right at eye level.

It has been a hard climb here, up crumbling talus slopes and over SUV-sized boulders, often on your hands and knees, your chest heaving in the thin, high-altitude air. This is a harsh environment of elemental rock and ice, far above the soft meadows and sparkling lakes of the valley below. It feels amazing to have made it to the pass. But this is just one of more than 30 such passes on your route, most of them, like this one, at the end of long, unforgettable scrambles in terrain with no signs or trail. This is the peaceful, rugged Sierra High Route (SHR), like the busy lower-altitude John Muir Trail (p138) put on steroids.

The SHR is a walk through the wilder side of the high Sierra, paralleling the John Muir and Pacific Crest Trails for much of its distance but keeping to higher elevations and continually veering off to follow the timberline, rarely dipping below 10,000ft. In many ways it's a lighter-traveled version of the JMT, sometimes routing just a few miles away from that trail but over harder, higher and more rugged ground – and therefore it's almost completely devoid of people. (It's also much easier to get a permit for, not coincidentally; just pick one up in Kings Canyon National Park at the Roads End Permit Station.)

Starting in Kings Canyon National Park and winding north to Yosemite and beyond, the route traverses two national parks, three wilderness areas, one national monument, 33 named passes and 11 major divides. It's not just off the beaten path – it's off any kind of path. Less than half of the total 195 miles

© Citizen of the Planet / Alamy Stock Photo; Right: Tomas Tichy / Shutterstock

Sleep here...

By and large, few official campsites await you over these high-altitude miles, making those options that appear seem like a wondrous mirage. Apart from these, it's all about Leave No Trace principles, careful campsite selection and exercising respect for nature on this untouched route.

Tuolumne Meadows Lodge
This lodge in Yosemite National Park has 69 canvas cabins with showers and stoves but no electricity. The Grill offers reviving cheeseburgers, and there's also a campground nearby.

Vogelsang High Sierra Camp
The collection of 12 tent cabins is the highest of Yosemite's five wilderness camps, offering meals but no showers, and there's a camping area for backpackers. Cabins are reservable by lottery in October.

Wilderness Camping
Dozens of stunning possible campsites entice from pristine mountain lakes along the trail, and unlike on the packed nearby John Muir Trail, you'll have them entirely to yourself. Be sure to Leave No Trace.

Parchers Resort
The resort requires a day's detour from the main route, over Bishop Pass to South Lake, but offers 20 cabins and a restaurant; Parchers will hold resupply buckets.

Toolbox

When to go
The months of July to mid-October are best. Before mid-July you'll find lots of snow. August has dramatic scenery, with snow at higher elevations but also mosquitoes. September and early October offer the best conditions, but snowstorms can arrive at any time after mid-September.

Getting there
From Fresno airport in California, it's a 90-mile drive to Copper Creek trailhead near Kanawyers; organize a shuttle. From the end point near Mono Village, you'll need to get 13 miles to Bridgeport, where Eastern Sierra Transit Authority buses run 110 miles to Reno airport.

Practicalities
Length in miles: 195
Start: Copper Creek trailhead at Roads End Permit Station, Kings Canyon National Park, CA
End: Twin Lakes, near Mono Village, CA
Dog friendly: No
Bike friendly: No
Permit needed: Yes, for backcountry access; pick up at Roads End
States covered: California

Cross-country skiing on Lower Twin
Lake in Mammoth Lakes, California.

is on an actual trail. The majority of the time you are navigating cross-country, finding your own way through massive glacier-scoured basins, sun-cupped snowfields and high alpine tundra.

It's this uncompromising terrain that makes the SHR such a tough proposition. You'll need strong boots and good-gripping soles to help you over unstable rockslides and talus slopes, and good poles to aid tension-filled descents over slopes with scree the size of ball bearings. High crossings like Stanton Pass and Frozen Lake Pass involve hands-on Class 3 scrambling, so you'll need to bring something to protect your hands, not just your feet.

Daily distance in this shattered mountain landscape is measured not in horizontal miles covered but in vertical ascent gained and basins crossed. The trail demands total engagement as you employ all your wilderness navigation and map skills to make your own route decisions and ensure your own safety. It's as much a mental challenge as it is physical. At the end of most days, you will reach camp bruised and exhausted. And grinning like a lunatic.

The ambitious route was first conceived and scouted by climber Steve Roper in 1977 and then publicized through his book *Sierra High Route: Traversing Timberline Country*, still a must-read guide to the trail and the only 'official' resource available on it. Every year a few hard-core adventurers tackle the entire monthlong trail in one bite, but the majority cover it in four main sections, resupplying and resting several times en route. From the typical starting point at Roads End in Kings Canyon, it's a five- to seven-day (40-mile) section to Dusy Basin, where a day's hike can detour across Bishop Pass down to Parchers Resort by South Lake, so you can pick up a resupply or catch a ride to the town of Bishop.

The second section onward from Dusy Basin winds for three to four days (42 miles) to sprawling Lake Italy. From here a second resupply or potential exit beckons, a day's walk away at Vermilion Valley Resort. You can also continue for another three to four days (37 miles) to Red's Meadow for an on-route resupply. From here things become a bit easier, with a four- to five-day section dropping you in beautiful, bustling Tuolumne Meadows in Yosemite National Park for another resupply; then it's a final three-day (28-mile) roller-coaster ride to the finish point at Twin Lakes.

It's hard to pin down specific highlights on such a scenically wondrous trek. The high, lake-filled bowls of the Upper, Palisades, Dusy, Evolution and Humphreys Basins in the first half of the walk are legendary. The climbs over Glacier Divide, Silver Divide and Mt Ritter are all wonderful too, as are the relatively relaxing sections of the John Muir Trail, notably through pretty LeConte Canyon. Large parts of the SHR involve easy walking over granite slabs and subalpine meadows, camping near groves of whitebark pine amid communities of mouselike pikas or fat-bellied marmots. In such a fragile, stripped-back environment, the principles of Leave No Trace are morally imperative.

The Sierra High Route is not for inexperienced backpackers unused to off-trail travel. But if you are an experienced trekker who wants to get beyond the routine maintained and signed trails, who loves the high country and is looking for one of the Lower 48's biggest adventures, this crazy route might just be for you.

Highlights

With fierce granite mountains standing watch over high-altitude lakes, the Sierra Nevada is a formidable but exquisite topographic barrier enclosing magnificent natural landscapes and an adventurer's wonderland. And this is its ultimate challenge.

EVOLUTION BASIN
The stunning line of Evolution, Sapphire and Wanda Lakes makes for a scenic springboard to Snow-Tongue Pass.

BEAR LAKES BASIN
Impressive Feather Pass leads to this remote basin, featuring Bearpaw, Ursa, Black Bear, White Bear, Brown Bear and even Teddy Bear Lakes.

PALISADES LAKES
Following the JMT, the trail drops down from views at Mather Pass to reach these two charming lakes below the Palisade peaks.

JOHN MUIR TRAIL
The SHR follows the JMT for around 30 miles over Mather and Muir Passes, offering the novelty of walking on a proper trail.

HIGH PASSES
There are 33 high points on the trail, some of them scary scrambles, others easy crossings; all offer incredible views.

53

Star-Spangled Banner National Historic Trail

Hike, bike and sail through the past on this trail that focuses on the War of 1812 and includes stops in richly historic Baltimore and Washington, DC.

Fort McHenry in Baltimore, Maryland. Right: The tall ship *Cisne Branco* from Brazil moored at Baltimore's Inner Harbor for a celebration of the 200th anniversary of the War of 1812.

Compared to other historic trails, some of which cover thousands of miles, the Star-Spangled Banner National Historic Trail can appear modest at first glance. It is only 560 miles – mostly in Maryland, though with portions in Virginia and the District of Columbia – and 373 of those miles are water routes. Despite its compact size, the trail fits a remarkable amount of history into its short length, as many key moments in America's early story played out on the Chesapeake Bay.

The namesake of the trail, the US national anthem, was written during the War of 1812, when the new nation's independence was tested by the country it had defeated in the American Revolution, the UK. Francis Scott Key, an American lawyer and sometime poet, was aboard a British ship on September 13, 1814. After dining with its officers (he was negotiating the release of an American civilian), they decided he should spend the night as a security precaution; he had learned details of British plans to bombard Baltimore's Fort McHenry. When he awoke the next morning to see the American flag still flying – showing that the fort had survived the assault – he was moved to write the verses that would become 'The Star-Spangled Banner,' and which give this National Historic Trail its name.

The trail, however, includes many more sites than Fort McHenry and covers a broader swath of history than just the War of 1812. Alexandria, Virginia, which is on a branch of the trail, was founded in 1749; some landmarks there, such as Carlyle House and Christ Church, where George Washington's family had a pew, are older than the US. The city of Havre de Grace on

Sleep here...

Prices are reasonable at Baltimore's stylish boutique hotels, though overnight parking fees increase the cost, and Annapolis and the Eastern Shore shine with quaint inns and historic hotels. Meanwhile, many DC lodgings are imbued with history that few other American cities can match: when rooms here are called the 'Roosevelt suite,' it's because Teddy actually slept in them. The best digs are monuments of opulence.

 Camping in Point Lookout State Park, Maryland
This point at Chesapeake Bay's entrance was used by Americans to monitor British ships, at least until the British seized it in 1814. Today this Maryland park has 146 campsites and six camper cabins.

 Hay-Adams Hotel, Washington, DC
Facing the White House across Lafayette Park, this hotel couldn't have a better location. Its bar is a favorite of Washington insiders, and President Obama slept at the hotel.

 Inn at Perry Cabin, Maryland
This Eastern Shore hotel in St Michaels, on 26 acres of waterfront property, is luxurious in a decidedly unpretentious way. It was originally a farm, established shortly after the War of 1812.

 Historic Inns of Annapolis, Maryland
These three inns under the same management date back to the 17th and 18th centuries. Maryland's capital feels like a living history museum, making the inns fitting places to spend a night.

Toolbox

 When to go
Annapolis, Baltimore, and Washington, DC, can be enjoyed in every season, but the Chesapeake Bay is especially wonderful in summer (though humid). However, that isn't an insider secret: keep in mind that millions of Americans flock to the area in July and August.

 Getting there
If you are flying in, it's easy to reach either end of the trail from Washington, DC's Dulles or Ronald Reagan airports as well as Baltimore's Baltimore/Washington International Airport (BWI).

Practicalities
Length in miles: 560 (187 on land)
Start: Solomons, MD
End: Baltimore, MD
Dog friendly: Yes, in portions
Bike friendly: Yes, in portions
Permit needed: Yes, some campgrounds
States covered: Maryland, Washington, DC, Virginia

➡ Sunrise through the lens of Concord Point Lighthouse in Havre de Grace, Maryland.

the trail in Maryland was also established in the Colonial era, though one of the most fascinating periods in its history was when it was an important stop on the Underground Railroad.

Unlike most historic trails, much of this one is on the water, which is fitting given its focus. The War of 1812 was a naval war that started with a blockade of the US, and many of its most important battles were fought at sea. The Chesapeake Bay was destined to be a flash point, as it was the route to Maryland's capital, Annapolis; the US capital, just up the Potomac River; and Baltimore, one of the young country's major ports. Some of the trail's sites, like Tangier Island, Virginia, (a British base of operations during the war) in the bay, can be reached only by boat. It famously became a destination for many slaves who, in the eyes of British law, became free men and women the moment they set foot on this outpost of the empire.

The land portion of the trail can be divided into three parts, along with some additional nearby destinations. The stretch of the trail south of Washington, DC, includes the Calvert Marine Museum in Solomons, Maryland, which provides an introduction to the bay's ecology and wildlife and offers river cruises on two vintage workboats. To its north, St Leonard's Creek was the site of the largest naval confrontation in the Chesapeake theater of the war, between a ragtag group of American ships and the Royal Navy: it pretty much ended in a draw. Croom and Upper Marlboro in Maryland date from the Colonial era, and the latter was occupied by British forces during the war.

In the capital of Washington, DC, sites on the trail include the White House, the original of which was burned by British forces in 1814; and the Octagon House, where President Madison moved until it could be rebuilt. The Francis Scott Key Memorial park in Georgetown is near the site of his family's home from circa 1805 to 1830 (the house is no longer standing). You can also see the famous Star-Spangled Banner itself, the oversize flag designed to be a provocative act of defiance, at the National Museum of American History on the National Mall.

After leaving the capital, head north to the end of the trail, Baltimore. Fort McHenry was built from 1798 to 1800 to defend the port of Baltimore. It proved successful on September 13–14, 1814, the night it resisted the assault by the British. The Fort McHenry Visitor and Education Center, in an environmentally innovative building, has displays that cover Francis Scott Key's life and the war.

The Star-Spangled Banner Trail also includes some sites that aren't on the land-based trail itself, like historic Annapolis, perhaps America's most charming state capital and home of the US Naval Academy. The Chesapeake Bay Maritime Museum is in St Michaels, a small fishing village reborn as a resort town.

Beyond the historical significance of its sites, this part of the mid-Atlantic is stunningly beautiful. Gracious estates reach the water's edge, parts of the Eastern Shore can feel lost in time, and you can end a satisfying day of touring with a cold drink and a basket of soft-shell crabs. Rather than following this as an end-to-end journey with a distinct start and finish, wend your way across the region, making ample use of waterways to explore by paddle or boat, and see why it was the key strategic zone of the war of 1812.

Highlights

The War of 1812 and its Chesapeake Campaign sometimes gets lost in the shuffle between the War of Independence and the Civil War conflagration, yet its rich history is worth rediscovering at these key sites.

GREENBELT PARK
This remarkable urban oasis in Maryland with 9 miles of trails and 174 campsites sits just 10 miles from downtown DC. It was newly renovated in the first half of 2020.

PATUXENT RIVER PARK
In August 1814, 45 British ships sailed up the Patuxent River to invade Washington. The 7500-acre Maryland park in Upper Marlboro is quieter today; it's a scenic place for a kayak excursion.

HAVRE DE GRACE
This Maryland town was almost the country's capital, losing to Washington, DC, by a single vote in Congress. Today its historic district draws travelers with about 1000 buildings in a range of styles.

FORT HOWARD PARK, BALTIMORE
The largest invasion of the US ever took place here in September 1814 when 7000 British troops landed before quickly returning to their ships when faced with resistance.

KENT ISLAND BIKE TRAILS
Kent Island off Maryland's Eastern Shore has 28 miles of bike trails for exploring on two wheels. Try the Cross Island Trail.

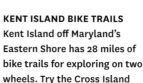

54

Superior Hiking Trail

Minnesota's premier trail runs parallel to Lake Superior for 310 miles and features stunning views of the lake, dramatic waterfalls and Split Rock Lighthouse, along with some of the North Shore's best camping.

Canoes on the rocky shore of a lake in the Boundary Waters Canoe Area Wilderness, accessible off the Border Route Trail extension. Right: The top of Oberg Mountain.

Like a lot of Minnesota, the state's Superior Hiking Trail (SHT) just wants you to have a nice time. You don't need to push yourself too hard, though you can, and you don't need to worry about what anyone else thinks – though if you're from Minnesota, that's a hard habit to break. This trail is good for everyone, accommodating hikers of all skill levels: families, adventurers, day hikers and thru-hikers.

Changing elevations (you can traverse the shore of Lake Superior to the cliffs that overlook the lake) are the biggest topographical concern, while most of the other challenges come with the elements. Mosquitoes and ticks are problematic during the thick of summer, and winter weather makes it dangerous for those who hope to thru-hike or camp from November through April. But with each challenge comes rewards: there are wild blueberries and raspberries that can only be found on the trail in midsummer. Some would argue that these alone are worth putting up with summer pests. Winter on the trail, meanwhile, provides a bright, crisp silence unlikely to be found anywhere else.

You don't need to hike all 310 miles of the SHT to know that the trail is a monument to Minnesota's core values: being a good sport, avoiding anything 'spendy,' and not being too 'showy.'

Minnesotan 'good sports' made the SHT. Those hiking the trail are often surprised to learn that they may be older than the trail itself, which dates only from 1986 when a group of naturalists, community members and local Department of Natural Resources (DNR) officials plotted out the trail sections. Good sports continue to maintain the trail, which is pristine, from the well-

Sleep here...

The North Shore region on Lake Superior has several one-of-a-kind properties, such as a hotel in a repurposed train and a lodge that used to be Babe Ruth's private club. Prices typically are midrange. Most of the state parks have campgrounds for both tents and RVs where sites cost $18 to $25. Lots of weekend, summer and fall traffic makes reservations essential for all accommodations. Smaller places close out of season.

Camping on the SHT
Using SHT-designated campsites ensures you don't have to worry about paying a park fee or being without water; there are mats, hammock hooks and backcountry latrines. Campsites are all near water.

Cascade Lodge
Watch the sun rise over Lake Superior in this North Shore base camp. Choose a cabin or a suite in the lodge, or rent one of the luxury homes. All the views are similar, and all are spectacular. The restaurant features a favorite Canadian import: poutine.

Superior Gateway Lodge
This happy log cabin lodge in Two Harbors has gleaming rooms and amenities that make even serious campers think twice about sleeping outside. Enjoy jetted tubs, a farm-to-table organic breakfast and a clean community kitchen for trail snack preparation.

Lutsen Resort
For those who appreciate the rigors of nature, but only to a point, the North Shore's Lutsen Resort is a haven. Accommodations range from rooms in the lodge to condos, villas and log cabins. It's dog friendly.

Toolbox

When to go
The trail is meticulously maintained and accessible year-round, though larger groups crowd it in summer. Winter on the trail is breathtaking but is not for inexperienced hikers. September is stellar. Whenever you go, get a copy of the wonderful *Guide to the Superior Hiking Trail*, one of the best trail guides in existence.

Getting there
Access the Superior Hiking Trail via any of the trailheads located every 3 to 11 miles along the trail. The largest city near the trail is Duluth, also home to the nearest airport. The city is about a 15-minute drive from the trail.

Practicalities
Length in miles: 310 miles (plus 16 miles of spur trail if section hiked)
Start: Jay Cooke State Park near Duluth, MN
End: The US–Canada border west of Grand Portage, MN
Dog friendly: Yes; leash required
Bike friendly: Only in marked sections of state parks
Permit needed: No
States covered: Minnesota

➡ Temperance River State Park holds a spur trail to the Superior Hiking Trail.

kept boardwalks and bridges right down to the backcountry latrines available at the campsites. Spendy isn't an issue, as the trail is free to use, including free parking at the trailheads, and there are no fees for camping at SHT campsites.

The showy part, however, is tricky for the Superior Hiking Trail. It has been ranked time and time again as a Top 10 North American hike. This trail is universally loved for its sights: gorgeous views of Lake Superior, a lighthouse that rivals any coastal competitors, and brilliant fall colors. Yet the trail rewards close attention; it doesn't gaudily grab you. The SHT and its attractions are marked, but they still require diligence. If you're not careful, you might miss a waterfall bustling on its way to Lake Superior or a particularly spectacular view.

One of the best things about the SHT is how easy it is to access. With most trails, you resign yourself to hiking half the distance you'd like to hike and then turning back, or else you bring two cars and leave one at the beginning and one at the end point. The SHT, though, has shuttle services. Whether it's Minnesota nice shining through or a profound call to share the SHT with everyone, shuttles (small fee) are available to take you to where you'd like to begin your hike. Even before you start, the enthusiasm of your shuttle driver will kick things off right. If you weren't excited to go on your hike before, driver extraordinaire Harriet will change that.

However you arrive at the start of your hike, be prepared to be wowed. At Judge CR Magney State Park, the scent of pine, spruce, and tamaracks is intoxicating. A stop at the famous Devil's Kettle Falls is a must, even if its great mystery has been solved. For years no one could explain why one of the forked branches of the river fell over the rocks and continued on its way as expected, while the other one fell into a rock hole halfway down. The seemingly bottomless vortex created by the so-called Devil's Kettle is thrilling, even if we now know that the water rejoins the rest of the river farther downstream. Hold on to your camera and your imagination, as both can get sucked into the water and be lost to the dark depths of Lake Superior.

At the right time of year, the SHT outshines any possible competition. One section, near Temperance River State Park, has so many ash trees that their golden leaves carpet the forest floor. The falls are also beautiful here, and Moose Mountain, a peak of Minnesota's Sawtooth Mountains, rewards those who scale it with the Summit Chalet, a cafe serving Minnesota staples like walleye. (The view from here is pretty great too.)

For those with FOMO, rest easy: There is no wrong part of the SHT. Even the sections that go through dense Duluth feature great views of Superior and its rocky shore. Farther up the trail, rivers, falls, scenic views and gorges are almost guaranteed; only their size and location differ. Wildlife can be tough to find beyond the trees, which change from oak, maple and basswood in the southern sections to balsam firs, pines, spruces, cedars and tamaracks further north. Maple ridges are also present throughout the trail, great for fall foliage watchers. Songbirds are usually heard, if not seen. Visitors who find themselves in the right place at the right time, however, can spot black bears, beavers, eagles and even the occasional Minnesotan moose.

Highlights

Trekking north from Duluth, follow a series of state parks with their own unique delights. You'll find twisting gorges and dramatic waterfalls at Gooseberry Falls and Temperance River State Parks, leading to a lonely lighthouse at Split Rock close by Two Harbors.

GOOSEBERRY FALLS STATE PARK
The five cascades, scenic gorge and easy trails draw carloads of visitors to Gooseberry Falls State Park. Several CCC buildings dot the premises.

DULUTH
The region's biggest city and port, Duluth, for decades, shipped the iron ore that fueled mills throughout the Midwest. You can still see the old ships here.

GRAND MARAIS
From artsy Grand Marais, the Superior Hiking Trail hugs the lake northward from Two Harbors. The town itself is a delight, with a naturally protected harbor that softens the waves.

SPLIT ROCK
The lighthouses of the East Coast have nothing on Split Rock. Get the best views of the beacon on the 4.4-mile loop trail.

TEMPERANCE RIVER STATE PARK
Follow the trails through the crashing Temperance River Gorge and up to Carlton Peak. In winter, snowshoeing takes center stage.

55

Tahoe Rim Trail

This two-week walk around beautiful Lake Tahoe in Nevada and California is a great first thru-hike, with the stunning 'Big Blue' never far from your shoulder.

➔ Sunset along the Tahoe Rim Trail. Right: Lake Tahoe framed by large granite boulders on the Tahoe Rim Trail.

The 165-mile Tahoe Rim Trail treks the lofty ridges of the Lake Tahoe Basin. Day hikers, equestrians and – in some sections – mountain bikers are rewarded by high-altitude views of the lake and Sierra Nevada peaks while tracing the footsteps of early pioneers, Basque shepherds and Washoe tribespeople. Stand below Nevada's South Camp Peak on a glorious summer day, and the views over the immense cobalt waters of Lake Tahoe are simply mesmerizing. At times the waters are framed by stands of fragrant Jeffrey pine, at others by the primary yellows of a field of mule's ear flowers. Wherever you stand, it's hard to pry your eyes away from the lake.

As might be expected, those lake views are the one thing you can count on when hiking the two-week Tahoe Rim Trail. The route follows the mountain flanks and ridgelines that encircle the continent's largest alpine lake; if you hike the trail clockwise, the lake will always be just over your right shoulder. For large parts of the walk, you can see your entire two-week itinerary laid out in one panorama, a view so huge that it feels as if you can see the crystal-clear waters bending with the curvature of the earth.

The stats of the Tahoe Rim Trail (TRT) are impressive: it takes in two mountain ranges (California's Sierra Nevada and Nevada's Carson Range), two national forests, three wilderness areas and two states, completely encircling the two-million-year-old Tahoe Basin and merging with the Pacific Crest Trail for 50 glorious miles. The terrain en route varies from forests of red fir and ponderosa pine to dramatic granite basins and stunning alpine tarns, but ultimately this hike is all about the

Sleep here...

Camping in Desolation Wilderness is by permit only, either reserved online at www.recreation.gov or picked up in person at one of the three USFS offices in South Lake Tahoe and Pollock Pines. In Lake Tahoe Nevada State Park, stick within the free established campgrounds. There's an array of lovely lodges on the north shore, plus an excellent hostel. Alpine charm is a keynote of Lake Tahoe's accommodations, from luxury places with spas to rustic log cabins.

Sorensen's Resort, California
Just off the southeastern corner of the trail and set in beautiful grounds, Sorensen's Resort has good food, cozy log cabins and a wood-fired sauna to revive those tired legs.

Granlibakken Tahoe, California
Splash out at this wellness retreat in Tahoe City, California, that offers a hearty hot buffet breakfast and a pool, spa and hot tub. It often holds resupply packages for free.

Mt Rose Campground, Nevada
This Forest Service campground on the northeast corner of the loop in Nevada has modest luxuries such as a vault toilet and running water, which you'll appreciate after a week of backpacking.

Dispersed Camping
Thru-hikers can camp almost anywhere within 300 yards of the Tahoe Rim Trail, giving you wonderful flexibility. In Lake Tahoe Nevada State Park, you can camp only at the established campgrounds of Marlette Peak, Hobart and North Canyon.

© Dalton Johnson / Shutterstock; © aaronjg / Shutterstock

Toolbox

When to go
The summer months of July to September are best, normally bringing reliably perfect California weather. Snowpack has generally cleared by the end of June but can linger. Water sources are most reliable earlier in the season.

Getting there
Lake Tahoe is an hour's drive from Reno-Tahoe airport in Nevada; a shuttle bus runs from the airport to South Lake Tahoe in California. You can start the trail at any of nine major trailheads, though most choose Kingsbury (Nevada), Echo Lakes or Tahoe City (both in California).

Practicalities
Length in miles: 165
Start: Any of nine major trailheads in CA or NV
End: Same as start if completing the circuit
Dog friendly: Yes, on leash
Bike friendly: Yes, outside of wilderness areas
Permit needed: Only in Desolation Wilderness
States covered: Nevada, California

lake. Hikers circle the water like Buddhist pilgrims; all that's missing is a string of prayer flags.

The Tahoe Rim Trail is a fun, forgiving trail. An ideal first thru-hike, it's long enough to challenge you physically and leave you with a sense of achievement, but free from the logistical hassles and tiresome sections that can mar tougher, more remote trails. The circular nature of the trail frees you from complicated vehicle shuttles, and the choice of nine major trailheads means that you can start the loop anywhere and hike in either direction. Even permits are a cinch; only the Desolation Wilderness demands an overnight permit, and even there thru-hikers are waived through the daily quota system.

It's also a great trail for rewarding yourself with the occasional luxury. Communities like South Lake Tahoe and Tahoe Vista lie just a short hitchhike or drive from several trailheads and allow you to swap the tent occasionally for a hot shower and a night in a soft bed. The TRT even leads right through Tahoe City, taking you less than a half mile from a supermarket and a fresh salad. The Brewery at Lake Tahoe ups the ante further by tempting hikers with a cold Alpine Amber Ale just 5 miles from the Kingsbury trailhead. This is how hiking was meant to be.

True trail heretics don't even have to camp at all if they don't want to. The circuit can feasibly be tackled as a series of 14 different day hikes, each ranging from 6 to 22 miles in length, allowing you to chip away at the loop over as much time as you want. And if you are nervous about tackling your first long-distance hike, the Tahoe Rim Trail Association runs guided thru-hikes and segment hikes for those organized

enough to sign up months in advance.

Ironically for a trail that offers continual views of the nation's second-deepest lake, the only logistical complication you might face is finding water. Particularly on the eastern section, you need to keep an eye on your next water source and maybe even cache a few gallons somewhere like the Spooner Summit trailhead in Nevada.

Needless to say, Tahoe scenery is epic. The northern trail section through Nevada's Humboldt-Toiyabe National Forest traverses the airy ridges and ancient lava flows of the Mt Rose Wilderness, cresting at 10,338ft Relay Peak, with an option to make a 1.5-mile detour to an even higher viewpoint at Mt Houghton. Sunsets over the lake from Picnic Rock to the west (in California) are legendary.

On the eastern side the spur at Christopher's Loop takes in almost the entire Tahoe basin from a cliff-top viewpoint. Further south, just after the trail crosses into California, hemlock-ringed Star Lake is one of a dozen superb lakes en route that offer perfect lakeshore camping.

Most dramatic of all is the 33-mile section shared with the Pacific Crest Trail (p228) along the rugged glacier-carved valleys, alpine lakes and granite slopes of the Desolation Wilderness in California. Many clockwise thru-hikers start from Tahoe City to save this section of trail for last, while others start in South Lake Tahoe and knock it off first, just in case they bail later. Either way, it's a highlight.

Wherever you start the Tahoe Rim Trail, after two weeks of hiking through unforgettable scenery, you finally end up exactly where you started. Mentally, emotionally and maybe even spiritually, though, you'll be in a whole different place.

Highlights

Shimmering in myriad shades of blue and green, Lake Tahoe is the USA's second-deepest lake and, at 6245ft high, also one of the highest-elevation lakes in the country. The peaks surrounding straddle the California–Nevada state line.

STAR LAKE
One of a dozen magnificent lakes on the trail, Star Lake near South Lake Tahoe nestles at the feet of three of the highest peaks in the Tahoe Basin.

DESOLATION WILDERNESS
Glaciers in this wilderness on the California side have stripped the land of earth here, leaving a rugged granite landscape of high lakes and epic views.

TAHOE CITY
This is a great place to refuel and recover in California, with supermarkets, restaurants, outdoor gear shops and craft breweries a stone's throw from the trail.

LAKE VIEWS
The sweeping views of crystal-line Lake Tahoe are the trail's recurring vision, allowing you to impress yourself with how far you've hiked.

EMERALD BAY STATE PARK
Along the shoreline, sheer granite cliffs and a jagged shoreline hem in glacier-carved Emerald Bay, a teardrop cove that will have you digging for your camera.

→ Sunrise overlooking Lake Tahoe's Emerald Bay, seen from Lower Eagle Falls.

Resources

01 The Tahoe Rim Trail Association
www.tahoerimtrail.org
Volunteers and members support the trail through this organization, which offers maps, information and ways to get involved.

02 US Forest Service
www.fs.usda.gov/ltbmu
The Lake Tahoe Basin Management Unit website of the USFS contains information about Desolation Wilderness permits and local conditions.

03 *Tahoe Beneath the Surface: The Hidden Stories of America's Largest Mountain Lake*
Readers love Scott Lankford's history of Lake Tahoe from the Ice Age to the modern era, unearthing many interesting facts and outlining its vulnerability to ecological threats.

Looking down on Lake Tahoe from the Flume Trail. Left: A Jeffrey pine in the Lake Tahoe Basin.

Hike this...

Lake Tahoe is a wonderland of polished granite peaks, deep-blue alpine lakes, glacier-carved valleys and pine forests that thin quickly at the higher elevations. In summer, wildflowers nudge out from between the rocks. All this splendor makes for some exquisite exploration.

➡ The Tahoe Rim Trail to the east of Lake Tahoe.

01
Christopher's Loop, Lake Tahoe Nevada State Park

The trail's most photogenic (and most photographed) viewpoint of Lake Tahoe's expanse can be found on the 1.2-mile Christopher's Loop, on the eastern slopes of the Carson Range within Lake Tahoe Nevada State Park, courtesy of 8840ft Herlan Peak. From here, hikers can take in almost all of the lake, looking down on Sand Harbor and the Marlette Flume Trail. Also known as the Sand Harbor Overlook trail on the Herlan Peak spur, Christopher's Loop is on the 23.3-mile stretch of the Tahoe Rim Trail from Mt Rose Summit/ Tahoe Meadows to Spooner Summit in Nevada, meaning the wildflower meadow views are a delight as well.

Want to add an extra level of difficulty? Try doing it by mountain bike. Although Christopher's Loop is relatively short, getting there takes more than a typical day hike's length. From the Tahoe Meadows trailhead on Hwy 431, stay overnight at the Marlette Lake campground, not too far away and with a useful water pump.

02
Echo Lakes, Desolation Wilderness

5.3 miles of out-and-back walking will let day hikers dip into the awe-inspiring Desolation Wilderness along Echo Lakes. Get your free, self-issued day use permit at the Echo Lakes trailhead in South Lake Tahoe (there's a 60-car parking lot here). You can also park at Echo Chalet, an ideal spot to base yourself for day tripping in the wilderness. Sculpted by powerful glaciers aeons ago, Desolation Wilderness is a relatively compact 100-sq-mile area spreading south and west of Lake Tahoe and is the most popular wilderness region in the Sierra Nevada. This moderate trail gives a taste of the wonders of the Desolation Wilderness while letting hikers rack up miles on both the Pacific Crest Trail and the Tahoe Rim Trail, which follow each other here along the northern edge of the lakes. Outside of April to October, snowpack can be too intense. During summer, however, the snow-fed alpine lakes are just the place for a cooling swim to relax after your hike. A boat even goes from Echo Chalet to the further-away Lake Aloha.

03
Van Sickle Bi-State Park

Near Nevada's Stateline casinos on Lake Tahoe's South Shore, and once the site of a Pony Express station, Van Sickle Bi-State Park is one of Lake Tahoe's most accessible parks. The trailhead starts in the parking lot behind Heavenly Village on Lake Dr. The Van Sickle Rim Trail Connector leads up to a waterfall (less than a mile from the trailhead) and views of Lake Tahoe. It's a very manageable 5 miles round trip up to and back from a viewpoint over Zephyr Cove, though that falls short of reaching the TRT, three and a half miles in. The trail crosses into both states (hence the state park's name; established in 2011, it's the first bi-state park in the country, though most of the acreage is in Nevada). The land was donated by a descendant of local rancher Jack Van Sickle, and the Van Sickle barn can also be visited on the property. Mountain bikes are welcome on this route, which they can descend on their rocky way off the Tahoe Rim Trail.

56

Trail of Tears National Historic Trail

Forcibly removed from their ancestral lands in the Southeast, trace the harrowing journey made by the Cherokee people when they were moved from west of the Mississippi to Oklahoma's Indian Territory.

Oconaluftee River overlook, Cherokee, North Carolina. Right: The Oconaluftee Visitor Center.

One of the most shameful episodes in a country not short on examples of racial injustice, the Trail of Tears was a tragedy whose scars are still visible. It began with the 1830 Indian Removal Act, signed into law by President Andrew Jackson. The act forced the tribes of the southeastern US to relinquish their lands to white settlers in exchange for new territory west of the Mississippi. After years of resistance, four major tribes – the Choctaw, Chickasaw, Muscogee Creek and Seminole – finally headed west. The Cherokee were last to go. In 1838, US Army soldiers and local militiamen rounded up some 16,000 into camps and then forced them on the trail. Thousands died along the way. The Cherokee named the journey Nunahi-Duna-Dlo-Hilu-I – 'the trail where they cried.'

While Trail of Tears is the term often used to refer broadly to the forced removal of southeastern tribes, the National Historic Trail specifically follows the routes taken by the Cherokee. Several routes are part of the official trail, including the water, northern, Taylor, Benge and Bell routes. These routes stretch across the country, covering many regions: the Great Smoky Mountains of Tennessee, the Ozarks of Arkansas, the swampy reaches of the Mississippi Delta and the hilly Green Country region of eastern Oklahoma.

For a traveler hoping to understand the Cherokee people's journey, an excellent starting place is the Museum of the Cherokee Indian in Cherokee, North Carolina. At the foothills of the Smokies, Cherokee is home to the Eastern Band of Cherokee Indians, descendants of some 800 individuals who hid in the mountains during the removals. The museum tells

Sleep here...

With over 5000 miles along various routes crossing nine states, the choice of lodging is yours. Try to make sure you spend some time in Tahlequah, Oklahoma, home of the Cherokee Nation. There are a handful of charming B&Bs downtown and plenty to keep you busy in not just experiencing the history of this route but also the immediate, vibrant life of Native American peoples today.

 Harrah's Cherokee Casino Resort, North Carolina
The luxury casino hotel in Cherokee, North Carolina, is owned by the Eastern Band of Cherokee Indians. At 21 stories high, it's the biggest building in this neck of the woods.

 Chattanooga Choo Choo, Tennessee
Many trail sites are day-trip distance from Chattanooga, Tennessee. This sweetly kitschy old railroad terminal hotel – you can really stay in a train car! – is a classic place to sleep.

 Camping in Shawnee National Forest, Illinois
The Northern route of the trail passed through this Illinois forest. It's one of many local, state and national forests and parks offering rustic campsites along the trail.

 Diamondhead Resort, Oklahoma
Tahlequah, Oklahoma, is a vacation destination for rafting down the Illinois River. This family-friendly spot has campsites, motel rooms, summer concerts and a bar; river trips run from the resort as well.

Toolbox

 When to go
Fall and spring are the most pleasant seasons for exploring outdoor monuments and historic sites. Autumn in the Appalachians and Ozarks is especially lovely. Winter in the mountains can create slippery roads.

Getting there
The trail consists of numerous routes both on land and on water. The easternmost point is Cherokee, North Carolina, an hour's drive from the Asheville airport. The western terminus is Tahlequah, Oklahoma, an hour from the airport in Fayetteville, Arkansas.

Practicalities
Length in miles: 5043 in total
Start: Varies by route
End: Tahlequah, OK
Dog friendly: Yes
Bike friendly: The NPS encourages you to explore the trail by bicycle, but it's not a great point-to-point ride
Permit needed: No
States covered: NC, TN, GA, AL, AR, KY, IL, MO, OK

the 13,000-year history of the Cherokee with gorgeous dioramas and artifacts – moccasins, pottery, beadwork, feather capes and more. The nearby Oconaluftee Indian Village is a re-creation of Cherokee village life circa 1760. See demonstrations of crafts like finger weaving, observe costumed interpreters going about their chores or watch a traditional dance.

Cross Great Smoky Mountains National Park through the deep green tree tunnel of US 441. In the town of Vonore is the Sequoyah Birthplace Museum. Born in the 1770s, Sequoyah was likely the son of a Cherokee woman and a German peddler. He created a syllabary (written characters used to represent syllables) to turn Cherokee into a written language.

Many Cherokee were held in camps around eastern Tennessee's Cumberland Plateau before the march west, and this area of the state has more than a dozen important sites, all within driving distance from Chattanooga. Red Clay State Historic Park holds the final Cherokee capital before removal. Deep in its forested valley is Blue Hole Spring, crystalline waters bubbling up from the limestone bedrock and once used as a water source during council meetings.

Most Cherokee took the brutal northern route of the trail, which began northeast of Chattanooga. Here the Cherokee Removal Memorial Park sits at the confluence of the Tennessee and Hiwassee Rivers, where the Blythe Ferry shuttled some 10,000 Cherokee across the water on their way west. They trekked across the green highlands of central Tennessee to Nashville. The trail passed within a few miles of the Hermitage, Andrew Jackson's plantation. Today visitors touring the house and expansive grounds can read about Jackson's destructive role in Indian history.

Passing into southwestern Kentucky, you'll come to the Trail of Tears Commemorative Park, where many northern route followers made camp. Two chiefs, Fly Smith and Whitepath, are buried here. At the border of Illinois, the Cherokee took flatboats across the Ohio River to Illinois at Berry's Ferry. This would prove to be one of the grimmest stretches of the northern route, with scores of people dying of cold and disease. The deceptively gentle hills are home to several cemeteries for the trail's victims. Of the survivors, nine groups crossed the Mississippi River from Illinois to Missouri in the brutal winter of 1838–39. In Missouri you can visit Trail of Tears State Park. Two miles of park road follow historic Green's Ferry Road, and visitors can walk in the footsteps of the Cherokee.

Finally, the travelers reached Oklahoma and the land they'd been promised. The survivors were exhausted, malnourished and footsore. They'd lost homes, friends, family and their tribal unity. But they would not be defeated. Instead, in the words of the Cherokee Nation: 'One will not hear the anguished voice of a forgotten and broken people. Instead one might hear the pride of people who faced overwhelming adversity and persevered.' Hear those voices at the Cherokee Heritage Center in Tahlequah, Oklahoma, capital of the modern Cherokee Nation and the United Keetoowah Band of Cherokee Indians. You'll see a reconstructed village, read firsthand accounts of the trail and see hundreds of artifacts. But you don't need to visit the museum to see the Cherokee people. They're all around Oklahoma – the state is home to more than 200,000 enrolled tribal members – proud despite their trials.

Highlights

This trip can be planned as an end-to-end drive, a short hike, or a visit to a few key sites. From Chattanooga's memorial The Passage westward, there is a rich history to engage with however you travel the trail.

LITTLE RIVER CANYON NATIONAL PRESERVE AND DESOTO STATE PARK
In northeastern Alabama's uplands, this 15,000-acre preserve is a landscape of cliffs, canyons, waterfalls and more.

GREAT SMOKY MOUNTAINS NATIONAL PARK
Hundreds of Cherokee hid in these mountains to escape removal. They call the land Shaconage, meaning 'place of blue smoke.'

MEMPHIS
The Bell and Water routes of the trail passed this Mississippi River city, beloved for its music – blues, rock and roll, soul and gospel – and barbecue.

Gourd Spoon

TENNESSEE RIVER MUSEUM
Several trail routes crossed the Tennessee River, while the Water route went down it. This museum in Savannah, Tennessee, has river-related artifacts from prehistory through modern times.

TAHLEQUAH
At the foothills of the Ozarks in Oklahoma, the western terminus of the trail became the new capital for trail survivors. Today it's home to several high-quality museums.

→ Cherokee National Homecoming parade, Tahlequah, Oklahoma.

Resources

01 **Trail of Tears National Historic Trail**
www.nps.gov/trte
The official trail website has interactive maps, historic information, opening times and more.

02 **Cherokee Nation**
www.cherokee.org
The website for the Cherokee Nation has a wealth of information.

03 *Trail of Tears: The Rise and Fall of the Cherokee Nation*
John Ehle gives a stirring account of Cherokee history before and after removal in this classic book.

04 *Walking the Trail*
This memoir by Jerry Ellis describes his 900-mile pilgrimage from Oklahoma back to Alabama.

Hike this...

Explore these important locations for the Trail of Tears by whatever conveyance is most convenient, from a raft to a bike, your two feet or a car to witness multiple sites in one day.

➡ Pedestrian bridge,
Chattanooga, Tennessee.
Left: Soco Falls near Cherokee,
North Carolina.

01
Upland Georgia

Thousands of Cherokee made their home in upland Georgia before the removal. Today you can wind your way down rural roads in Chatsworth to the Chief Vann House State Historic Site, a park surrounding a brick mansion built by wealthy Cherokee James Vann in the early 1800s. See exhibits and artifacts from a family whose elite status did not protect them. Further south is the New Echota State Historic Site, a former capital of the Cherokee Nation. You can visit several period buildings, including a council house, courthouse and print shop.

A half hour southwest in Rome is the Chieftains Museum, a leafy 6-acre property once home to Cherokee leader Major Ridge (given name Ca-nung-da-cla-geh), born in 1771. Visit the grand two-story home and its outbuildings, which tell the story of Ridge and the Cherokee people with artifacts, including some found on-site. The land was given to a white widow by lottery in 1832.

02
Water Route

Some 2800 Cherokee traveled to Indian Territory on steamboats and barges, moving along the Tennessee, Ohio, Mississippi and Arkansas Rivers. Though it might sound easier than walking, this route was plagued with overcrowding and sickness. The boats departed from Ross's Landing in Chattanooga, where now you can stand in a park overlooking the Tennessee River, the city humming behind you.

Once the crafts were underway, the river cliffs at Columbus-Belmont State Park in Kentucky saw boats pass by; this was also an encampment for the Benge route. Today you can camp and picnic amid the oaks, and walk the 2-mile loop trail on the bluffs over the Mississipi River. Later it would be a strategic location in the Civil War. Another worthy lookout on the Water route is atop Mt Nebo State Park in Arkansas, with views over the Arkansas River, Lake Dardanelle and the mountains. The Cherokee – those who survived – disembarked at Fort Coffee in Oklahoma.

03
Chattanooga, Tennessee

Chattanooga is now one of America's greenest and hippest cities. It has a half-dozen Trail of Tears sites within the city; more are within easy day-trip driving distance. Audubon Acres in the city is a serene forest preserve on what was likely once Cherokee land. All plants are marked with both English and Cherokee names. You can also visit the Spring Frog log cabin, named for a Cherokee naturalist. Nearby, the Brainerd Mission was a Christian mission to the Cherokee. It's now paved over with a shopping mall; a tiny cemetery is all that remains. On the city's breezy riverfront, tucked between the Tennessee Aquarium and the Tennessee River, the patch of greenery known as Ross's Landing was the embarkation point for the Water route travelers. Featuring a weeping wall and seven large ceramic discs that share the stories of the Cherokee, The Passage on this spot is a memorial walkway linking the park with downtown. You can walk or bike for miles along the bluffs.

5.7

Historic Union Pacific Rail Trail

This 28-mile historic multiuse trail is worth including on your trip if you are visiting Park City, Utah, and have more than the slopes on your agenda.

➔ Ski runs and a star-filled sky above Park City, Utah. Right: Union Pacific Railroad building.

The year 1869 marked a turning point for westward expansion in the US, when the famous Golden Spike was nailed into the railroad tracks at Promontory Point in Utah. This historic site, not too far from the rail trail, sits to the north of the Great Salt Lake. There the Central Pacific and Union Pacific lines met, and soon the age of wagon trails would recede into memory. That first transcontinental railroad ran from San Francisco to Council Bluffs, Iowa – a city served by other rail lines to many points throughout the Midwest and East Coast. In the years that followed, however, the network of rail lines would spread rapidly. From 2175 miles of track in 1860, the number would increase to 72,389 miles by 1890, including several additional transcontinental routes.

Now one stretch of the historic old Union Pacific line from Park City to Echo Reservoir has been reborn as a trail for bikers, hikers and joggers – as well as horseback riders and, in the depth of winter, cross-country skiers. In short, as long as you aren't on a motorized vehicle, you're welcome on the trail. Just as railroads reshaped the American West, making it faster and cheaper than ever to travel across the country, they too would eventually be replaced (in large part) by the automobile and air travel. Some of the space the railroads left behind has been creatively repurposed for locals and visitors alike.

The 28-mile multiuse trail is well worth including on your trip if you are visiting Utah with more than the slopes on your agenda, or if you want to do your cross-country skiing on storied ground. While the original transcontinental railroad passed through the town of Echo, this spur to the

Sleep here...

As a seasonal resort town, Park City gets busy. Mid-December through mid-April is winter high season, with minimum stays required; rates rise during Christmas, New Year's and the Sundance Film Festival. Off-season rates drop 50% or more. A complete list of condos, hotels and resorts in Park City is at www.visitparkcity.com. For budget options, consider staying down in Salt Lake City, Heber Valley or at the Park City Hostel.

Stein Eriksen Lodge
This Deer Valley resort's upgrades include a spiffy family pool. Its spa is one of the best in the area, a perfect first stop after a day on the trail.

Washington School House
Park City has many luxury options for those on special-occasion trips. This hotel near Main Street is in a meticulously restored 19th-century building and has just 13 guest rooms.

Camping at Echo Reservoir
The sites are primitive and you'll essentially be picking a spot that looks appealing on the shore of the reservoir, but the price is right – $20 per night.

Camping at Rockport State Park
The state park has campsites on the shores of Rockport Lake. Its range of options – developed, primitive, RV and boat-in sites – is greater than what you'll find at Echo Reservoir.

Toolbox

When to go
From April to November, you can usually count on the trail being free of snow. July and August in Park City offer almost perfect warm days with cooler temperatures at night.

Getting there
Park City is just 35 miles from Utah's Salt Lake City International Airport, a major hub in the West served by 15 airlines. From the airport, take I-80 to Kimball Junction and continue on UT 224 south to Park City.

Practicalities
Length in miles: 28
Start: Echo, UT
End: Park City, UT
Dog friendly: Yes
Bike friendly: Yes
Permit needed: No
States covered: Utah

Ice fisherman on a frozen lake, Echo Reservoir, Utah.

north of it was constructed a little later. It was opened in 1880 to take coal up to Park City to fuel the mining machinery there, and then the cars would be filled with ore from the mines for the return trip. Once Park City's mines were exhausted, the rail line lost its purpose. It did have a second life as part of a route for a ski train, bringing winter travelers from Salt Lake City to the slopes. By 1989, Union Pacific had abandoned the line completely, and it was closed. The rails and ties were removed and the land given to the Utah Division of Parks and Recreation. In 1992 the line was reborn as the Historic Union Pacific Rail Trail.

The trail starts (or ends) in Echo, where it makes its way along the eastern side of Echo Reservoir, one of Utah's newest state parks. While it only became an official state park in 2018, it has long been a popular spot for local boaters and campers. At the opposite end of the reservoir, you'll reach Coalville. The name sums up the town's early history, though it was actually founded as Chalk Creek. The discovery of coal in the area in 1860 changed the course of its history. Today Coalville is a quiet town of some 1300 people – its main claim to fame these days is that it sits on this trail, though the museum at the Summit County Courthouse is worth a visit.

From Coalville you'll travel south with the Weber River and I-80 to one side and farms stretching out on the other. Around the trail's halfway point, Wanship is a small town with a convenience store and about 400 residents. If you want to extend your day of hiking, you can access the Wanship trailhead here, which leads south to nearby Rockport Reservoir.

The main trail continues from Coalville to Promontory, a gated community with some of Park City's most expensive real estate. After you pass Promontory, I-80 and the trail part ways, and you'll continue your ride, run or walk with Silver Creek alongside your route. As you get close to Park City, the trail goes from gravel and dirt to paved again. Finally, you'll arrive on Bonanza Drive in Park City, and you can end your trek with a drink or a meal, though it's still about another 20 minutes on foot (or five on bike) before you reach Main Street, where most of the town's restaurants and cafes, as well as galleries and boutiques, are concentrated.

Among the country's historic and scenic trails, the Historic Union Pacific Rail Trail is definitely on the shorter side. It would be easy to travel the length of it in three to four hours by bike. If you are on foot, you might want to run or hike only a portion of it – at 28 miles, it's a little longer than a marathon. Keep in mind that Park City sits at an elevation of 7000ft, while Echo is at 5777ft. Most of that descent is in the portion from Park City to Wanship. It's a fairly steady 2% grade, and the ride down from Park City is decidedly easier than traveling the other direction.

Now that you've conquered the trail, head to Golden Spike National Historical Park. On May 10, 1869, the westward Union Pacific Railroad and eastward Central Pacific Railroad met at Promontory Summit. Golden Spike National Historical Park, 32 miles northwest of Brigham City on Hwy 83, has an interesting museum and films, auto tours and several interpretive trails. Steam-engine demonstrations take place May through mid-October. Aside from Golden Spike National Historical Park, few people visit Utah's desolate northwest corner, but it changed the West forever.

Highlights

A one-time silver boom-and-bust town, pretty Park City is now lined with condos and mansions in the valleys to take advantage of the great local skiing. But that earlier history lingers, nowhere more prominently than on the old Summit County Union Pacific line.

PARK CITY MAIN STREET
You'll find 64 historic buildings on Main Street and the Park City Museum, which provides an introduction to the history of the town and region.

DEER VALLEY RESORT
Great in winter, Deer Valley Resort is also hopping in summer, with open-air concerts and unusual ways to hit the slopes, like on a mountain bike.

UTAH OLYMPIC PARK
The Park City site of the 2002 Winter Olympics is open year-round, with summer activities like zip lines and summer bob-sled rides (wheels are added to the bottom of the sleds).

KIMBALL ART CENTER
The museum in Park City has an outstanding collection and also offers classes and special events, many intended for kids. Its art festival in August is a highlight of summer.

HIGH WEST DISTILLERY AND SALOON
This Park City distillery offers tours and introductions to the process used to create its whiskies and vodkas. Note: the saloon is limited to those 21 and older.

58

Washington-Rochambeau Revolutionary Route National Historic Trail

This historic trail from Rhode Island to Virginia cuts across classic Eastern Seaboard scenery and highlights the crucial, and often overlooked, contributions of French forces to American independence.

Independence Hall in Philadelphia, Pennsylvania. Right: Men dressed as British soldiers march on Battle Road in Concord, Massachusetts.

When many Americans think of the Revolutionary War, it is as a confrontation between the American rebels and British forces. That's true overall, but it overlooks the contributions of other countries, especially France and Spain, on behalf of the Americans. And of the French military leaders who played key roles in the war, the Marquis de Lafayette has overshadowed the Comte de Rochambeau. You don't have to go far in America to find a street, square or school named in Lafayette's honor – 17 states have Fayette or Lafayette counties. Rochambeau, on the other hand, hasn't been memorialized to the same degree. The French nobleman and military commander does, however, share top billing with George Washington on this National Historic Trail.

Established in 2009 to honor this collaboration, the Washington-Rochambeau Revolutionary Route National Historic Trail follows the route of French troops from Rhode Island to Yorktown, Virginia, in 1781. Rochambeau departed from Providence that July with some 450 officers and 5300 troops, heading across Connecticut to meet up with Washington and his forces in Dobbs Ferry, New York. They would then make their way down through New Jersey, Pennsylvania, Delaware and Maryland before joining with Lafayette's forces in Virginia.

This trail named in honor of the two military leaders, one venerated and the other far less well-known, passes by Revolutionary War battlefields and other sites of southern New England and the mid-Atlantic. Rochambeau's route would stop in the Colonial capitals of Providence, Rhode Island; Hartford, Connecticut;

Sleep here...

Camping options exist along this route, but it's those who like creature comforts and sleeping on a bed at night who'll love the overnights on this historic trail. All along the densely populated mid-Atlantic corridor are endless options, though Newport is pricey during the summer.

Stone Arches B&B, Connecticut
The inn dates from 1694 and sits just to the north of the trail in Storrs, Connecticut. French troops surely would rather have stayed here than camping by the roadside.

Camping in Washington Crossing State Park, New Jersey
A 15-minute detour from the trail will bring you to Washington Crossing in New Jersey, where you camp at the state park near where Washington crossed the Delaware River.

Thomas Bond House, Pennsylvania
This 1769 house that was owned by a friend of Benjamin Franklin is an ideal base for exploring Colonial and Revolutionary War sites in Philadelphia.

Camping in Elk Neck State Park, Maryland
Few battlefields include campsites, but this state park is on the Elk River in Maryland, where British ships gathered before invading Chesapeake Bay in 1777. Rochambeau passed near here in 1781.

Toolbox

When to go
As this is typically a driven route, it's good for all seasons. Many of the trail's highlights are museums and historic houses in cities, and you can visit them at any time of year. The battlefields along the route, however, may be wet and cold in the winter.

Getting there
Providence, Rhode Island, is served by its own airport, though it's also possible to fly into Boston and drive (just under two hours) to Newport, Rhode Island. At the other end of the trail, Newport News, Virginia, is your best airport option. Amtrak and regular long-distance buses also run along this corridor.

Practicalities
Length in miles: 680
Start: Newport, RI (another branch starts in Boston, MA)
End: Yorktown, VA
Dog friendly: Yes, in portions
Bike friendly: Yes, in portions
Permit needed: Some campgrounds
States covered: MA, RI, CT, NY, NJ, PA, DE, MD, VA, DC

Philipsburg Manor along the trail, Hudson Valley, New York.

Trenton, New Jersey; Philadelphia, Pennsylvania; and Annapolis, Maryland. In all these cities significant sites from early US history, including ones that aren't related specifically to Rochambeau, await.

In Lebanon, Connecticut, the nearly mile-long Lebanon Green was the winter headquarters for many French soldiers before they began their long journey south. The town is also home to the so-called War Office, where Governor Jonathan Trumbull oversaw the Revolutionary War efforts in the state. Rochambeau, Washington, Lafayette and other military leaders met with Trumbull here. If you want to explore further, you can visit some of the more than 40 other buildings of historic significance in Lebanon, though not all of them are from the Revolutionary War period.

In New York, the John Odell House in Hartsdale, currently in the process of being restored, served as Rochambeau's headquarters. The Elijah Miller House in White Plains was used as Washington's headquarters at several different points during the war. White Plains was also the site of a major battle in 1776, and a portion of the battlefield is maintained as a park. A founding father who has fallen in and out of favor over different periods, the still-controversial Thomas Paine, lived in a cottage in New Rochelle from 1802 to 1806.

In Trenton, New Jersey, the Old Barracks served as a hospital for wounded soldiers from the Battle of Yorktown (so you'll see this site out of chronological order if you're traveling south along the trail). Nearby, the William Trent House was a headquarters of the British army at the beginning of the war and then later seized for use by Washington's army.

Some French troops camped in the northern part of Philadelphia, and the city has dozens of other sites related to the Revolutionary War, some well-known (Independence Hall) and others not. Declaration House is the building where Thomas Jefferson wrote the Declaration of Independence – he had rented the second floor of the building. The Thaddeus Kosciuszko National Memorial honors another foreigner who rallied to the side of the Americans, and it has the added distinction of being the country's smallest national park unit.

The trail ends at Yorktown, Virginia. The American Revolution Museum tells the entire story of the war, not just the crucial battle that took place here in October 1781. That event, however, was in many ways the culmination of the conflict; it was the defeat from which the British would never recover. The degree to which that victory was due as much to the French as to the Americans is sometimes forgotten.

At sea, a French fleet under the direction of the Comte de Grasse and additional ships under the command of the Comte de Barras were essential to keeping the Royal Navy in check. On land, the troops led by Rochambeau combined with Washington's and Lafayette's to form a force of some 20,000. This force faced off against an estimated 9000 British and Hessian soldiers. Around half the soldiers on the American side during the siege were, in fact, French. On October 19, General Charles Cornwallis surrendered; Britain would begin to negotiate an end to the war, and its recognition of the US. Armchair historians who have traveled the entire trail to reach Yorktown's excellent museum will have a special thrill from reliving the war's final end.

Highlights

To succeed on the battlefield, General Washington needed help, and in 1778, Benjamin Franklin persuaded France to ally with the revolutionaries. The French went on to provide the troops, material and sea power that won the war at the sites below.

HISTORIC BOSTON
While most of Rochambeau's troops marched south to Virginia, some headed north to Boston and then sailed south. See Boston's Revolutionary War sites along the Freedom Trail (p100).

NEW WINDSOR CANTONMENT
After the victory at Yorktown, Washington moved his headquarters to this New York state historic site, where he issued the final cease-fire.

COLONY HOUSE
After the French expelled the British, this building in Newport, Rhode Island, was used as a hospital. Rochambeau also held a banquet welcoming Washington when he visited in 1781.

PRINCETON
Rochambeau's route passed through Princeton, New Jersey, which was already the home of a college. Nassau Hall here served as the new country's first capital for six months in 1783.

YORKTOWN AND COLONIAL PARKWAY
This is where America – and its French allies – won the war. The 23-mile Colonial Parkway connects Yorktown and Jamestown.

59
Wonderland Trail

Walk around awe-inspiring Mt Rainier, Washington's iconic mountain, on this 10-day loop past lakes, glaciers, wildflowers and incredible volcano views.

▶ Mount Rainier summer colors. Right: Hiker pauses on a trail to look at the snow-capped peak of Mt Rainier.

Mt Rainier (Rain-eer) dominates the Wonderland Trail. Rising from the lush temperate forests of the Pacific Northwest, it towers above everything, the highest point of a chain of snowcapped volcanoes that runs from Mt Baker to Mt Hood. At its feet lie fields of lupine and Indian paintbrush (also called prairie fire), as well as dripping forests of red cedar and Engelmann spruce. And around it all winds the Wonderland Trail, 10 days of unrivaled scenic magnificence, circling the famous peak through the very best of Mt Rainier National Park.

The USA's fifth-highest peak outside Alaska, majestic Mt Rainier is also arguably, America's most astonishing mountain. Part of a 368-sq-mile national park (inaugurated in 1899), the mountain's snowcapped summit and forest-covered foothills boast numerous hiking trails, swaths of flower-carpeted meadows and an alluring peak that presents a formidable challenge for aspiring climbers. For most hikers Rainier exerts an irresistible pull. Its hulking form dominates the skyline, pulling them into its orbit and dragging the helpless, ecstatic hikers around the mountain. For 93 miles the Wonderland Trail climbs and descends the mountain's lateral ridges like a roller coaster, crossing raging rivers that pour off the mountain's glaciers like spokes from a hub.

However many times you see them, the views of Rainier never seem to get old. The mountain's multiple faces constantly reveal different characters, shifting in differing light and changing weather – sometimes reflected serenely in a mirror lake, at other times disappearing behind its glacial arms. The trail passes a huge variety of climatic zones, from old-growth rainforest along

Sleep here...

There are campsites and lodge options in the park and plenty of other types of lodging from hostels to B&Bs outside, mostly along the Longmire entrance route. A wilderness permit is required to hike the Wonderland Trail and camp in the backcountry. There are 18 trailside camps. Once you have a permit, make wilderness camping reservations: the backcountry camps are extremely popular, understandably.

 Paradise Inn
This imposing example of 'parkitecture' in the southern Paradise section of Mt Rainier National Park was built in 1917 and features modest rooms but huge fireplaces, big views and great nearby trails.

 Cougar Rock Campground
One of the park's three front-country National Park Service campgrounds, the campground is the closest to the popular hub and starting point of Longmire, so be sure to reserve in advance.

White River Campground
Near Sunrise, the front-country park campground on the northeast corner of the trail is a good place to overnight before starting the trail nearby. There are no reservations, but it accepts food caches.

 Wilderness Campsites
Lining the Wonderland Trail are 18 wilderness campsites between 3 and 7 miles apart, each equipped with bear poles and pit toilets but rarely a view.

Feng Wei Photography / Getty Images; Galyna Andrushko / Shutterstock

Toolbox

 When to go
Mid-July to September are the most reliable months in terms of weather. July can have a lot of lingering snow, depending on the snowpack from the preceding winter, and has the worst of the mosquitoes. August is the prime month for wildflowers.

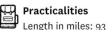 **Getting there**
Mt Rainier National Park is 87 miles south of Seattle, Washington, and 135 miles north of Portland, Oregon. Both cities have international airports; Seattle-Tacoma International Airport is even named, in part, after the mountain's name among the Puyallup people. You will almost certainly have to get to the park by car.

Practicalities
Length in miles: 93
Start: Longmire, Sunrise, White River or Mowich Lake trailheads
End: Same as start
Dog friendly: No
Bike friendly: No
Permit needed: Yes
States covered: Washington

Sunrise Lake, Mt Rainier National Park.

low-lying Ipsut Creek at 2450ft to barren talus slopes and snowbanks at 7000ft Panhandle Gap. In between, hikers pass flower-strewn meadows, cross swaying suspension bridges, skirt rubble-filled glacial moraines and stare open-mouthed at the snow-domed peak. If you are lucky, you'll spot the occasional black bear grazing on patches of huckleberries, or mountain goats scrambling the fractured slopes above. Perhaps most visually striking of all are the half-dozen lakes that reflect the mountain in the serene, magenta-hued waters of dawn and dusk.

To the Native Americans, Rainier has always been known as Tahoma or Tacoma (the Mother of Waters). To most climbers and hikers it is simply 'the mountain.' At 14,411ft the peak is the highest point in the Washington Cascades, but the eye-catching scale of the peak really comes from the fact that it rises higher from the surrounding land than any other comparable mountain, towering an incredible 12,000ft over the nearest flat land. Its hulking mass is twice the size of Mt St Helens and holds more snow and ice than the combined ice mass of every other volcano in the Lower 48. On a clear day Rainier dominates the horizon for a hundred miles. It is an awesome mountain.

The Wonderland Trail that encircles Rainier was originally built in 1915 as a ranger patrol trail, but within a year a group from the Mountaineers club of Seattle became the first people to walk it as a recreational route. In the 1930s the trail was briefly slated to become a paved ring road for cars, a plan that thankfully came to nothing. The surrounding national park, America's fifth, dates from 1899, thanks in part to the efforts of

environmentalist and wanderer John Muir, who reached the summit the year before.

So just how tough is the Wonderland Trail? Well, the trails are in excellent shape, navigation is easy and there are some excellent camping spots. At around 10 days, it's not especially long. The real challenge comes from the constant elevation gain, a total of around 23,000ft, which is equivalent to climbing to the summit two and a half times. This is one trail that requires you to get in shape to really enjoy it. The one thing the park service omitted mentioning when coining the phrase 'Wonderland' was the region's weather. Summer months bring the clearest skies, but this is the Pacific Northwest – rain, fog and clouds can descend at any time and obscure the mountain for days. Spend enough time soaked in a low-visibility downpour and you'll swear Rainier was named after the weather, not the 18th-century British admiral. Pack plenty of waterproof gear.

If the threat of rain hasn't put you off, you'll need to read the small print. The Wonderland Trail is a popular route, and before April 1 you must secure a hard-to-get permit through the park's online lottery system. If you are refused, not all is lost, as 30% of backcountry campsites are reserved for walk-ins. Most people start from the park hubs at Longmire or Sunrise, but your exact route and overnight stops will likely be determined by the availability of backcountry campsites. Most people hike the route clockwise, largely because counterclockwise entails steeper ascents (but easier descents if you have bad knees). Finally, carrying 10 days of food is too much for most backpackers, so you'll have to leave a cache on the loop.

Highlights

An active stratovolcano that recorded its last eruptive activity as recently as 1854, Rainier harnesses untold destructive powers. Not surprisingly, the mountain has long been imbued with myth, and its dangerous potential only increases the perception of its beauty.

LITTLE TAHOMA PEAK
Accessible from Summerland, this satellite peak would be the third-highest peak in Washington if considered on its own.

SUMMERLAND
Offering some of the best sunrise views of Rainier, Summerland's meadow is surrounded by snowfields, glacial tarns and, if you are lucky, mountain goats.

INDIAN BAR
What is perhaps the best wilderness camp spot in the park has stunning views of towering rock walls, dense forests and lush meadows.

SPRAY PARK
This alternative route adds a few thousand feet of ascent and descent but rewards with great views of Rainier's north-western face.

EMERALD RIDGE
Epic views of Rainier's western Tahoma and South Tahoma Glaciers and Puyallup Cleaver ridge are beautiful framed in late summer wildflowers.

60

El Yunque Peak

Ascending through tropical rainforest in Puerto Rico to the magical peak of El Yunque, you have views of the Atlantic Ocean and jewel-like islands.

→ Mist in El Yunque National Forest. Right: An El Yunque cascade.

The only tropical rainforest in the US National Forest System, El Yunque covers almost 29,000 acres in the northeastern corner of Puerto Rico. Diminutive it may be for a national forest, but exploring its 36 miles or so of trails will immerse you in four distinct forest ecosystems. The mix of rugged terrain and tropical climate means that there's a trail to suit every hiker.

More than 240 species of trees – more than 20 of which are found nowhere else – and about a thousand species of plants, including 50 kinds of flamboyant orchids and 150 varieties of ferns, thrive in this mist-wreathed, rain-drenched forest. It's also home to some 60 bird species, such as the critically endangered Puerto Rican parrot, as well as anole tree lizards, the 7ft-long Puerto Rican boa and myriad bats and insects.

The forest has a long and fascinating history, serving as a sacred place of worship for Puerto Rico's indigenous Taíno people, who inhabited the island long before the Spanish arrived. During WWII El Yunque was a military outpost, with its tallest peak a perfect radar site for the Caribbean, giving early warnings of German aircraft and submarines.

Puerto Rico was a Spanish colony when King Alfonso XII proclaimed the forest a Crown Reserve in 1876, making it one of the Western Hemisphere's earliest forest reserves. Almost 30 years later, with the island already under US control, President Theodore Roosevelt named it the Luquillo Forest Reserve. Over the years it grew in size, and in 2007 President George W Bush signed an executive order renaming it El Yunque National Forest.

Much of the trail system and the park's

Sleep here...

There are several boutique accommodations on the fringes of otherwise still-wild El Yunque National Forest. Proximity to the rainforest means you'll be lulled to sleep by the sound of chirruping coquí and wake to tropical birdsong. Lodging to the north means easy access to Luquillo's beaches – the south is more isolated but both areas are within reach of Fajardo and Vieques. Unfortunately, there are no campgrounds in El Yunque.

Yuquiyú Treehouses
At this rustic retreat just north of El Yunque, complete with an organic garden, secluded treehouse terraces overlook El Yunque Peak. Post-hike, you can walk down to the river and go for a swim.

Dos Aguas
Tucked in a towering forest of bamboo in Río Grande, this stylish B&B gives you easy access to Luquillo's surfing beaches, Fajardo's bioluminescent bay and San Juan, as well as El Yunque.

Rainforest Inn
Bordering the national forest, the romantic boutique lodge in Río Grande comes with clawfoot tubs, gourmet food and a private trail leading to a stunning waterfall pool.

St Regis Bahia Beach Resort
If you want to combine forest and beach, the luxe retreat just 20 minutes from El Yunque is set on a sweep of icing-sugar sand with two pools, a pampering spa and gourmet restaurants.

Toolbox

When to go
The trail is open year-round, but visit from mid-April to June to avoid the winter season rush and the rainy summer. Remember that it's called the rainforest for a reason – you can expect showers every day. Access to the trail closes at 6pm. Check trail conditions beforehand.

Getting there
The nearest airport is in Puerto Rico's capital, San Juan, around a 30-minute drive from El Yunque. There are two entrances to the park; the one in the north, close to the beach town of Luquillo, takes you to this trail.

Practicalities
Length in miles: 6.3/7.4 miles round trip, including El Yunque Rock, Los Picachos and Mt Britton Tower
Start: Caimitillo trailhead or Mt Britton, Puerto Rico
End: Caimitillo trailhead, Puerto Rico
Dog friendly: No
Bike friendly: No
Permit needed: No
Territory covered: Puerto Rico

➡ Panoramic view over
the hills in Puerto Rico's El
Yunque National Forest.

structures were constructed by the Civilian Conservation Corps –affectionately known as the 'tres Cs' – between 1935 and 1943. Many of the original trails are still in use, including the popular trail to El Yunque Peak. If you want to mix up your hiking experiences, you can take a few fascinating detours, including to El Yunque Rock, the Mt Britton observation tower and the Los Picachos Trail.

The trail to El Yunque, the second-tallest peak in Puerto Rico, begins at the Palo Colorado Information Center at an elevation of 2047ft. It steadily climbs to 3496ft as the trail passes through Palo Colorado forest, where ancient trees are laden with vines and orchids. The trail then heads up through Sierra Palm forest, dominated by mountain palms, eventually reaching a surreal and beautiful area of cloud forest known as dwarf forest. Here, the stunted, twisted trees are draped in moss and festooned with water-loving bromeliads.

Along the way you'll cross streams, pass waterfalls and explore trails flanked by luxuriant ferns and vibrant flowers, such as hibiscus and heliconia. The soundtrack to your hike will be the incessant chorus of 'co-kee' from Puerto Rico's tiny but highly local endemic tree frog, the coquí, symbol of the island.

El Yunque Peak is often shrouded in clouds that sweep up the hillside and bathe you with a cool, refreshing mist. It's why the Taíno are thought to have named it Yuqué, or 'white lands,' believing that Yuquiyú, the god of light and life, dwelled at the top. The trail is best done in the morning for a cloud-free experience with panoramic views from the top of its observation tower, a structure that looks like something between a castle, with its turrets, and a church, with a cross engraved in the stone inside. On a clear day, as you look out over the lush green canopy, the views stretch to the northern coast, all the way to San Juan, surrounded by the cobalt-blue waters of the Atlantic.

From El Yunque Peak, you can see El Yunque Rock, often wrapped in clouds. This enduring icon of the island stands at 3412ft above sea level, and the final scramble is over a jumble of often-slippery boulders. Still, the rewards are views reaching as far as the Atlantic Ocean and San Juan.

The barren, anvil-shaped rock – yunque means 'anvil' in Spanish – is enshrouded in clouds as it protrudes through old-growth forest. Buffeted by trade winds and swept by three showers a day on average, this spot receives more than 14ft of rain every year.

From there you can return to El Yunque Trail and hike to the 68ft Mt Britton Tower, named, like the peak it stands on, after the famous botanist Nathaniel Britton, who had identified numerous endemic plant and tree species in the region a decade before. Look north toward El Yunque Peak, east toward Pico del Este and south to El Toro Peak, the tallest peak in the forest in the designated wilderness area.

Another detour from the main trail is the short but rewarding out-and-back hike to Los Picachos Peak. A strenuous climb up a 60-step stairway leads to a flat, grassy summit with great views over the forest. From this easternmost lookout, you can see the islets and cays off Fajardo on the island's northeastern tip, as well as stunning vistas from the Yokahú Observation Tower – a 65ft, Moorish-looking stone tower, built as a lookout in 1962 – and the Mt Britton Tower.

Highlights

El Yunque National Forest is one of Puerto Rico's crown jewels. It boasts nearly 29,000 acres of lush mountainous terrain, with waterfalls, rushing rivers and gurgling brooks, bromeliads clinging to trees and groves opening to spectacular ocean views.

PANORAMIC VIEWS
On a clear day, the showstopping views stretch from San Juan in the north to the small islands of Vieques and Culebra to the east.

LOCAL FLORA
Take time to stop and metaphorically smell El Yunque's vibrant flowers – from hibiscus to heliconias, torch ginger to red ginger, orchids and more.

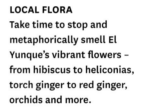

MT BRITTON TOWER
Climb the 98 steps of the stone Mt Britton Tower, built in the 1930s by the Civilian Conservation Corps and named after botanist Nathaniel Britton.

SWIMMING HOLES
Start – or end – a hike with a dip in Baño Grande or Baño de Oro, two beautiful man-made swimming holes close to the Palo Colorado Information Center.

FOREST ECOSYSTEMS
In El Yunque you can explore four different forest ecosystems at different elevations, from Tabonuco up through Palo Colorado to Sierra Palm to the cloud forest.

Index

Acknowledgments

Published in May 2020
by Lonely Planet Global Limited
CRN 554153
www.lonelyplanet.com
ISBN 978 1788 68938 0
© Lonely Planet 2020
Printed in China
10 9 8 7 6 5 4 3 2 1

Managing Director, Publishing
Piers Pickard
Associate Publisher Robin Barton
Editor Nora Rawn
Art Direction Daniel Di Paolo
Layout Kristina Juodenas
Illustrations Holly Exley
Print Production Nigel Longuet

Front cover: Feng Wei Photography / Getty Images.
Back cover: MIHAI ANDRITOIU / Alamy Stock Photo.

STAY IN TOUCH lonelyplanet.com/contact

AUSTRALIA
The Malt Store, Level 3, 551 Swanston St, Carlton, Victoria 3053 T: 03 8379 8000

USA
Suite 208, 155 Filbert Street, Oakland, CA 94607
T: 510 250 6400

IRELAND
Digital Depot, Roe Lane (off Thomas St), Digital Hub, Dublin 8, D08 TCV4

UNITED KINGDOM
240 Blackfriars Rd, London SE1 8NW
T: 020 3771 5100

Paper in this book is certified against the Forest Stewardship Council™ standards. FSC™ promotes environmentally responsible, socially beneficial and economically viable management of the world's forests.

MIX
Paper from responsible sources
FSC® C021741

Contributors

Austin Aslan (AZT)
Diane Bair & Pam Wright (Crawford Path, Derby Wharf, Freedom Trail, NET)
Amy Balfour (El Camino Real de Tierra Adentro, Pony Express)
Catherine Brody (AK trails)
Gregor Clark (Long Trail)
Ron Eid (ADT)
Bailey Freeman (Natural Bridge)
Ethan Gelber (ECG)
Sarah Gilbert (El Yunque)
Emma Hileman (MTS)
Emily Matchar (AT, Cumberland Trail, FT, Mormon Pioneer, Overmountain, Santa Fe, Trail of Tears)
Bradley Mayhew (Hayduke, JMT, MDH, SHR, TRT, Wonderland)
John Mock & Kimberley O'Neil (NCT, PCT, Potomac Heritage)
John Newton (California NHT, Captain John Smith Chesapeake, El Camino Real de los Tejas, Juan Bautista, Nez Perce, Old Spanish, Old Rag, Oregon NHT, Star Spangled Banner, Union Pacific, Washington-Rochambeau)
Meghan O'Dea (OCT)
Elizabeth Paulson (IAT, SHT)
Trisha Ping (C&O, Selma to Montgomery)
Zuzanna Sitek (OHT)
Sarah Stocking (CT, CDT, Grays Peak, Natchez Trace)
Kaidi Stroud (ICT, PNT)
Jan Wizinowich (HI trails)
Alexia Wulff (GET, R2R)